MAKING SCHOOLS WORK FOR UNDERACHIEVING MINORITY STUDENTS

Making Schools Work
for Underachieving
Minority Students ⸻

NEXT STEPS FOR
RESEARCH, POLICY,
AND PRACTICE

EDITED BY
Josie G. Bain
AND
Joan L. Herman ⸻

Center for Research on Evaluation, Standards, and Student Testing
UCLA Center for the Study of Evaluation

CONTRIBUTIONS TO THE STUDY OF EDUCATION, NUMBER 36

Greenwood Press
New York • Westport, Connecticut • London

Library of Congress Cataloging-in-Publication Data

Making schools work for underachieving minority students : next steps
  for research, policy, and practice / edited by Josie G. Bain and
  Joan L. Herman.
    p.   cm. — (Contributions to the study of education, ISSN
  0196–707X ; no. 36)
  Includes bibliographical references.
  ISBN 0–313–26889–4 (alk. paper)
  1. Minority students—Education—United States—Congresses.
  2. Underachievers—United States—Congresses. I. Herman, Joan L.
  II. Series.
  LC3731.M35 1990
  371.92—dc20   89–48904

British Library Cataloguing in Publication Data is available.

Library of Congress Catalog Card Number: 89–48904
ISBN: 0–313–26889–4
ISSN: 0196–707X

First published in 1990

Greenwood Press, 88 Post Road West, Westport, CT 06881
An imprint of Greenwood Publishing Group, Inc.

Printed in the United States of America

∞

The paper used in this book complies with the
Permanent Paper Standard issued by the National
Information Standards Organization (Z39.48–1984).

10 9 8 7 6 5 4 3 2 1

The development of this work was supported by a grant from the Office of Educational
Research and Improvement/U.S. Department of Education. However, the opinions
expressed herein do not necessarily reflect the position or policy of that agency and no
official endorsement should be inferred.

Contents

Background and Overview

JOSIE G. BAIN AND JOAN L. HERMAN

For quite some time, serious concern has been expressed about the quality of education that is provided for our youngsters. Fueling public interest, *A Nation at Risk*, the *Carnegie Report*,[1] and other published reports recorded strong disenchantment with public education and gave legislators, educators, and parents a challenge that could not be ignored. As a result, reforms have been launched and much has been done in subsequent years to address the challenge. However, while some progress has been noted, the performance of our minority students remains a disturbing problem.

During the planned process for the Center for Research on Evaluation, Standards, and Student Testing (CRESST), the staff articulated its commitment to assuring educational quality for all students. It was that belief, confirmed by the conference from which this book arose, that the efforts of any one group, such as educational researchers, were clearly insufficient to the scope and importance of the problem. We believed that we needed to be a part of a larger effort, drawing from teachers, parents, community organizations, and government, from people who had recent and direct insight on the problem. We wanted a gathering where information would be shared, positive courses of actions could be evaluated, and collaborative efforts could be created. Consequently, the idea of bringing such people together evolved.

We broached this idea when we participated in the 1986 annual meeting of the Council of the Great City Schools in New York, where the magnitude of the problem was reinforced. At this meeting members concurred with the need for action and raised such questions as: What are the intergenerational issues? How much investment is society willing to make in the illiterate? What kinds of jobs will be available for the underachiever, and in what quantity will they be available? What role ought research and evaluation play in solving the dilemma? And finally, what really works? Where can we find processes and programs that actually and consistently address the problems of the underachiever?

Members of the council agreed that there were many promising educational practices in the field, but some questioned whether such practices had been validated sufficiently and whether they truly could be replicated in other localities. The council, through its president, Dr. Richard Green, and its executive director, Dr. Samuel Husk, expressed great interest in the problem and offered all possible assistance to efforts that might be made. This concern added impetus to CRESST's desire to offer suggestions for intervention through planned research and evaluation.

Pursuing the problem further, we discovered that many individuals, community groups, and organizations were approaching the problem of underachieving minority students with a sense of urgency. Most felt something could and should be done. Two such groups were the National Urban League and the National Council of La Raza.

The Urban League has launched a five-year national educational initiative designed to improve the educational performance of Black students. John Jacob, president of the National Urban League, in the formal announcement on September 30, 1986, described the program by saying:

Our educational initiative will mobilize the community to define key issues, maximize the use of existing resources, build coalitions and support for change, and implement concrete action plans. Our initiative is not an exercise in confrontation, but a program that mobilizes citizens and institutions in a collaborative effort to make the public schools work better for our children. We have no illusions that a quick fix can solve the crisis.

Similarly, demonstrating its serious commitment, the National Council of La Raza has established a multiyear effort, the Innovative Education Project, that is designed to develop, demonstrate, evaluate, and replicate five innovative community-based approaches to reduce the dropout rate and improve the quality of education available to Hispanics. La Raza's president and chief executive officer, Raul Yzaguirre, says about the project: "There is an overwhelming need for community-based educational programs which can supplement school offerings, work with youths who have dropped out or been pushed out of school systems, and help parents and teachers increase their ability to help Hispanic children learn."

Building on these shared interests and as a first step in an intervention process, CRESST initiated a national conference in collaboration with the Council of the Great City Schools, the National Urban League, and the National Council of La Raza, with principal financial support from the U.S. Department of Education, Office of Educational Research and Improvement.

Held at the UCLA Faculty Center on June 25–26, 1987, *Making Schools Work for Underachieving Minority Students: Next Steps for Research, Policy and Practice* was planned to further a number of critical goals:

- To focus national attention on the problem of underachieving minority students and call for action to improve their educational achievement.
- To share and promote dialogue on promising practices that can help solve the current educational crisis for these students.
- To foster active collaboration on creative solutions among practitioner, policy maker, and researcher constituencies.
- To identify critical R&D needs and collaborative arrangements as important next steps toward problem solution.
- To collaborate on CRESST's research agenda by specifically identifying significant testing and evaluation issues for the subsequent inquiry.

The conference brought together a distinguished group of approximately 200 educators, policy makers, and researchers to share the best of what we know about how to improve educational opportunities for minority students and to deliberate on their implications for research, policy, and practice. Those who served as keynoters and presenters were leading figures in the field of education. They represented a broad range of viewpoints, experience, and academic training, and each participant had keen interest in the topic and felt that change was possible.

The agenda featured a provocative mix of keynote addresses, special topic panels, small working discussion groups, and opportunities for more informal interaction and conversation. The first session, "Our National Dilemma," commenced with consideration of the current status of education for underachieving minority students and the special problems that underlie it. Distinguished researchers presented their views of the roots of this national dilemma and of the critical and sustained action required for its resolution with reactions from two school superintendents.

"Bridges to Change: More Effective Practices" featured smaller group panels that presented brief overviews of promising approaches for addressing specific problem areas. Each conference participant chose two from among five available problem-focused panels. Composed of both researchers and practitioners, the panels dealt with Creating Effective Instructional Programs for All Students, Reducing the Drop-Out Rate, Preparing Students for Success at the Postsecondary Level, Assuring Effective Programs for Language Minority Students, and Improving Teacher Quality.

Issues of evaluation and testing, subthemes during the first day, became primary foci on the morning of the second day. Keynote addresses on "The Role of Testing and Evaluation in Effective Schools," were followed by a number of small group panels that focused on: Creating Better Evaluation Strategies to Monitor and Improve School Effectiveness, and Developing

Alternative Strategies for Better Diagnosing and Meeting Individual Student Learning Needs.

The final activities were designed to encourage conference participants to actively synthesize what they had learned from the conference and to identify next steps, including consideration of potential collaborations among conference attendees and the constituencies they represented. Following brief keynote presentations on a variety of models of collaboration, participants were assigned to small working groups to discuss the implications of the two-day proceedings for future school improvement efforts; to identify implications for local, state, and federal action; and to articulate implications for national R&D, particularly in the areas of testing and evaluation.

This book's organization follows the same structure. The chapters that compose the book give a sense of the substance of the conference presentations. What is more difficult to convey is a sense of the enthusiasm, urgency, and commitment of the assembled group.

NOTE

1. National Commission on Excellence in Education, *A Nation at Risk: The Imperative for Educational Reform. A Report to the Nation and the Secretary of Education* (Washington, DC: U.S. Department of Education, 1983); and Carnegie Foundation for the Advancement of Teaching, *The Condition of Teaching: A State-by-State Analysis* (Princeton, NJ: Princeton University Press, 1988).

PART I

Our National Dilemma

ONE

The Educationally Disadvantaged Are Still Among Us

HENRY LEVIN

Most of the recent reports on reforming American education ignore the problem of the educationally disadvantaged. Pupils defined as educationally disadvantaged lack the home and community resources to fully benefit from recent educational reforms as well as from conventional schooling practices. Because of poverty, cultural differences, or linguistic differences, they tend to have low academic achievement and experience high secondary school dropout rates. Such students are especially concentrated among minority groups, immigrants, non-English speaking families, and economically disadvantaged populations.[1]

The educationally disadvantaged begin their schooling with lower standardized achievement than their nondisadvantaged peers. Typically, they rank at about the 15th percentile in achievement performance throughout their schooling careers. Unfortunately, that standard of performance means that such students fall farther and farther behind in achievement and are about three years behind grade level by the end of secondary school. As a consequence of both their poor achievement and other factors, educationally disadvantaged students have exceedingly high dropout rates, approaching 50 percent according to recent data.

The War on Poverty, launched some two decades ago, made the educationally disadvantaged a central target of educational policy. In stark contrast, recent policy statements such as that of the National Commission on Excellence in Education *A Nation at Risk* or the report by U.S. Secretary of Education William Bennett, *First Lessons: A Report on Elementary Education in America* virtually neglect the disadvantaged as an educational priority.[2]

Unfortunately, few congratulations are in order. The vanishing of the disadvantaged from policy reports and the media is a reflection of political expediency or wishful thinking rather than an educational triumph. The battle to overcome educational disadvantage did not end in victory, but in neglect and disarray. At present the educationally disadvantaged are estimated to constitute about 30 percent of elementary and secondary enrollments, a far higher proportion than in the 1960s. And their numbers are increasing more rapidly than the nondisadvantaged. In states such as California and Texas they will account for the majority of enrollments during the next decade. Moreover, gains in educational achievement for the disadvantaged have been so marginal, that their educational situation is as serious today as it was in the 1960s.

Why are the disadvantaged increasing so rapidly? First, the groups that constitute such populations are relatively young and have far higher birthrates than nondisadvantaged populations. Second, the United States is experiencing a wave of documented immigration that is unprecedented since the turn of the century, and added to this are huge numbers of undocumented immigrants. Most of today's immigrants to the United States derive from rural and impoverished circumstances where little schooling was provided. Third, the proportion of children in poverty families—many of them female-headed—is higher today than it was a decade ago. Together, these three factors are fueling the rapid upsurge in disadvantaged students. This phenomenon has overwhelmed the schools of the largest cities in the United States where a majority of their enrollments are disadvantaged.

SOCIAL CONSEQUENCES OF INACTION

In the absence of substantial educational interventions, the rapidly increasing population of educationally disadvantaged students will ultimately emerge as a large and growing population of disadvantaged adults. The potential consequences of ignoring the needs of these students will afflict not only the disadvantaged but also the larger society as well. These consequences include: (1) the emergence of a dual society with a large and poorly educated underclass, (2) massive disruption in higher education, (3) reduced economic competitiveness of the nation as well as states and industries most heavily impacted by these populations, and (4) higher costs for public services that are a response to poverty.

As the disadvantaged population increases without appropriate educational interventions to improve its situation substantially, this group is likely to form the underclass of a dual society. Composed of racial and ethnic minorities and persons from economically disadvantaged origins, its members will face high unemployment rates, low earnings, and menial occupations. At the same time the political power of the disadvantaged will increase as its numbers and potential votes rise. The specter of a dual society suggests great political conflict and potential social upheaval. Economic and educational inequality in conjunction with equal political rights are the ingredients for future polarization and intense political, social, and economic conflict and instability.

The implications for higher education are also severe. Larger and larger numbers of educationally disadvantaged will mean that public institutions of higher education will have to become more restrictive in their admissions criteria or more devoted to remedial academic work. Either direction is fraught with problems. Substantial remedial activities will require additional university resources, and student programs will take longer to complete their degrees. All of this means that costs to universities and students will spiral. The increase in remedial functions will alter the character of public higher education with a tendency to water down the overall curriculum and reduce standards as pressures increase to improve the application of such courses to degree programs.

Alternatively, the universities may seek to restrict admissions through greater reliance on standardized test scores and more academic course requirements so that fewer persons from disadvantaged populations can participate in higher education. Even now a disproportionately small share of minority and educationally disadvantaged students are eligible to participate in public higher education because of their high dropout rates and their poor academic records in secondary school. But these disproportions will be exacerbated by creating an elite system for admissions, a result that flies in the face of the democratic mission conferred upon public systems of higher education supported by tax revenues collected from the entire population. At the same time that higher education would become more exclusive, those who were increasingly excluded would be expanding their political power at both the state and federal levels. Clearly, such a policy will lead to political and social turmoil, both on and off the campuses.

A further consequence of the present treatment of the educationally disadvantaged will be a serious deterioration in the quality of the labor force. As long as the disadvantaged were just a small minority of the population, they could be absorbed into seasonal and low-skill jobs or relegated to unemployment without direct consequences for the overall economy. But as their numbers grow and they continue to experience low achievement and high dropout rates, a larger and larger portion of the available labor force will be unprepared for available jobs. Here we refer not only to managerial, professional, and technical jobs, but to the huge and burgeoning numbers of lower level service jobs that are characterizing the economy. Clerical workers, cashiers, and salespeople need basic skills in oral and written communications, computations, and reasoning—skills that are not guaranteed to the educationally disadvantaged. A U.S. government study in 1976 found that while 13 percent of all 17 year olds were classified as functionally illiterate, the percentages of illiterates among Hispanics and Blacks were 56 and 44 percent, respectively.[3]

The United States is already facing great difficulties in maintaining a

competitive economic stance relative to other industrialized and industrial-
izing nations. As the disadvantaged become an increasing and even a dominant share of the labor force in some states and regions, their inadequate
educational preparation will undermine the competitive position of the industries and states in which they work and our national economic status.
Employers will suffer lagging productivity, higher training costs, and competitive disadvantages that will result in lost sales and profits. State and
federal governments will suffer a declining tax base and loss of tax revenues,
thus curtailing funds for improving education and other services.

Finally, the economic losses will come at a time of rising demands for
public services. More and more citizens will rely upon public assistance to
meet their needs, and increasing numbers of undereducated teens and adults
will rely upon illegal activities to fill idle time and obtain the income that
is not obtainable through legal ones. The inability to find regular employment
that is remunerative enough to overcome poverty will require greater public
interventions to support the rising poverty population and to counter drugs,
prostitution, theft, and other activities associated with poverty. This development will not only make the United States a less desirable place to live,
but it will also increase the costs of police services and criminal justice as
well as public assistance. Pressures will be placed on the middle class to pay
higher taxes at the same time that incomes are threatened by a flagging
economy, creating an additional source of political conflict as besieged tax-
payers resist tax increases.

THE NEW REFORMS AND THE DISADVANTAGED

Although the rhetoric of the recent state reforms stresses the improvement
of the education of all children, including the disadvantaged, this emphasis
is not supported by the substance of the reforms. The educationally disadvantaged are systematically neglected. The reforms stress raising standards
at the secondary level, without providing additional resources or new strategies to assist the disadvantaged in meeting these higher standards. Any
strategy for improving the educational plight of the disadvantaged must begin
at the elementary level and must be dedicated to preparing children for
doing high-quality work in secondary school. Simply raising standards at the
secondary level without making it possible for the disadvantaged to meet
the new standards is more likely to increase their dropping out.

Two of the most typical recent state reforms are the setting of competency
standards for a diploma and raising course requirements for graduation.
Paradoxically, both of these may contribute to increasing dropouts of disadvantaged students who already have difficulty in meeting the old standards. Disadvantaged students enter secondary school with achievement
levels that are two years or more below those of their nondisadvantaged
counterparts. Even present standards are difficult to meet with this handicap.

Unless this gap can be closed prior to entering secondary school, the higher standards will serve to further discourage the disadvantaged rather than improve their performance.

In this respect, the current wave of reforms may be meritorious for many nondisadvantaged students, while actually serving as obstacles for improving the education of the disadvantaged. Reforms for the disadvantaged must address their needs directly, rather than assuming that a rise in general standards will automatically solve the needs of all students.

WHAT NEEDS TO BE DONE

Twenty years of experience have shown that there do exist instructional interventions that promise at least modest improvement in the achievement of the disadvantaged. For example, peer tutoring, cooperative learning, mastery learning, computer-assisted instruction, preschool programs, and new curricula have all shown some success in this regard. The major challenge is that these successes have been exceedingly modest relative to the achievement gap that exists. While each of these might systematically close some of the achievement gap—for example, raising achievement from the 15th to the 20th percentile—gains of this magnitude do not provide a substantial improvement in the educational or occupational fortunes of the disadvantaged.

Progress toward further improving the education of the disadvantaged is limited by the very way in which we think about and address the problem. We know that disadvantaged children begin school with a learning gap in those areas valued by schools and mainstream economic and social institutions. But remedial interventions are not adequate unless they ultimately contribute to a substantial narrowing or closing of that gap by bringing the disadvantaged up to the same range of academic performance as their non-disadvantaged peers.

The existing model of intervention assumes that disadvantaged students will not be able to maintain a normal instructional pace, that the mere provision of remedial services will close the learning gap, and that no time-table is required. Thus the remedial model consists essentially of placing such youngsters in a less demanding instructional setting without a time limit. Although this may appear rational and even compassionate, we must consider its consequences.

First, this process reduces learning expectations on the part of both the child and the educators who are assigned to teach them functions, and stigmatizes both groups with a level of inferiority. Such a stigma contributes to weak social support for the activity, low social status for the participants, and negative self-images for the persons engaged in remediation. The combination of low social status and low expectations is tantamount to treating such students and their educators as educational discards who are marginal to the agenda of mainstream education. These are the unhealthiest of all possible conditions under which to expect significant educational progress. *In contrast, an effective approach focuses on creating learning activities which are characterized by high expectations and status for the participants.*

Second, the usual treatment of the educationally disadvantaged is not designed to bring students up to grade level. There exist no timetables for doing so, and there are rarely any incentives or even provisions for students to move from remedial instruction back to the mainstream. In fact, since students in compensatory or remedial situations are expected to progress at a slower than "normal" pace, a self-fulfilling prophecy is realized as they fall farther and farther behind their nondisadvantaged counterparts. The result is that once a disadvantaged student is relegated to remedial or compensatory interventions, that student will be expected to learn at a slower rate, and the achievement gap between advantaged and disadvantaged students will grow. While the gap may be measured in months of achievement in first grade, it will have grown to years of difference by secondary school. *A successful program must set a deadline for closing the achievement gap so that ultimately educationally disadvantaged children will be able to benefit from mainstream instruction.*

Third, by deliberately slowing the pace of instruction to a crawl, a heavy emphasis is placed on endless repetition of material through drill and practice. The result is that the school experience to the disadvantaged lacks intrinsic vitality, and the slow rate of progress just reinforces low expectations. Interesting applications and assignments are omitted in favor of drudgery, on the premise that these fundamentals must be learned before anything more challenging can proceed. Both language skills and mathematics are virtually substanceless, emphasizing mechanics over content. Such a joyless experience further negates the child's educational experience and diminishes the possibility that the child will view the school as a positive environment in which progress can be made. *An effective curriculum for the disadvantaged child must not only be faster paced, but must actively engage the interests of such children so that they will be motivated to learn.*

In addition to these shortcomings, most compensatory educational programs do not involve parents sufficiently or draw adequately upon available community resources. Furthermore, the professional staff at the school level are often omitted from participating in the important educational decisions that they must implement. Such an omission means that teachers are expected to dedicate themselves to the implementation of programs that do not necessarily reflect their professional judgments, a condition that is not likely to spur great enthusiasm. *The implementation of successful educational programs to address the needs of the educationally disadvantaged will require the involvement of parents and the extensive participation of teachers in formulating the interventions that will be provided.* Given the severity of these impediments to the effective schooling of the educationally disadvantaged, it is little wonder that even the most successful programs have produced modest results. These outcomes persist despite the good intentions and efforts of the many educators who work with the disadvantaged. It is the basic approach and its underlying assumptions that are at fault.

A NEW APPROACH

What we have learned from the experience of the last twenty years is that an effective approach to educating the disadvantaged must be characterized by high expectations, deadlines by which such children will be performing at grade level, stimulating instructional programs, planning by the educational staff who will offer the program, and the use of all available resources, including the parents of the students. At its heart, the educational intervention must be viewed as transitional. That is, the intervention will be designed to close the achievement gap so that such students can benefit from regular instruction after some period of intervention.

In order to meet these goals, I have been working with a group of colleagues at Stanford University's School of Education to design a program of Accelerated Schools for the Disadvantaged. The Accelerated School is a transitional elementary school that is designed to bring disadvantaged students up to grade level by completion of the sixth grade. The goal of the school is to enable disadvantaged students to take advantage of mainstream secondary school instruction by effectively closing the achievement gap in elementary school. The approach is also designed to be a dropout prevention program by eliminating the most important single cause of dropping out: serious achievement deficits.

The school is based upon an accelerated curriculum that is designed to bring all children up to grade level. The entire organization of the school will focus on this goal rather than limiting interventions for the disadvantaged to "pull out" sessions in a school where the dominant agenda addresses other goals. This approach requires an assessment system that evaluates the performance of each child at school entry and sets a trajectory for meeting the overall school goal for that child. Periodic evaluations on wide-spectrum, standardized achievement tests as well as tailored assessments created by school staff for each strand of the curriculum will enable the school to see if the child is on the anticipated trajectory.

Major curriculum aspects include a heavily language-based approach, even in mathematics. Language use will be emphasized across the curriculum, with an early introduction to writing and reading for meaning. An emphasis will also be placed upon applications of new tools to everyday problems and events in order to stress the usefulness of what is being taught and learned.

Parents will be deeply involved in two ways. First, they and school representatives will be asked to sign a written agreement that clarifies the obligations of parents, school staff, and students. The agreement will be explained to parents and translated, if necessary. Second, the parents will be given opportunities to interact with the school program and to be given training for providing active assistance to their children. Parents will be asked to set high educational expectations for their children and to support their success as well as to encourage reading.

Other features include the implementation of an extended-day program in which rest periods, physical activities, the arts, and a time period for independent assignments or homework will be provided. During this period, college students and senior citizen volunteers will work with individual students to provide learning assistance. Since many of the children are latchkey children, the extension of the school day is likely to be attractive to parents. Instructional strategies will also include peer tutoring and co-operative learning. Both have been shown to be especially effective with disadvantaged students.

These broad features of the accelerated school are designed to make it a total institution for the disadvantaged, rather than just grafting on compensatory or remedial classes to elementary schools with a conventional agenda. However, the actual choice of curriculum and instructional strategies will be decided by the instructional staff of the school. That is, the decision-making approach is a school-based one in which those who will be providing the instruction will make the decisions. Each school will have a site team composed of instructional staff and a representative of the central office of the district. The Stanford group will assist in the planning process by providing information, technical assistance, and help in initiating a school-based governance model. But each school will set out a program that is consonant with the strengths of the district and the local staff. In this way, the reform will be a "bottom-up" approach in which the professionals who are providing the instruction will make the decisions they will implement and evaluate.

During the 1986–87 school year, the Stanford group developed a full information clearinghouse on the Accelerated School, training capabilities for staff, and an assessment model. At the same time they worked with site teams at schools in San Francisco and Redwood City, California, to plan programs for Accelerated Schools that opened in the autumn of 1987. We believe that this approach has a high probability of success because of its emphasis on the instrumental goal of bringing students up to grade level by the completion of sixth grade; its stress on acceleration of learning and high expectations; its reliance on a professional model of school governance that is attractive to educators; its capacity to benefit from instructional strategies that have shown good results for the disadvantaged within the limits of existing models of compensatory education; and its ability to draw upon all of the resources available to the community including parents and senior citizens.

In large measure we believe that the approach can be implemented within existing resource constraints, including federal and state categorical grants.

The only aspect that will have obvious, additional cost implications is the extension of the school day. Finally, this approach does not require new legislation at either the state or federal level, but can be implemented with local initiatives by educators and parents.

By solving much of the problem of the educationally disadvantaged at the elementary level, we hope to reduce the risk of dropping out and to save much of the cost of secondary school dropout programs. We believed that improved levels of school achievement and self-concept will also go far to reduce problems of violence, drugs, and teen pregnancies of secondary school students. Finally, it must be stressed emphatically that unless we take a bold stand to intervene now in behalf of the disadvantaged, we will soon be reaping the distasteful harvest of our neglect.

NOTES

1. A fuller review of the issues that are covered in this chapter and the evidence supporting them is found in Henry M. Levin, *Educational Reform for Disadvantaged Students: An Emerging Crisis* (Washington, DC: The National Education Association, 1986). Critical and comprehensive views of what we have learned from twenty years of research on the education of the disadvantaged are found in a group of papers prepared for the Conference on Effects of Alternative Designs in Compensatory Education, sponsored by the Office of Educational Research and Improvement of the U.S. Department of Education (June 17–18, 1986). See particularly: Penelope Peterson, "Selecting Students and Services for Compensatory Education: Lessons from Aptitude-Treatment Interaction Research"; Thomas A. Romberg, "Mathematics for Compensatory School Programs"; and Jere Brophy, "Research Linking Teacher Behavior to Student Achievement: Potential Implications for Instruction of Chapter I Students."

2. *A Nation at Risk: The Imperative for Educational Reform. A Report to the Nation and the Secretary of Education* (Washington, DC: U.S. Department of Education, 1983); and W. J. Bennett, *First Lessons: A Report on Elementary Education in America* (Washington, DC: U.S. Department of Education, 1986).

3. National Assessment of Educational Progress, *Functional Literacy and Basic Reading Performance* (Washington, DC: Office of Education, U.S. Department of Health, Education, and Welfare, 1976).

TWO

Building Quality Relationships

JAMES COMER

There is probably no more critical an issue facing our country from the standpoint of individual students, their families, their community and society, than that of improving our schools for underachieving minorities, and yet, as we all know, we are not giving the issue the kind of attention that it deserves. I would like to share my understanding of the problem in several ways. First, I will describe just a little bit about my own background, because it raises some of the questions that got me interested in the problems of education in the first place, and mention some of the insights I have gained from this personal background. Then I will talk about the nature of the problem as I understand it, and the impact of science and technology on community, family, and the development of children over the past 70 years. I will stress its impact on education in particular. I will talk about why minorities have been most adversely affected by the technological and social changes that have been taking place. Finally, I will briefly describe our intervention and research project in New Haven, Connecticut—not as a model, but as the source of my recent insights concerning the education of minority students.

MY OWN BACKGROUND

I am from a low-income family, and a disproportionate number of the underachieving young people that we are concerned about are from low-income families, although too many middle-income minority students are also underachieving, for reasons I will discuss. Both of my parents were from the rural South: my mother from Mississippi, my father from Alabama. My mother worked as a domestic in the North and had absolutely no education. My father worked in a steel mill and had only a sixth-grade education. Nevertheless, together the two of them sent their five children to college, where we earned 13 college degrees among us.

As I describe in a book about my family that will be coming out very soon,[1] my three best friends from elementary school days, who were from the same kind of background as I was, who were just as able on the playground, in the church, and a variety of other places, did not do well in school and had a downhill course in life. One died early of alcoholism, one spent a good part of his life in jail, the other has been in and out of mental institutions all of his life. The only difference between my friends' and our own family's experience was that my parents, through their connections with the church and other affiliations, developed attitudes, values, and interactive skills that allowed them to interact with our schools and school people in a way that supported us and taught us interactive skills and ways of managing ourselves in schools that enabled us to succeed. I was interested in the fact that those former classmates did not succeed although they had the ability, and that interest led me to my career in this field. The question I have always had is, "Why can't the schools provide children with what they do not receive at home and make it possible for them to achieve at the level of their ability?" That was in the back of my mind when I began my work in schools.

THE NATURE OF THE PROBLEM

Let us turn now to the impact of science and technology on our society and the changes over the years that I feel have led to the academic underachievement in this country until the 1950s, when education became the ticket of admission to living-wage jobs. You needed that job to be able to provide for yourself, your family, and carry out all your adult responsibilities. Prior to that point, you could drop out of school and still meet all your responsibilities. After the 1950s, a disproportionate number of people who left school were on a downhill course.

Now, if this is true, why can't we just show young people the light and convince them to stay in school? Unfortunately, it takes more than understanding that there are undesirable outcomes of not achieving well in school to keep students from failing. It really requires adequate support for the students' development, from infancy onward, and it requires adequate schools—schools functioning in such a way that they can promote the success of young people. That is the problem.

In the society of yesterday, it was not a great problem because we were a nation of small towns and rural areas. Even our cities were basically collections of small towns. Work and play were local and often communal. There was a low level of mobility and communications were limited. People had social interactions in their churches and clubs and a variety of other activities within their localities. There was an on-going interaction among authority figures to develop a great deal of trust in one another. They at least knew what to expect from one another. There was a sense of place. Even though your place might not be a desirable place in the society, you had a sense of place. Life was very predictable. There was a sense of community as a result of past conditions. The school was a natural part of the community and there was an automatic transfer of authority from home to school as a result of the interactions that authority figures had on a regular basis.

Those authority figures were really the source of all truth for young people. Everything they knew about the world came to them from those important authority figures, who could censor the truth and censure you for not behaving in certain ways. They spoke with a common tongue about what was right or wrong, good or bad, and if you asked one what was right or wrong, good or bad, you might as well have asked them all, because they were all saying the same thing.

One example of this was when I would go to the A & P store with my parents every Friday, and there was never a time that I did not bump into someone from my school—the custodian, a teacher, the principal, the clerk. Someone from the school was there, and there was always an exchange of information between them and my parents about how I was doing in school, and what was expected, and what would happen if I did not do well. I always knew that there was only so much acting up that was possible in school, given the fact that I was going to meet them on Friday in the grocery store.

One day, when I was eleven years old and about to get into trouble, a "sister" from our church saw me and before I even got home, my father knew what I was up to. Now, I was fortunate. I had one of those progressive fathers who didn't spank me, but who pointed out to me that if I wanted to be respected by the people in my church and my neighborhood, there were certain things that I could do and certain things I could not do. Since I wanted to be respected, I did not do those things, at least not where anybody could see me. My point is that the home, the school, the neighborhood, everybody involved was aiding my social development and that of all the children in my community.

After World War II, science and technology were applied to every aspect of life. As a result, we became a nation of metropolitan areas with high mobility. You could, and often did, work long distances from where you lived, and you would not interact on a regular basis with parents, teachers, administrators—all of the traditional authority figures in society. In addition, there was massive visual communication as a result of television.

Society became more complex as a result of these conditions, and there was less trust because people did not get to know each other on a regular basis. There was less of a sense of place, less of a sense of community. There was increasing distrust and alienation developing as a result of overall social conditions. Youngsters received more information than ever before in the history of the world from television. Television brought attitudes, values, and ways from around the world right to the children without any censorship or explanation by their parents or community. Very often these attitudes, values, and ways were in conflict with what parents were trying to teach their children.

I became personally aware of this situation when my daughter was about four years old. My wife and I were both working, and we had a housekeeper who liked to watch the "soaps." I was packing to go on a trip when my daughter came to me and very solemnly shook her finger at me and said, "Now don't you have an affair!" She was four. I was sixteen before I knew what an "affair" was.

Given these conditions I have briefly outlined, the complexity of the world, the amount of diversity of information that young people receive, it is understandable that they need the highest level of development than ever before needed to gain the necessary competence to function well as adults. They need more sustained and skilled adult help for development than has ever before been required. They need institutions that support their development over a longer period of time than ever before. In fact, they have less support today than in the past. There are many more families in which both parents are working than in previous years. There is more divorce today. There is more social stress. There are more parents who, because of past social conditions, are without the kinds of skills that would allow them to help their children function well.

Schools have not responded adequately to the challenge. Schools remain hierarchical and authoritarian, inadequately flexible. They can not respond to the problems right in front of them. The training of teachers and administrators is such that many really do not understand children and do not understand the behaviors that they are confronted with.

The transfer of authority from home to school is no longer automatic. It is conditional, it depends on the quality of relationships between home and school. A teacher pointed this out to me recently when she said that a six year old in her class, after she explained the expectations of the school, raised his hand and said, "Teacher, my momma said I don't hafta do anything you say." Very different from in the past when there was an automatic transfer of authority from home to school.

Thus the problem is that students need the highest level of development to achieve well in school and to achieve well in life, and yet we increasingly have families that are unable to support such development and schools that have not been responsive. In fact, there has been very little understanding of the relationship between good personal development and academic learning. We still think of academic learning in a very mechanical fashion. It is something that is merely put in (the child), the learning machine (brain) acts on it, and the child is then "educated." We often view behavior solely as a willful act; thus troublesome behavior, as a willful bad act, deserves to be punished. In light of these misconceptions, I would like to review very quickly the whole issue of human development, how it relates to academic learning, and why it is the problem that I think is central and must be addressed if we are to help underachieving minority children.

Our society, like all societies, has certain tasks that we ask everybody to be able to accomplish by the time they are adults. We ask people to get specific training so that they can hold the kinds of jobs that are available today so that they can live successfully in families and neighborhoods, and so that they can participate as responsible citizens of society. But children are not born capable of carrying out any of these things. They are born totally dependent, with only the biological potentials that must be developed over time. They are born with aggressive energy that can be destructive to themselves and everybody around them unless it is very carefully channeled into the energy of life survival.

They are born with the capacity for relationships and we must act on this to make it possible for children to develop and learn. The caretakers— parents, in particular, teachers and others—must interact with and provide for the basic needs of the child in a way that the child establishes an emotional attachment and bonding that allows the parents then to lead the child across developmental pathways that lead to mature development. There are many pathways, but several are crucial for academic learning: social-interactive, psycho-emotional, moral, speech and language, and intellectual, cognitive, or academic. I include academic at the end of that list because the academic is really a function of overall good development. When children are developing well, they have the highest potential for learning in school.

Let me give just a couple of examples of what I mean by adult-child interactions that help children grow. A two year old who wants to play with the ball another child is playing with does not know that he or she cannot just take that ball. They will do it, and if the other child resists, they will often simply hit him in the mouth and take the ball anyway. Now the parent who is present has to say, "Michael, you cannot take Johnny's ball. You'll have to go do something else 'til Johnny is through, or maybe you can work it out and you can play together." The parent spells out the options and because of the close parent-child relationship, the child wants to please the parent and acts appropriately. In the process, the child begins to develop along all those developmental pathways—the social rules of the game, controlling the impulse to hit, and handling any feelings about that situation. What is right and what is wrong is learned in that situation. Speech and language are involved, as are thinking, learning, and cognitive development.

Parents who are functioning well and understand the importance of reading will often read to their children at the end of the day, an emotionally good time when the child has the parent to himself or herself in the big, busy world. Reading, and that moment, becomes emotionally charged and a positive emotional experience. Many children's stories are designed to deal with fears and anxieties that children have, and so they want to hear them again and again. After a few times hearing the story, the child has associated the page, the picture with the words he hears, and begins to "read" from memory and his parents get all excited. "Look Mom, Johnny can read!" And when grandma calls on weekends, "Guess what Grandma? Johnny can read!" Johnny hears all of these important, powerful adults excited about the fact that he can read, so he wants to read more and more. He wants to master everything in his environment to please those powerful adults until it becomes important to please himself on his own. And that is the beginning of the motivation for learning to read and to becoming an achiever.

In addition, that child probably notices that his parent starts reading at the top of a page and reads from top down, reads from left to right, and explains the story in certain ways. All of those are prereading skills, and that child goes to school already reading or at least prepared to learn to read. This impresses the teacher. Teachers like bright kids who seem curious, who seem to have skills, and who seem to be able to handle themselves and behave well. These characteristics make it easier for teachers to relate well to such a child, and for the child to make an attachment to them. A similar attachment or bonding that took place with parents takes place with school staff, and that allows the school staff to motivate and support the child for development in school. It allows the child to imitate, internalize, and identify with the attitudes, values, the ways of school people, and things that are going on in school.

The child who is able to have such experiences develops a sense of competence and confidence, wins the approval of the people around him or her, develops personal esteem, and is motivated to continue to grow and develop and learn. The opposite occurs for children who have not had preschool experiences that prepare them to go to school and present themselves in a similar kind of way. Those children very often have experiences in groups and families that lead to a downhill course.

Now, the question is: Who are these families? The answer is: A disproportionate number of them are Blacks, Hispanics, and Native Americans, because the experiences of those groups have been very different from other groups. I will discuss these experiences very briefly, not to accuse or excuse, or to blame, or to promote guilt, but to think in terms of understanding what has happened and how we can develop effective interventions. I will talk only about the Black experience because that is the one I know most about, but there are similarities among all three groups.

I will start with the Black experience in West Africa. Most Black Americans are from West Africa, where there was a tight-knit political, economic, and social system that was integrated into the kinship system of those areas. Out of the relationships and the social organizations, families developed a sense of direction and values, were motivated to perform in certain ways, and were able to rely on certain qualities of relationships that were prescribed and expected. These were largely communal societies, with relationships, sharing, and a sense of belonging being very important.

Slavery resulted in the dislocation of people, the disruption of kinship systems and all of the guiding, supporting institutions, the discontinuity of culture and loss of social cohesion. This is very different from the White American immigrant's experience, and it is important to talk about the White immigrant experience briefly because consciously and unconsciously, we use that as a model of the way all groups in our society adjusted and the way all families functioned.

Immigrants came to America with their religion largely intact. They came with their language intact. Many came in groups from the same hometown and relocated to the same town, operating as homogenous ethnic enclaves until they were able to make it into the mainstream of the society. Educational and social opportunities were available almost instantly, and all of these conditions promoted family stability. Those families were able to undergo a kind of three-generational upward movement and development.

The prevailing economic conditions allowed people to work, provide for their families, and provide family stability. Conditions allowed those parents then to help their children grow and to learn in school. The opportunities in the mainstream of society almost immediately made it possible for them to want to gain an education and to gain skills and contacts in order to make it into the mainstream of the society. The men could vote almost immediately. They had political, economic, and social power. The educational-social opportunities made it possible for tremendous progress within the three generations. The first generation (the immigrants who arrived before 1900) could be uneducated and unskilled, but adequately provide for their families, which created the stability that allowed one to achieve moderate education and skill during the next generation, 1900 to 1945. Stability in the job market, with moderate education during that period, allowed those families to provide their children with experiences that made it possible for them to function well during that next (third) period, between 1945 and 1980, when one needed a high level of education and skill to be successful in the job market. During this postindustrial era, when even with a high level of education and skill many adults are in some difficulty in the job market, finding a job became highly competitive.

The Black experience in America made this type of three-generational movement impossible. Slavery was a system of forced dependency. Food, clothing, shelter, and all of the basic needs were provided by an outside force, the master. There was no future. No matter how hard you worked, the achievement was for the master, not for your family, not for your group. There was no sense of control. Profound powerlessness is a major social-psychological strike. Even one's sexual experience and major social relationships could be determined and supervised by the master. These conditions affected the functioning of the group and the family.

There were behavioral consequences as well, such as acting up and acting out behavior on the part of many, and violence and aggression often against other slaves. There was passive-aggressive behavior, doing as little as one could, working slowly without being punished, leaving a plow out in the field to rust. There was apathy, withdrawal, and depression within and among the slaves. All of these situations created troublesome attitudes, and in some families the attitudes and behaviors were transmitted from generation to generation.

After the Civil War, conditions were not much better. Through subterfuge and terror, Blacks were denied the vote, and as a result of that, political, economic, and social power was not possible. The Black family and community could not develop mainstream knowledge, skills, or contacts. Only limited education was available. Even as recently as the 1940s, four to eight times as much money was spent on the education of a White child as on that of a Black child in the eight states that had 80 percent of the Black population. This was a significant problem because the period of 1900 to the 1940s was when most of the United States was preparing for the last stage of the industrial revolution, a time when one needed a high level of education and skill to be successful.

The same problem existed in higher education. As late as the mid–1960s, two prestigious White women's colleges had an endowment that was about one-half the endowment of Harvard. And that one-half endowment of Harvard was more than that of all the more than 100 Black colleges put together. Thus there was massive undereducation of the Black community well into the 1960s.

In spite of these negative social, economic, and political conditions, the church culture allowed many Black families to function relatively well and provided them with organization, a sense of direction, values, and motivation, and allowed them to achieve adult tasks regardless of their low income. The Black church culture also led to the creation of an educated nucleus of Blacks, which eventually led to the Civil Rights Movement. But by that time we were already into the 1960s, the middle of the third stage of the industrial era, and much of the Black community had by then been closed out of opportunities to obtain living-wage jobs. One needed mainstream knowledge, skills, and contacts to overcome the racial discrimination and problems that existed.

Blacks had been excluded from high-quality educational institutions and from the mainstream of economic and political contacts. Yet many Black families were still functioning well through the 1950s, at which point 80 percent of all Black families were two-parent families, and Black communities were largely safe places. Since the 1950s we have begun to see many families that once functioned well begin to function less well.

What we see now are Black families going in opposite directions. Most of those who were able to organize and be successful prior to the 1950s are functioning better than ever before; those who were not able to do so are having more difficulty than ever before. In addition, because of identity problems, because of racial barriers and social network pressures, many middle-income Black children are not functioning as well as they should, not achieving at a high enough level. In too many cases, achievement has been associated with being White, and nonachievement has been associated with being loyal to one's Black identity.

INTERVENTION AND RESEARCH PROJECT
IN NEW HAVEN

These were some of the most serious problems that we were confronted with when we started our intervention/research program in New Haven, Connecticut. In 1968, our Child Study Center team, which I directed with a social worker and special education teacher, began working with two schools that were 99 percent Black and almost all the children were poor. They were 32nd and 33rd out of 33 elementary schools in reading, language arts, and mathematics achievement; 19 and 18 months behind in those areas by the fourth grade. They had the worst attendance in the city, they had the worst behavior in the city. By 1984 the children in these two schools were tied for third and fourth, respectively, in the city in language arts and mathematics achievement, a year above grade level in one school, seven months above in the other, with no change in the socioeconomic makeup. In six of the previous seven years they were first or second in attendance, and we have not had a serious behavior problem in over a decade.

In our method of intervention, we thought about the conditions that had been a part of the Black community, and how we had to acknowledge what had changed in the society. Then we had to develop an intervention that dealt with dependency, that dealt with the feeling that there was no future and no sense of control. We also focused on the underdevelopment of the children who came from families that were under severe pressure. We realized that we had to empower all who were involved in the school, which is what I meant by school power, as described by my book with that title.[2] We had to involve students in active learning, not passive learning, in order to allow for self-actualization. We had to create something that would allow them to see that they had a future, and that they were in school to prepare for a positive future.

We therefore developed a major focus on the organizational management of the school that would give us flexibility to respond to the problems as we found them, and to develop a sense of trust to cope with the major problem of alienation, anger, distrust, hopelessness, and despair. We developed a governance and management group that was representative of all the adults in the school. They worked together on the social program to create a good climate of relationships that would allow teaching and learning to take place, and on the academic program of the school.

We developed a way to utilize mental health knowledge and skills and positive ways of relating to and supporting the development of the children without saying to people, "You don't know how to work with children." The new approach was carried out by a "mental health team" that focused not only on treating individual children, but also on helping the system function and create. The fundamental idea was to give teachers and other school staff members the kinds of skills that would allow them to understand children and to support their development. These ways of working decreased the behavior problems, allowed the teachers to feel better about themselves, caused them to have more energy and more time to focus on the teaching and learning tasks.

We also realized that we had to create a sense of future and a sense of opportunity, so we created a program called the Social Skills Curriculum for Inner City Children. We asked the parents in what areas they felt the children would need skills to be successful as adults, focusing toward adulthood even in elementary school. We came up with four areas: politics and government, business and economics, health and nutrition, and spiritual-leisure time activities. We then developed units that integrated teaching of basic skills, arts, and social skills. Our assumption was that many of the children were from families that were disconnected from the mainstream of society, and that many of the children had not received the kinds of experiences that would allow them to impress their teachers and make the ties that were necessary to be motivated for tomorrow.

We developed this approach first at the elementary school level and got dramatic improvement in achievement. We are now also doing it in the middle school and in high school. In the high school we are focusing very much on tying the young people into the real world. We are also bringing the real world—adults in many occupations and representing many mainstream agencies—into the school. The program seeks to help the real world understand what the students will need, and to help the students develop the skills and ties that have been generally denied the Black community. With knowledge of the real world, children can then be motivated to develop the skills that are necessary to be successful throughout their lives.

My final comment, about research and evaluation, is really a challenge to everyone. I think that the field of education has been very much influenced by psychology, with the focus on the individual. It has also been very much influenced by the results of experimental research, which has dominated the field so much that when we were trying to get support from the National Institute of Mental Health, they wanted to know about our independent variables, our dependent variables, and what was it specifically that we did that made the difference. I could not convey to them that it was a structure operating on a daily basis in the school that influenced the climate of relationships that made it possible for people to plan and that one could not put a finger on exactly what made the difference.

To understand our program, we really need an ecological perspective, because what we really did was to change the ecology of the school. We changed the quality of the relationships, the nature of the relationships, the way people interacted with each other. So the challenge is to find a way to evaluate our kind of approach and to understand what goes on in systems that allows them to change and allows the children to develop in a way in which they can achieve academically and develop the skills and the motivation to become responsible citizens, responsible family members, responsible and competent childrearers. Unless we do that we really have not achieved the mission of the school, because the mission of the school is not simply to teach basic academic skills, it is not simply to provide employers with future competent workers, but it is to prepare children to be responsible citizens of a democratic society.

NOTES

1. J. P. Comer, *Maggie's American Dream: The Life and Times of a Black Family* (New York: New American Library, 1988).

2. J. P. Comer, *School Power: Implications of an Intervention Project* (New York: Free Press, 1980).

THREE

Understanding the Dimensions of Our Problem

SAMUEL BETANCES

Through the years I have worked with school systems as a consultant on issues that have to do with curriculum and bilingual and multicultural education. Lately, I have introduced humor as a force in helping us, as educators, to set a tone and create a climate for the exchange of ideas about educational reform. We can laugh our way into accepting new ideas about serious issues in our profession. It is interesting that the people who are abusive to minorities have always used humor to mock people. Those of us who claim to be the friends of minorities are not as good at using humor as an ally. And I'd like to make a distinction between humor that amuses and humor that abuses.

Diversity, or how to make our society safer for differences, is my theme. There are some lessons about this issue from my past. When I began attending schools in New York City I was about 11 years old. Having just arrived from Puerto Rico, my only language was Spanish. My teachers thought they knew exactly what they needed to do in order to prepare me for the future, so the first thing they told me when I came from Puerto Rico was: "Learn English." So I said, "Si, si." Then, in the same vein, they came up with, "Forget Spanish." And interestingly enough, before I learned English I forgot Spanish, and soon I was illiterate in two languages.

One of the things that we have to do in this business of preparing children for the world of work and for the world of becoming good citizens in a democratic society is how to distinguish when teachers are basically wrong and when they tend to be right. When they told me to learn English, they were right on target, because anybody who says you can get along without English in the United States of America is a fool! English has replaced German as the language of science and French as the language of diplomacy.

It is the *lingua franca*; it is the most useful instrument in the world as the foreign language that makes it possible for people to have access to the world of technology. But more importantly, it is the language of American citizens that binds us together. Therefore, when they said "Speak English," they were right.

However, when they said "Forget Spanish," they were wrong, because you cannot argue in the name of education that it is better to know *less* than more. So in that sense, my problem with educators is that teachers and school systems, who are very good about giving minorities advice about what students need to do in order to make it, often are only half right. We have to figure out how we can get teachers to be right a lot more often. Because of that, you need the insight of some of us who are freelance troublemakers in the circuit of the exchange of ideas.

My accent is a "Spanglish" one, and it comes out of an interesting social reality. How I managed to learn to speak middle-class English is very revealing, since I come from what can best be described as a troubled background. My mother had five children, about a fourth-grade education, and she hails from a rural background in Puerto Rico. She migrated, with my father, to New York City, and later with my stepfather to Chicago. My father is an alcoholic. He became an automobile mechanic, but did not do well economically. My mother is a very white, European-looking Puerto Rican woman. My father is a very Afro, Black-looking Puerto Rican man. And they had some of the most *beautiful* children you have ever seen.

We can talk about Black being beautiful now; but we lived at a time when the concept of Black being beautiful was not there. Women were not pushing back the night. Handicapped people did not have a parking space. In a sense, the gifted were not recognized as a unique possible track. Gay people were not, at least collectively, deciding that somehow the society had to be at least more humane about how they would be treated as people. Senior citizens were not organized as Grey Panthers. Even though I look at myself now, and think of myself as an attractive human being, I remember a time when I actually thought that I was ugly.

I came out of a poor background and my language reflected growing up on public welfare. Let me dramatize what I mean to say about how poor we were by telling you a true story from my past. I used to live with my folks on the West Side of Chicago on Harrison Street and Independence Boulevard, near the Eisenhower Expressway. Not long after we moved into our little apartment, someone forced the door and broke into our home. Because I spoke the best English in our family, I was told by my mom to call the police and report the crime. And so I called. After all, I had watched television and remembered "Dragnet." I knew that they would come out and investigate and solve the problem.

I called the police and said, "I want to report a robbery." And the desk sergeant said, "No you don't." I said, "What do I have to report?" He said,

"A break-in." "Okay," I said, "I want to report a break-in." I said, "Could you send somebody to investigate?" He said, "No, we won't." I said, "Why not?" He asked, "What did the thieves take?" I started to think about what they took. And it dawned on me that while they had gone all through our things, and had made a big mess, that they hadn't taken *anything*. If you think being a victim is bad when they take the stuff that you really treasure, you are a real victim when they break into your house and don't take anything. We were poor.

I lived in poverty; my vocabulary skills were poor; I was illiterate in two languages; I never earned a grade higher than a D in English. I did poorly in math and I was a high school dropout. Need I tell you about my poor self-esteem? But then I met Mary Yamazaki, a Seventh-Day Adventist, and she got me turned around and put me on the right track.

Mary Yamazaki is Japanese-American. I went to work for her at Hinsdale Hospital, just outside of Chicago. She became like a surrogate parent in the arena of education. She was a tiny lady with a long bony finger. She told me that I needed to finish my education. She helped me go to a boarding prep school, Broadview Academy in Lafox, Illinois. It was there that I learned middle-class English by memorizing the speeches of the preacher Peter Marshall, or the sermons of Billy Graham, or the political speeches of Jack Kennedy. And by doing that, I empowered myself with middle-class language skills. I learned, interestingly enough, often in spite of the school system, not because of it.

I will never forget attending school at Broadview. Living in a dormitory meant taking showers with other boys. Six at a time was not unusual. Looking at other young men naked was very revealing. I noticed young adolescents whose bodies did not have one scar. I remember looking at this dude, six foot two, gifted with a beautiful mop of blond hair. This young man was to me the epitome of what the mainstream WASP society must project as a handsome man.

So, how did this Puerto Rican kid—a kid from a broken home, on welfare, from a racially mixed background, with not many resources, whose relatives own not one thing that others would want to steal—eventually wind up at Harvard University? What happened? How was I able to earn my Master's and Ph.D. degrees?

Basically I was intelligent, but I was incompetent until Mary Yamazaki intervened in my life. Because of her religious faith, which made her believe that God could do all things, she said to me, "God has great work for you to do. But you've got to prepare yourself." This person not only introduced me to the idea or the option of education, she also helped me to manage my money matters to save for my entrance fee at the academy. At Hinsdale Hospital I was an orderly in her Central Service Department. I was earning about a dollar an hour. I used to commute from the West Side of Chicago to the suburb of Hinsdale. She knew that I could not save for my education, paying a big chunk of my income on train fare every day. So Mary Yamazaki fought with the housing administration at the hospital to let me live on the hospital grounds. Racist policies did not encourage Black and Latino lower level workers to find housing in the elite suburban hospital. But Mary Yamazaki fought for me and won. In fact, she got the hospital to allow me to share a room with six Korean students. They spoke very little English, and I didn't speak any Korean, but we slept in the same room—we snored in the same language, I guess. So that's how it began for me, the road to success in the educational arena. I had someone in my corner fighting for me in order to remove obstacles that the system puts in the way; while she fought with me, so that I could be the best that I could be by taking advantage of the new opportunities.

Thinking about my Korean roommates brings the thought about new immigrants and success in education. While many of the newcomers are poor and from the Third World, others are not. Some are not poor; even if they happen to be from the Third World. The Filipinos, the Hindus, the Koreans, and some Vietnamese—many of them come through a process known as select immigration. Educators give a wrong meaning to their achievement in education. Teachers often beg to take credit for what these students are able to achieve in schools, when their achievements often are related to what these students bring from their native culture. Yet, teachers will often look down on U.S. minority students and scold them, telling them "Why can't you be like these new kids?" The thing is that "these new kids" are the way they are precisely because they did not go through our system.

I took my children to do a little homework at Northeastern Illinois University, and I said, "Who do you think comes to Northeastern?" And my daughter looks at me and says, "Koreans." They are less than 1 percent of the population of the university, but they seemed to be the majority of the people who used the library at night and on weekends.

Interestingly enough, now that Asians are doing very well, MIT and Stanford want to put a limit on how many Asians they will accept. So while the Asians go about doing what they are supposed to be doing to achieve in education, they now may be facing what Jews experienced for a long time. The core society will put some obstacle in their way to limit their success rate in the society. Stephen Steinberg in his book, *The Ethnic Myth*, has documented how testing and the process of conducting entrance interviews were put into practice at Harvard when Jews were getting into that elite university in greater numbers than the core society felt prudent.[1] Testing as a process was introduced to limit the entry of Jews into Harvard. Some new criteria will no doubt be introduced soon to limit Asian progress. It seems that the core society wants the best and the brightest to succeed in education as long as these talented students are not the racial minority in our time; just as they were not to be from a religious minority group many years ago.

Let's stop comparing minority young people in the United States with people who come through a select immigration process. Let's ask the question: Are there people like Samuel Betances, who are high school dropouts in places like the West Side of Chicago, who are Harvard material? How do we find them and develop them to reach their full potential? For me the opportunity came a a result of a national tragedy. Through Mary Yamazaki's effort I had graduated from college. I didn't have the best grades; but I earned a B.A. When Martin Luther King was assassinated, Harvard was embarrassed that they did not have many Blacks and Hispanics. In order to honor Dr. King, Harvard recruited minority men and women. Recruiters, like Beatrice Miller, found people working in the cities for positive social change and had them apply to enter Harvard to do graduate work. When I got to Harvard I found that the biggest problem was getting in.

Once we minority students got in, we had some responsibility but we could meet the responsibility. We were able to create networks of interest, not of color, in order to achieve certain goals. Now, I did not graduate cum laude or summa cum laude, but I graduated. There were times when we had to read a book a day just to get ready for certain classes. But, we did it! We've got to stop this nonsense that says minority people lack the intelligence to succeed. What we see is that doors are not open wide enough. When the doors open in the major universities, there are people in staff and faculty positions who do not know how to work with people like myself.

We need to provide incentives for minorities. We can say to them, "Hey, we know that you have come here with some deficits." I tell my students, if you read two extra books, your letter grade is going to go higher. This is an incentive. We can create incentives. It takes a little extra work, but if we're in this business about equity and excellence, then we've got to do some of that. Also, don't forget that one of the things that minority people experience in the United States is rejection. Don't talk about academic and testing issues impacting minority young people and not talk about rejection. Many minority young people have experienced and are experiencing rejection. They have internalized a negative vision of themselves. They think there is something wrong with their eyes, or that they're ugly, or that they have been cursed by God or something. Somewhere along the line, when we talk about making schools work for underachieving minorities, they've got to empower those children to reject rejection, not to reject themselves. And that means that you need to hire people in those universities that not only look like those minorities, but who have a track record for a conscious experience of battling rejection. Then you can really have role models. I don't mean finding some Black scholar who does not relate to the Black experience. I'm talking about finding some Black scholar who relates to the Black experience and who may not be as published and polished academically, but who may, in fact, be published and polished in the ability to empower Whites and Blacks in those institutions to learn how to be extensions of those things that universalize the human spirit.

At one time I thought there was something wrong with our hair. We need folks to talk to students about the way they thought about themselves before capturing a positive vision of their real worth. We need faculty members and counselors to teach by illustrating, and confessing how wrong they were not to value themselves. Some of us wanted to cook our hair. Remember the days? I used to cut my hair real short and get a skull cap and put some Posner products on my very short hair, and sleep real stiff. The next day I would remove my cap, and my pressed hair resembled the "good hair" that I so desperately wanted. We were like shadows of what we could not be. How often I hid in the shadows of bus stop signs so I wouldn't get darker from the sun. There's nothing wrong with our hair. It's the meaning that society puts on hair. It's just like we take a piece of cloth and we call it a handkerchief, and it collects waste, and we blow our nose into it. Or we can take a piece of cloth and it can be a flag, and we salute it. The meaning is not in the cloth. The meaning is in the culture. Unfortunately, we live in a culture that says that some groups are handkerchiefs, and some groups are flags, and what we've got to teach those young people by simple illustrations like the one I am using is, that in God's sight, we are all flags, and if we are good enough for God, then we are good enough for America.

We must confront the national dilemma that says to students be thankful and proud that you are an American. But what do we tell an American Indian to be thankful for on the eve of the Thanksgiving holiday season? The fact is that some people see the society as hostile and others see it as a host society. When we teach those who experience life as hostile to be thankful from the perspective of those who experience it as host, we've got a problem.

In Puerto Rico, the Americans came and said, "We're going to get rid of the Spaniards." And they did. So we said, "Hooray for the Americans." And then the Americans stayed. On the eve of World War I, they said that we were now American citizens. The American Indians were not made citizens to give them access to power, they were made citizens so that they wouldn't sign treaties. So citizenship was made to conquer people, not to liberate people.

For Black Americans who became citizens after the Civil War it meant the end of slavery. Citizenship became a plus for Blacks. To be a teacher from a Greek, Polish, Ukranian, Lithuanian, Armenian background is to view becoming a citizen always as a blessing. It's hard to imagine, if you look at the issue of citizenship as a stride toward freedom and/or the end of persecution and oppression, why some students would not value citizenship, why some students walk around with what appear to be chauvinistic cultural chips on their shoulders.

The society portrays Mexican-Americans in the media as though they came to this country last night, and illegally. Mexican-Americans or Chicanos didn't come to this country as much as this country, through conquest, took over what used to be Mexico. So if you tell a Mexican-American "go back where you came from," and if they take you up on it, they would go back to Texas, California, Arizona, New Mexico, Colorado.

Don't forget in your research agenda to focus on the role of teachers and educators who come to the challenge of teaching minorities from dominant/ host society enclaves. These instructors face the challenge of educating our people to accomplish two things: (1) to empower them with skills of going into the world of work, and (2) at the same time, with the skills to reject rejection. The minority students should not put a negative meaning on their hair, on their Negroid or dark skin features, because that's not the problem. The problem has to do with meaning-making. Black folks came up with a beautiful idea when they declared that "Black is beautiful," which did not mean that White was ugly. When Black people reached the conclusion that indeed Black was beautiful they decided to let their hair grow. They knew that the problem did not have to do with their hair, but with the meaning that was put in their hair. Blacks made a political statement with their hair. The "Afro" was born.

When I see people look to Japan for guidance it scares me, because I've been to Japan, and Japan is full of Japanese people. How in the world do you find solutions for a country that's multicultural from a country that's homogeneous? That worries me. It worries me because their assumptions and their cultural base are just different. Do you realize that there are more Black people living in the United States than there are people in the country of Canada? There are more than 20 million Americans of Italian descent. In Chicago there are more than 1 million Americans of Polish descent. The United States is now the fifth-largest Spanish-speaking country in the world.

When you put it all together with the Scandinavians, the French, the Germans, the Greeks, and so on, this is a country of multicultural diversity where too many groups are viewed as handkerchiefs and some of them are blouses and some of them are towels. When you take a look at all of that diversity, U.S. education needs to educate our people on how to consistently affirm the value of all of us together. This is good for Whites, good for Blacks, and good for all of us who are in between.

In Japan, because getting into college is so competitive, Japanese mothers get textbooks so they can learn how to tutor their children. In Israel, in terms of homework for the newly arrived Jews from Morocco or Ethiopia, the students from Ben Gurion University earn their scholarships by living in the housing compounds of newcomers. The students from mainstream Israeli society help the newly arrived Jews because educational leaders in Israel know that the parents of Moroccan and Ethiopian Jews cannot help their own children. In the United States, at least for the middle class, it is the parents who help.

My three children attend the public school system in Chicago. My 16-year-old daughter said to me: "Daddy, I need some work with my homework on Shakespeare." We did a little bit of research; I helped her to do the three-by-five cards, how to do quotes, how to do the whole thing. We did a fantastic job and it brought me closer to my daughter. We worked very hard on her paper. When she took it to school the teacher liked it. The paper had the five sources required and the encyclopedia. The teacher looked at her and said, "This is fantastic." Then she called Pedro to the front of the class, who had moved to Chicago from Mexico. She said, "Pedro, why did you copy from the encyclopedia? Why didn't you do what Cristina did?" Pedro had plagiarized because the only resource that he had available was, in fact, the encyclopedia. Christina Betances had the resources of her father, who is a university professor.

Yes, Pedro was passing himself off as a student, when in reality he was taking credit for work he had not done. In a sense Pedro is a fraud. But his teacher was also a fraud. She was taking credit for work she had not done. She was saying, "Cristina did what I told her." Cristina did not do what she told her. Cristina did what the resources made available to her at home enabled her to do.

In many instances, the problems facing American urban education can be understood in this type of illustration. Kids are not competing with other kids; but social class families are competing with social class families. Love in each family can be constant and abundant; but if the class resources are very uneven the outcome in the area of achievement will also be uneven.

In California there is a lot of talk about the business initiatives in the adopt-a-school program. What we ought to do is ask businesses to do something very simple: hire some of the kids who are doing very well in urban schools to become the tutors of those students who are not doing very well. Let's establish communal homework centers in our school districts. From Monday through Thursday from 3:30 p.m. to 9:00 p.m. in selected places throughout our cities, there will be places where young people can get help with their homework. A particular business can adopt a school by paying the wages of the tutors. The tutors can wear the logos of the sponsoring company on sweatshirts provided by the company. Instead of flipping hamburgers, young people can flip ideas and provide help to those who need it. The students who tutor will become stronger in the process. Those who are earning Cs can earn As. The achievement rate of all involved will go up. There are a lot of parents out there who love their children, but who cannot help them with their homework.

Teachers are always dumping on parents, saying they don't care. Even if you care but you don't know the new math and science, even if you show up at school, even if you create the climate, even if you turn the television off, even if you get them to bed on time, those kids are still in need of technical assistance with the know-how in terms of being competitive with the curriculum of the school system. If parents know that there is a center that they can send their kids to where they are going to be safe, the parents will send those kids to get the help they need, so that they don't have to plagiarize. Let's see if we can get the teachers' unions to join with principals and parents' groups and businesses to establish communal homework centers so that those kids can get help in their neighborhoods. If it isn't possible to hire other students to be tutors, provide computers or other incentives to increase homework skills. Don't build a volunteer tutoring program; they don't work. My point is this. My mother loved me, but she could not help me with my homework. I love my daughter, I can help her with part of her homework, but in her math and in her science, I cannot help her. Let's figure out how we can take those kids and build the kind of base that the homework centers can give us.

When people say that Hispanics don't care about education and point to our high dropout rate, don't believe that we don't value education. Take another look at the meaning that's being put on the statistics. It's a big lie that we don't value education. Our dropout rate is 55 percent. Now that's not acceptable. However, for the children of the nineteenth-century White immigrants, the dropout rate was 94 percent. The difference is that those people came with strong backs and a willingness to work, and they could get into the job market. While the schools rejected them or did not accept them, the economy did. They had a high dropout rate of 94 percent, but a zero dropout problem.

Today when my people come to this society, with the same intelligence in the farming area, we face agribusiness. Consequently, it's not that we lack intelligence or interest, it's that we lack opportunity. When the schools reject us, so does the economy. Because when the earlier immigrants came, they could talk to the cows in Swedish and they gave milk; they could talk to the corn in German and it would grow. But we don't face the corn or the cows, we face the computer.

It's not that we don't value education, but there is a myth that says White people made it through education. Not true. If you check back in your families, your parents may have had less education than you did. Your grandparents probably had less education than your parents did. And the further you go back, the less formal schooling you'll find. What this means is that because they were able to get into the economy without formal education, you and I were able to get, and our children are going to get, more. The dropout problem is not that we lack values, but that the economy has changed.

All of these issues demand our attention. All of us must agree that part of our agenda will be to eradicate racism and sexism and intolerance—to increase diversity—in order to make this country safer and stronger and freer than when we found it.

NOTE

1. Stephen Steinberg, *The Ethnic Myth: Race, Ethnicity, and Class in America* (New York: Atheneum, 1981).

PART II

Promising Practices

SECTION A

Developing Effective Instructional Programs

FOUR

Effective Education for Underachieving African-Americans

BARBARA SIZEMORE

In his report issued by the Institute for Educational Leadership, Inc., Harold L. Hodgkinson (1985) presents some stark demographics of education for us to consider.

For example, it is clear that Cubans (1.3 children per female) and Whites (1.7 children per female) will be less numerous in our future since a group needs about 2.1 children per female just to stay even, which is the case for Puerto Ricans. However, Blacks (2.4 children per female) and Mexican-Americans (2.9 children per female) will be a larger part of our population (p. 3).

Moreover, he points to major changes in the American family, reporting that in 1955, 60 percent of U.S. households contained a father who worked, a mother who stayed home, and two or more school-age children. We came to know them as Mother, Father, Dick and Jane, Spot and Puff—or the Rockwell Family. In 1980, only 11 percent of American families fit this pattern; by 1985 that figure had dropped to 7 percent. Of every 100 children born today, Hodgkinson reports, 12 will be born out of wedlock; 40 will be born to parents who divorce before the child is 18; 5 will be born to parents who separate; 2 will be born to parents one of whom will die before the child reaches 18; and 41 will reach age 18 "normally."

To be sure, Hodgkinson says,

the United States is confronted with an epidemic increase in the number of children born outside of marriage and 50 percent of such children are born to teenage mothers. Although the percentage of Black teenage girls who have children outside of marriage is higher than that of White girls, comparisons with other nations indicate that a White teenage female is twice as likely to give birth outside of marriage as in any other nation studied. The situation is most striking with very young mothers, age 13 and 14. Indeed every day in America, 40 teenage girls give birth to their third child (p. 3)

Two other aspects of family life are important to us in our deliberations about education for underachieving African-American children. One is the increase in the number of children who are at home alone after school when adults are not present. Hodgkinson reports at least 4 million "latchkey" children in the United States of school age. The second is that the increase in children in one-parent families also increases the number in poverty— 90 percent of the children that are represented in the increase live in one-parent households. Two of three poor children are White, but the percentage of poor Black children who live in one-parent homes is much higher. In addition, Hodgkinson reports, although only one in three poor children live in impoverished conditions for more than three years, those who do are likely to be Black.

"A child under six today is six times more likely to be poor than a person over 65," says Hodgkinson (p. 5). This is because we have increased support for the elderly and government spending for poor children has actually declined during the past decade. The result is an increase of over 2 million children during the decade who are "at risk" from birth. Almost half of the poor in the United States are these children.

The important thing to remember, however, about these demographic changes is this: "In the year 2000 America will be a nation in which one of every three of us will be nonWhite; and minorities will cover a broader socio-economic range than ever before, making simplistic treatment of our needs even less useful (p. 7)." In addition, the baby boomers, those born between 1945 and 1965, will be coming to old age. The retirement income for these baby boomers will be provided by a much smaller age group. In 1950, for example, 17 workers paid the benefits of each retiree. By 1992 only 3 workers will provide the funds for each retiree and one of the 3 will be minority.

If the baby boomers do not want interesting interactions with poverty in their golden years, they will find the money now to educate the high school dropouts whose work is necessary to pay their pensions. High school dropouts have a rather typical profile.

They are usually from low-income or poverty settings, often from a minority group background (although not often Asian-American), have very low basic academic skills, especially reading and mathematics, have parents who are not high school graduates and who are generally uninterested in the child's progress in school, and do not provide a support system for academic progress (p. 11).

Hodgkinson reports that male dropouts tend to leave school to find work, although the job often turns out to be a failure; female dropouts tend to leave school to have a child. More males drop out than do females. In general, dropouts are bored with school. They have accurate perceptions of themselves as failures in school, and they usually feel quite alienated.

ADDRESSING THE PROBLEM

State have attempted to address this problem by raising the standards but few have given the same amount of attention to providing remediation or counseling to those who cannot meet the higher standards. We must look more carefully at this problem. Moreover, we must review what we know about making elementary and middle schools more effective in order to prevent this problem before the student arrives in high school.

Effective schools' research gives us much information about how to make these changes, especially in elementary schools. The five correlates of effective schools are: (1) strong leadership, (2) positive school climate, (3) high expectations for student performance, (4) intense instructional focus, and (5) some kind of consistent measurement. The most important factor is the strong leader or principal (Sizemore, 1987). Recently, researchers have inserted teacher decision making and parental involvement in the number although the author's research generally does not reflect these two findings.

According to this research, the school leader or principal, as well as other educators, must have the profound belief that all children can learn and must have high expectations for the academic performance of all students. Such expectations have not been well served by much of implicit causality in research on the underachievement of African-American students. In particular, at least three of the five main categories of cause-effect arguments advanced in the literature could be seen as detrimental to high expectations: (1) African-Americans are genetically inferior in intelligence; (2) African-Americans are culturally deprived; (3) African-Americans have deficient, indifferent, unstimulating, and immoral families, homes, and community environments; (4) African-American students are served by schools and/or school systems that are inefficient, underfunded, and ineffective; and (5) the larger social order dictates through its value systems a racial/caste system that perpetuates itself through the schools (Sizemore, 1985, 1989).

The first category was fueled by the work of Arthur R. Jensen of Harvard University (Jensen, 1960, 1981; Sizemore, 1989). Defining intelligence as whatever the intelligence test (IQ) measured, Jensen set out to show that African-Americans as a population score significantly lower on IQ tests than the White population and attributed these lower scores to their genetic heritage (Jensen 1960; Eysenck and Kamin, 1981). Jensen's propositions have been criticized by those who found fault with the validity of his scientific methods and his use of the discredited work of Cyril Burt (Gould, 1981). Others further noted that science could not begin to differentiate hereditary variations in intelligence from environmental ones until social conditions had been equal for both races for several generations (Bodmer and Cavalli-Sforza, 1970; Eysenck and Kamin, 1981). Gould (1981) argues that scientists have been too often distracted by their biases and searched for what they knew to be true before the data were in. In his review of three books on the IQ controversy, Chase (1980, p. 218) says:

We are not in a position to state conclusions about intelligence; sweeping general-izations are clearly premature. Instead, we should be posing hypotheses that can be tested. The data in favor of the genetic view are too vulnerable, but the environ-mentalists have not formulated an appropriate theory of their own.

Certainly, this is the proposal accepted by most African-Americans.

Howard and Hammond (1985) relate the inferiority argument to the power of expectations. They hypothesize that Black performance problems are caused in large part by a tendency to avoid intellectual competition, which in turn is a psychological effect arising from Black people internalizing the larger society's projection of Black intellectual inferiority. Imputing intel-lectual inferiority to genetic causes, especially in the face of data confirming poorer performance, intensifies the fears and doubts that surround this issue. Howard and Hammond cite the powerful effect of expectancy on behavior and cognition and conclude the following:

Expectations of Black inferiority are communicated, consciously or unconsciously, by many Whites, including teachers, managers, and those responsible for the often demeaning representations of Blacks in the media. These expectations have sad consequences for many Blacks, and those whose actions lead to such consequences may be held accountable for them. If the people who shape policy in the United States, from the White House to the local elementary school, do not address the problems of performance and development of Blacks and other minorities all Amer-icans will face the consequences: instability, disharmony and a national loss of the potential productivity of more than a quarter of the population (p. 21).

They also surmise that Blacks must recognize their own responsibility in solving this problem.

In a recent article Lemann (1986, p. 35) argues that their distinctive cul-ture is now the greatest barrier to progress by the Black underclass, rather than either unemployment or welfare. He says: "Today the bedrock of the economic arguments of both left and right is eroding: the value of welfare benefits is declining, and the northern industrial cities are not rapidly losing jobs anymore. Still the ghettos get worse and the power of culture seems to be the reason why." Lemann sees the increasing isolation of the Black underclass as a dominant source of the problem:

The plight of the ghetto is due to two mass migrations: The first was from the rural South to the urban North and numbered in the millions during the forties, fifties and sixties before ending in the early 1970's. This migration brought the Black class system to the North virtually intact, though the underclass became more pronounced in the cities. The second migration began in the late sixties, a migration out of the ghettos by members of the Black working and middle classes, who had been freed from housing discrimination by the civil rights movement. Until then the strong leaders and institutions of the ghettos had promoted an ethic of assimilation (if not into White society, at least into a Black middle class) for the underclass, which worked up to a point. Suddenly most of the leaders and institutions (except criminal ones) left, and the preaching of assimilation by both Blacks and Whites stopped. What followed was a kind of free fall into what sociologists call social disorganization (p. 35).

While Lemann does not deny that both welfare and unemployment are factors in the rising disorganization of the Black family and community, he believes that the rapid urbanization of most Blacks, followed by the isolation of the Black lower class in the cities, may be more significant (Sizemore, 1989).

McGhee (1985), on the other hand, sees three major problems facing Black families today that account for most, if not all, of the difficulties they encounter: divorce and separation, which dissolve large numbers of married couple families every year; teenage pregnancy, which creates new families in which all members are at risk; and nonemployment and unemployment, which are the most serious of all problems faced by Black families because they are the primary reason for their poverty (see Sizemore, 1985, 1989).

Some selected figures tell a dire story. In October 1985 the U.S. Bureau of Labor Statistics reported that the Black teenage male unemployment rate was 41.4 percent and the female rate was 37.9 percent. The rate for White teenage males was consistently lower at 18.8 percent and the female rate was 15.5 percent. Increasingly, many of these unemployed Black youth, who are frequently unskilled, are the parents of young children. Chronic unemployment for adolescent males and pregnancy for adolescent females are increasingly becoming the twin social problems that afflict Black youth, each of which renders hundreds of thousands impotent to cope with the exigencies of day-to-day living and the future (Ladner, 1986).

In fact, Staples (1987, pp. 277–78) argues that the dominant force in the decline of the Black nuclear family can be found in structural conditions: "The basis of a stable family rests on the willingness and ability of men and women to marry, bear and rear children and fulfill socially prescribed familial roles." While abundant evidence exists to show that Black women are willing and able to fulfill their roles, data show that Black men are thwarted in their efforts to be economic providers and family leaders. The prerequisite for providing, protecting, and leading is holding a steady job or being gainfully and regularly employed.

Based on 1982 statistics, Joe and Yu (see Staples, 1987) found that 1.2 million Black men were unemployed, 1.8 million had dropped out of the labor force, 186,000 were in prison, and 925,000 were classified as missing in the 1980 U.S. Census, likely to be transient and unemployed. One consequence of these factors is that unemployed males do not make good marriage prospects. Therefore, the percentage of Black women heading families alone in 1982 (42 percent) corresponds closely to the percentage of Black males not in the labor force (46 percent) (Staples, 1987). Staples says the crisis of the Black family is the crisis of the Black male and his inability to carry out the normative responsibilities of husband and father in the nuclear family. At the same time, it is important to remember that over one-half of Black families are intact, married-couple families and such families represent the most economically viable family units where usually both parents work.

Regardless of the source of the problems, we must look toward an effective solution. Machado (1980, pp. 22–23) makes the case:

When a student does not learn, the fault, in some way, belongs to the system in which he learns. Any system that does not form intelligent men, whatever its other achievements, is an inevitable social failure. Every student with an undeveloped intelligence is a censure of the systems that did not know how to educate him. Education makes us free. . . . It is the most powerful tool for the attainment of equality among men.

Nationally, people look to the schools for some kind of significant contribution to the solution of these persistent chronic problems. There have always been some schools with Black and/or poor students demonstrating high achievement (Jones, 1981; Sowell, 1972; Hundley, 1965; Sizemore, Brossard & Harrigan, 1983). But these schools have been the exception rather than the rule. More often than not, Black inner-city schools have rested at the bottom when ranked in achievement with other schools in the same school system. However, as noted earlier, a body of literature has accumulated on effective schools (Sizemore, 1985), which has identified the five correlates of effectiveness.

RECENT RESEARCH ON AFRICAN-AMERICAN SCHOOLS

During the 1979–80 school year there were five predominantly Black elementary schools in the Pittsburgh Public Schools (PPS) where 51 percent or more of the student body scored at or above the national norms in reading and mathematics on the standardized achievement tests given in April of the school year. These schools anomalies at the time. After a political struggle for control of the school board by the Black and liberal White community, the priorities of the school system changed. First the schools were desegregated and then the pursuit of excellence commenced. The goal was to elevate achievement in every school and especially those where large numbers of Black and/or poor children were enrolled (Sizemore, 1987).

In the PPS during the 1985–86 school year there were three elementary schools that narrowed the achievement gap between Whites and Blacks in reading by bringing the Black students to or above the White norm in the system and three that did so in mathematics. During the 1984–85 school year one school accomplished this feat in reading and four in mathematics. In 1985–86 the schools that reached this goal ranged from 8 percent to 99 percent Black.

School board members and administrators in Pittsburgh know that nothing improves the chances more for at-risk students than the elevation of their achievement. Success gives these youngsters an improved self-esteem, which generates confidence and a sense of belonging. With this belief, the PPS have established several programs for changing the routines in their schools. If a school is low-achieving, this outcome is the result of the routines in progress in the school. In order to make the school high-achieving, the routines must change. A routine is a series of activities designed and implemented to reach a goal. A routine that reaches the goal is functional; one that does not is dysfunctional. A scenario is a series of routines. A process is a series of scenarios.

First, in each school that has narrowed the achievement gap the principal as instructional leader has set the tone for high expectations for student achievement, established accelerated growth and high achievement as a priority, and developed consensus among school factors around this priority. Then the principal implements processes for handling student discipline and parental involvement. Next the principal and teachers by methods of arriving at consensus set up a monitoring system that informs them about their progress in achieving their goals (high achievement in reading and mathematics). To make this systemwide, the PPS has developed two programs for effective monitoring: the Pittsburgh Research-Based Instructional Supervisory Model (PRISM) and the Monitoring Achievement Plan (MAP).[1] Although these need not be the plans every school district should use, a pre- and posttest measurement process must be designed and implemented to determine what objectives are reached and how well. This measurement and monitoring process is the heart of the implementation of effective schools programs. The principal and teachers must establish assessment, placement, pacing, monitoring, discipline, instructional, staff development, evaluation, and decision-making routines that differ from those already in place if the school is low-achieving.

INSTRUCTIONAL THEORY

Moreover, these routines must be undergirded by belief systems that inspire the learner and motivate him or her. Old systems and routines that relied on parents for prior instruction and socialization must be abandoned, since many parents will be single, teenagers themselves, and/or working full time jobs that prevent school volunteer work and attendance at meetings during school hours. To motivate at-risk students, a teacher must know his or her subject and how to teach it. Bruner (1960) in his book, *The Process of Education*, argued that the main objective of instruction should be to present subject matter effectively—that is, with due regard not to coverage but to structure. Structure for him meant the underlying principles and concepts that defined a discipline when their basic relationship was understood. He used the following example to explain his position:

[A]lgebra is a way of arranging knowns and unknowns in equations so that the unknowns are made knowable. The three fundamentals involved in working with these equations are commutation, distribution and association. Once a student grasps the ideas embodied by these three fundamentals, he is in a position to recognize wherein "new" equations to be solved are not new at all, but variants on a familiar theme. Whether the student knows the formal names of these operations is less important for transfer than whether he is able to use them (pp. 7–8).

The second point in Bruner's theoretical framework is that any subject can be taught to any child in some honest form if it is taught structurally and tied to the experiences the learner brings to the situation:

If one respects the ways of thought of the growing child, if one is courteous enough to tempt him to advance, then it is possible to introduce him at an early age to the ideas and styles that in later life make an educated man. We might ask, as a criterion for any subject taught in primary school, whether, when fully developed, it is worth an adult's knowing, and whether having known it as a child makes a person a better adult (p. 52).

The third focus of Bruner's theories states that intellectual activity anywhere is the same whether in the scientist's laboratory or the primary classroom; therefore, the training of intuition or the ability to generate intellectual hunches, or best guesses about the answers to problems, must be taught so that school children can master this gift. "The shrewd guess, the fertile hypothesis, the courageous leap to a tentative conclusion . . . these are the most valuable coin of the thinker at work, whatever his line of work" (p. 14).

The last idea stressed by Bruner is that of motivation for learning. He argues that teaching aimed at the average student in order to provide something for everybody is inadequate: "The quest, it seems to many of us, is to devise materials that will challenge the superior students while not destroying the confidence and will-to-learn of those who are less fortunate" (p. 70). If the at-risk is to be rescued from failure, he or she must experience some success. In order to provide this success, the teacher must know his or her subject from its undergirding principles and be able to plug that knowledge into the experimental baggage the learner brings to the situation.

FEELING GOOD ABOUT LEARNING

In their study of 200 high schools and 400 elementary schools for desegregation effects, Crain, Mahard, and Narot (1982) investigated two aspects
of academic success among others: achievement and self-esteem. They found
that most students felt reasonably good about their academic abilities and
Blacks were as confident as Whites despite their generally lower test scores.
Two-thirds of both races said they had the ability to complete college. Students resisted labeling themselves as poor students. Some 35 percent of
Whites and 21 percent of Blacks said that they were above average, and
only 5 and 9 percent, respectively, said they were below. One important
finding, however, was that the racial climate of the desegregated school was
central to a Black's feelings about the school, and for Black males their
feelings about the school were critical to their ability to do school work well.
For Whites, school race relations were secondary; for Blacks they were not.
The important finding for the researchers was the negative relationship
between high interracial contact and racial tensions. Racial tensions rose
where interracial contact was highest.

Significantly, they also found that Black students in predominantly Black
high schools had higher academic self-esteem than others. Even the White
students in predominantly Black schools had higher self-esteem than others.
Researchers suspect that Black schools often make a special effort to provide
a good school experience for their White student minorities and that this
explains the higher test scores of Whites in such schools, but the high White
withdrawal from these schools makes it hazardous to try to interpret the
scores for the students who remain (p. 55). Predominantly White schools
are most threatening to Blacks when the White students are working-class,
since working-class Whites are most prejudiced and more openly aggressive
in the main. Both busing and school racial mix have stronger effects on Black
students than on Whites.

In any of these schools where achievement is high for Black students, the
principal is the key factor and can cause a change in behavior before attitude
change occurs. Crain et al. (1982) also found a close association between
prodesegregation attitudes and higher teacher expectations. While the investigators argue that school behavior can be changed without challenging
belief systems, another approach is to hire more Black and liberal teachers
to change teacher behavior.

For most students their only interaction with Whites is at school, so race relations
at school are of enormous importance. This is not true for Whites. Their feelings
about the school's race relations have less to do with whether they like school. For
Blacks and especially for Black males, achievement is strongly affected by the racial
climate of the school (p. 130).

The investigators found that human relations workshops, courses and materials were useful in promoting behavioral change, and also minority history was useful but not as a course. They recommended the integration of minority history into the regular curriculum. The investigators in this study found that a knowledge of Black history, life, and culture had an effect on Black self-esteem. Students who study their heritage learn to realize its worth and think more highly of Blacks in general and of themselves in particular. This favorable self-opinion extends to feelings of academic competence.

CHANGING THE ROUTINES

To educate the at-risk learner, many of whom are minority and Black, the routines of low-achieving schools must be changed and the racial climate of desegregated schools must be improved. Routines must result in the elevation of achievement (scores at or above the national norms on achievement tests as a minimum floor and parity between Black and White scores). Minority history, especially Black history, must be integrated into the regular curriculum so that all of the students can learn it. The principal must be an instructional leader aggressive in pursuit of the five correlates of effective schools, strong in his or her expectations for student performance, and energetic in his or her attempts to implement the necessary routines. Needless to say, this principle can work most efficiently with the full support of the central administration and the school board.

The rescue of the at-risk learner begins in elementary school. There are many schools that are predominantly Black and poor where 70 to 80 percent of the students are achieving at or above the national norms in mathematics and reading on standardized tests. The Charles Rice Elementary School and the Maynard Jackson Elementary School in Dallas, Texas, are two; the Robert L. Vann Elementary School and the Madison Elementary School in Pittsburgh, Pennsylvania, are two more.

Staff development programs must be implemented to train teachers in their subject matters. All teachers should be given refresher courses in basic algebra, reading, and Black and minority history and reading. Additionally, teachers should be taught the basic principles of mastery learning and cue enhancement. And teachers should be trained to create word problems from the experiences of their learners and their understanding of the subject to teach their learners critical thinking and higher intellectual skills. The teacher must always keep in mind that learning in any classroom is the same as learning in the scientist's laboratory.

How does a school start to make these changes? More cross-grouping instruction must be provided based on sequential skills that have been designed by teachers who understand the subject and know the skills that must be learned and their order. Expect 80 percent mastery of these skills although there are some skills, like knowing one's name and address, where expectations are 100 percent. Give pre- and posttests in order to determine whether or not this had indeed occurred. Schedule a time for the mastery of these skills, say 20 every 9 weeks. Where this mastery does not occur, provide for reteaching, more reinforcement, and feedback. Under mastery learning principles if thoroughly understood and implemented, students learn the subject matter with formative tests giving feedback followed by corrective procedures and parallel formative tests to determine the extent to which the students have mastered the subject (Bloom, 1984, p. 4).[2]

To accelerate achievement, the teacher must be prepared, that is, know what skills the learner must master, know their sequential order, understand the learner and his or her experimental baggage, and understand the relationship. The teacher must then organize the content so that objectives are stated and clear and the mastery level expected known to the learner and his or her parent. Then the teacher must create a bank of activities for each objective so that reinforcement and feedback are possible. After this, the teacher must educate the parents about these activities, especially when assigned as homework so that parents can reinforce school plans if possible.

Next, to motivate the at-risk student the racial climate of schools must be improved. To do this, discipline routines must describe practices and referral systems in the school. These should be analyzed by a committee of school actors (teachers, parents, and students). Help from central administration for staff development should be available where necessary in areas like human relations or classroom management. Any disparities in referrals between Whites and Blacks should be carefully studied and special counseling for Black males who are most critically affected adversely by perceived racial injustices should be in place.

CHANGING THE CURRICULUM

Although teachers may not know it themselves, staff development should provide them with a knowledge and an understanding of minority history, life, and culture, especially when these youngsters comprise the largest number of at-risk students. It may be necessary for school boards to hire writers to write textbooks if publishers insist on currying to the prejudices of their largest customers. Whatever is done, the appendage of Black history to the regular curriculum as an elective or supplement is not the answer. It is not just for Black children, although it boosts their self-esteem and thus helps to motivate them. But all children should know the real history of our country.

African-Americans' life in the New World began with the voyages of African people from Nubia and Mali. Thus the first period of this history is the Era of African Explorers, beginning with the Nubians, who sailed to the New World and influenced the Olmec culture in Central America (700–800 B.C.), and Abubakari II of Mali, who sailed toward the New World in 1310

A.D. from West Africa (Van Sertima, 1976). Columbus's arrival commenced the second period of African-American history in the New World, the Era of African and European Explorers. Many Africans accompanied the Europeans in their explorations of this continent (Franklin, 1947; Sizemore, 1987). Their knowledge of the sea, navigation, agriculture, exploration, and mining is documented (Williams, 1974). Consequently, their presence reflected the revival of learning that took place in the fifteenth and sixteenth centuries in Songhay's principal learning centers in Jenne, Gao, and Timbuktu (Williams, 1974, p. 219). In 1517 Bishop Las Casas encouraged immigration to the New World by permitting Spaniards to import 12 Negroes each, and the slave trade to the New World began. It became an important factor in European economic life as the colonies in the New World grew and demonstrated an insatiable need for labor.

In 1619, 20 Negroes were left at Jamestown, Virginia, beginning the importation of human beings that was to evolve into the most inhumane form of slavery known (Franklin, 1947). This act brought an end to the Era of African and European Explorers and commenced the Slavery Period, which lasted until 1865 when the Civil War ended. The first Reconstruction Period commenced when the Thirteenth, Fourteenth, and Fifteenth Amendments were added to the U.S. Constitution, the first abolishing slavery, the second granting citizenship rights to the former slaves and the right of due process, which was subsequently revoked by the U.S. Supreme Court in *Plessy v. Ferguson*. Homer Adolph Plessy was a light-skinned Negro on an eastbound Louisiana train on June 4, 1892. He was stopped by a conductor and told to go to the Black car, which was the car directly behind the locomotive. He refused and was promptly arrested. He sued the state of Louisiana for violation of his Fourteenth Amendment rights and lost his appeal to the U.S. Supreme Court, which ruled in 1896 that a state could separate the races as long as the facilities provided were equal. This Separate but Equal ruling reinforced the first Jim Crow period, which had begun in 1876 when Rutherford B. Hayes withdrew the military from the six military districts in the South in exchange for the electoral votes of three former Confederate states during his campaign for the presidency.

The First Jim Crow Period lasted from 1876 until 1954, when the U.S. Supreme Court ruled in *Brown v. Topeka* that segregation was unlawful. The Second Reconstruction Period commenced on May 17, 1954. During this period the great civil rights struggles occurred and Martin Luther King, Jr. arose as the Black national leader. This period ended in 1978 when the U.S. Supreme Court ruled in *Bakke v. the University of California Medical School at Davis* that a seat could not be denied a White in favor of a Black if the credentials of the former were better; but institutions could consider race in individual cases. This history should be known in detail by teachers in order to better explore the experiential baggage brought by Black learners to the classroom (Sizemore, 1986).

CONCLUSION

We have the technology to rescue at-risk learners from failure. It is no longer an educational question. It is a political problem. Politics is the management of the conflict of groups at war over scarce resources. Power is the central concept. When those who have power decide that we should educate the at-risk students, we will do so on a grand scale. Maybe that time has come. For if the baby boomers do not educate the young minority students in school now, there may be no one to pay for their old age pensions.

NOTES

1. PRISM is a staff development effort designed to improve the instructional leadership of administrators, the effectiveness of teachers, and the learning of students. PRISM is an adaptation of Dr. Madeline Hunter's Effective Teaching Model, which includes: the four elements of effective instruction, the lesson design for effective instruction, supervisory skills for instructional growth, and adult learning theory for effective inservice. PRISM was initiated during the 1981–82 school year in Pittsburgh.

2. Bloom shows that students who develop good study habits, devote more time to learning, improve their reading skills, and so on, will be better able to learn from a particular teacher and course—even though neither the course nor the teacher has undergone a change process. The Mastery Learning Feedback Corrective Approach (ML) is addressed primarily to providing students with the cognitive and affective prerequisites for each new learning task. Teachers must identify the initial cognitive entry prerequisites at the beginning of the course. The procedure was to take the final examination in the prior course, say Algebra 1, and have a committee of four to six teachers in the subject area independently check each test item that they believed measured an idea or skill that was a necessary prerequisite for the next course in the subject. Then students are taught the specific prerequisites they lacked. This corrective process took about three to four hours during the first week of the course. After the students completed the corrective process, they were given a parallel test. As a result of the experiment conducted by Bloom et al., most of the students reached the mastery standard (80 percent) on the parallel test given at the end of the first week of the course (see Bloom, 1984).

REFERENCES

Bloom, B. S. (1984). The two sigma problem: The search for methods of group instruction as effective as one-to-one tutoring. *Educational Researcher*, June/ July, 4–16.

Bodmer, W. F. & Cavalli-Sforza, L. L. (1970). Intelligence and race. *Scientific American*, October, pp. 19–29.

Bruner, J. S. (1960). *The process of education*. Cambridge, MA: Harvard University Press.

Chase, C. (1980). Three views in the complex controversy on the origin of intelligence. *Phi Delta Kappan*, 61(11) (November), 217–18.

Crain, R. L., Mahard, R. E., & Narot, R. E. (1982). *Making desegregation work*. Cambridge, MA: Ballinger.

Eysenck, H. J. & Kamin, L. (1981). *The intelligence controversy*. New York: John Wiley.

Franklin, J. H. (1947). *From slavery to freedom: A history of Negro Americans*. New York: Alfred A. Knopf.

Gould, S. J. (1981). *The mismeasure of man*. New York: W. W. Norton.

Hodgkinson, H. L. (1985). *All one system: Demographics of education, kindergarten through graduate school*. Washington, DC: Institute for Educational Leadership.

Howard, J. & Hammond, R. (1985). Rumors of inferiority. *The New Republic*, September 9, pp. 17–21.

Hundley, M. G. (1965). *The Dunbar story: 1870–1955*. New York: Vantage Press.

Jensen, A. R. (1960). How much can we boost I.Q. and scholastic achievement? *Harvard Educational Review*, Winter, pp. 1–123.

———. (1981). *Straight Talk About Mental Tests*. New York: Free Press.

Jones, F. C. (1981). *A traditional model of educational excellence: Dunbar high school of Little Rock, Arkansas*. Washington, DC: Howard University Press.

Ladner, Joyce (1986). Teenage pregnancy: The implications for black Americans. In *The State of Black America, 1986*. New York: National Urban League.

Lemann, N. (1986). The origins of the underclass. *The Atlantic Monthly*, June, pp. 31–55.

Machado, L. A. (1980). *The right to be intelligent*. New York: Pergamon Press.

McGhee, J. D. (1985). The Black family today and tomorrow. *The State of Black America 1985*. New York: National Urban League.

Sizemore, B. A. (1985). Pitfalls and promises of effective schools research. *The Journal of Negro Education, 54*(3).

———. (1986). The limits of the black superintendency: A review of the literature. *The Journal of Educational Equity and Leadership, 6*(3) (Fall).

———. (1987). The effective African American elementary school. In G. W. Noblit and W. T. Pink, eds., *Schooling in social context: Qualitative studies*. Norwood, NJ: Alex Publishing Corporation.

———. (1989). Curriculum, race and effective schools. In H. Holtz, I. Marcus, J. Dougherty, J. Michaels, & R. Peduzzi, eds., *Education and the American dream*. Granby, MA: Bergin and Garvey Publishers.

Sizemore, B. A., Brossard, C. A., & Harrigan, B. (1983). *An abashing anomaly: Three high achieving predominantly black elementary schools*. National Institute of Education, Grant #G–80–0006.

Sowell, T. (1972). *Black education: Myths and tragedies*. New York: David McKay.

Staples, R. (1987). Social structure and black family life: An analysis of current trends. *Journal of Black Studies, 17*(3) (March), 267–87.

U.S. Bureau of Labor Statistics. (1985). The employment situation. In *Current Population Survey*. Washington, DC: Author.

Van Sertima, I. (1976). *They came before Columbus*. New York: Random House.

Williams, C. (1974). *The destruction of Black civilizations*. Chicago: Third World Press.

FIVE

Equity, Relevance, and Will

KATI HAYCOCK

A lot of people interpret the title of this part of the book—"Promising Practices: Developing Effective Instructional Programs"—as suggesting that minority youngsters need something quite different from other youngsters. The notion here somehow is that we educate all kids the same. But somehow, Black kids, Brown kids, and poor kids don't learn as much. That is a serious misconception. In fact, we do not educate all children the same way. Into the education of minority and poor youngsters we put less of everything that we believe makes a difference in terms of quality education. We put in less instructional time. We put less in the way of well-trained teachers; less in the way of rigorous higher order curriculum; less in the way of interesting books. Perhaps most important of all, we put less in the way of teachers who believe students can learn. How does this happen? What about equal opportunity: don't we have equal opportunity? No, we don't, and it occurs primarily in two ways.

The first way is that despite what we thought had happened with *Brown v. (Topeka) Board of Education* and the numerous desegregation decisions that followed it, we continue to educate most minority youngsters separately from other youngsters. The amount of racial isolation that we see in California has actually increased over the last several years. Why is this important? It is important because the schools that serve minority youngsters have fewer resources or resources of a lesser quality than other schools. They tend to have poor facilities, broken-down buildings, boarded-up windows. They have less experienced teachers. They have unbalanced curricula, especially at the secondary level: balanced away from college preparatory subjects in the direction of what at best might be considered vocational or quasivocational in nature.

For those minority kids whom we don't *get* in this way, we have another practice, and that's called grouping and tracking. We *get* those students by sorting them into lower ability groups and educating them quite differently than we do other students. Those in the lower groups, as all of us know, get educated primarily by ditto. Ditto after ditto after ditto, throughout the years. It is hardly surprising, as a result of these two practices, that no matter what index of academic achievement one uses, minority students show up on the bottom. And the longer those youngsters remain in school, the wider the gap grows. In California, at the first-grade level we see very few, if any, differences in actual achievement between minority youngsters and other youngsters—generally no more than about 10 percentage points.

By the time those youngsters reach sixth grade, the gap has grown quite a bit larger—many times on the order of about 30 percentage points. By the time those youngsters reach the twelfth grade, if they reach the twelfth grade at all, they've fallen enormously behind. In many California school districts, there are gaps of about 60 percentage points on tests like the Comprehensive Test of Basic Skills between the average Anglo youngster and the average Black or Hispanic youngster. Many do not graduate and among those who do, there are very, very few high-quality postsecondary opportunities. A recent study of California schools suggests that Blacks and Hispanics who graduate from high school attain eligibility to enter one of our four-year public institutions at about one-quarter the rate of the average Anglo graduate.

Once they enter our four-year institutions, what happens? Typically, because their levels of preparation are considerably lower, they wash out of college at higher rates. The cumulative effect of all of this is that what comes out of our education systems looks very, very different from what went in. Those who are prepared for white-color professions are disproportionately Anglo and from affluent homes. Those who are prepared, at best, for blue-collar jobs are disproportionately minority and from poor families. Not a pretty picture considering we have been at all of this for about 25 years.

The question we asked, however, was: Is all of this inevitable? All of us have heard the success stories. Stories about schools that take the kids nobody else seems to think can learn and somehow manage to produce striking achievement gains. When we looked at the data for California, we found that some schools were doing a much better job than others at educating minority and poor students. Some schools were doing a much better job at helping them to prepare for or gain entry into good four-year colleges. Some were doing a better job at helping them to prepare for and find good jobs. Some were doing a better job of helping them to prepare to achieve at or above grade level. But in all of that, the basic answer to our bottom line question was very, very clear. Minority and poor youngsters can achieve at the same high level as any other youngsters in this nation. And schools absolutely *do* make a difference in whether that happens or whether that does not.

We looked carefully at the schools where students were achieving at much higher levels. What is it that made them different? First and perhaps foremost is a determined principal. What we saw at successful schools around the state was not always the classic turnaround principal style. But we always saw determined school leaders: leaders who believed not only that kids *could* learn at the highest levels, but that they *had* to learn at the highest levels. And that determination was clear in everything those leaders did. The second thing we saw was a clear focus on academics throughout the school—a quality instructional program. What are the pieces of such a program? I want to give you a few hints from what we've seen around California.

The first is bound up in the notion that all students should be in grade-level materials. It is interesting what a simple, but controversial, proposition that is. I was talking recently to a principal from a junior high school in Oakland who was telling me that for years the children in her school, most of whom were Black, had performed at very low grade levels. Typically those who entered at grade seven had fourth-grade-level skills. And the response to that, as the response nationally tends to be, was to put them in fourth-grade-level readers.

While they were doing that, they wondered why those kids never improved—why they never achieved at grade level. Finally it dawned on them: they didn't achieve at grade level because they were never exposed to grade-level materials. So what they decided to do, in one fell swoop, was to put all kids in grade-level materials. They provided them with some help during school and with a lot of help after school. In one way or another, they made sure that kids who were having some difficulty got help. What happened? Scores went up tremendously and students felt better about themselves. The school has soared. A very simple idea but, surprisingly, rarely used.

Second, especially at the elementary level, we need to look carefully at what kinds of books we use. A lot of studies have come out recently suggesting that in the inner city our tendency is to use considerably less rich materials than we use elsewhere. Books at the first- and second-grade-levels tend to introduce about half as many new words as books that are used in the suburbs. That choice of books alone makes a major difference in what kids learn. We need to get the richest possible materials in order to have a quality instructional program.

Third, schools that succeed tend to have virtually all of their students in a common core curriculum, and a rigorous curriculum at that. They have very, very few branches to divide students. Experience and the literature both tell us that when you confront youngsters with a choice, to go to the next highest class or go to a less difficult class, poor kids will almost always opt into the lower class. The more branches you have, the more often you push kids apart and the less likely low-income children are to learn. By reducing those branches in your curriculum—or where you must have branches, by reexamining standards for entry and by pushing as many youngsters as possible up into the higher curriculum rather than allowing them to choose on their own—schools are more likely to give more kids the kind of education we know makes a difference in terms of achievement.

Fourth, the schools that work have figured out that educators don't communicate very well across levels. What happens in many cases is that kids don't do well in a particular subject because they didn't get through the requisite chapter in the previous year, but the teacher never knew that. By bringing teachers together across levels within a discipline, to talk about what kids need to know and what those teachers need to do together to make sure they learn it, we generally get a much more closely sequenced curriculum and a better learning process for the student.

Fifth, as is probably obvious in the concept of a core curriculum, there is much more heterogeneity in classrooms in schools that work than there is in schools that don't. The general rule of thumb is: Even if you can't mix kids across achievement or ability levels all the time, the more you do of it, the more likely you are to have improved achievement. This is especially true if your teachers are trained to use available instructional strategies like cooperative learning.

Sixth, there's also something to the very simple notion that you get what you ask for, you get what you demand. What we see in successful schools' programs is teachers who demand a lot from their students. High expectations are something we talk about all the time, but in effective schools they are translated into demands. Many times when we talk to the teachers about what they ask of kids—because we've seen that they're asking so much more in successful schools of the same age kids as is the case elsewhere—they say that they too had not been convinced kids could master these kinds of skills. But the teachers found that the more they asked, the more the kids delivered. So their own expectations kept rising, and the kids kept learning more. Again, a very simple notion, but a powerful one.

Finally, there is the matter of parent communication. There has been a lot of talk about parent involvement in education, such as volunteers in classrooms and increased attendance at back-to-school nights. But the one thing that is not commonly discussed is communication from the school to the home about how the youngsters are doing in school. The fact is that parents cannot help their kids if they don't know until the semester mark, or at least until the halfway mark, that their children are having difficulties. Successful schools have found that if they communicate with parents more regularly, if parents know early on that the youngsters are having some difficulty, even the poorest families, and the families with the least education, will somehow find ways to get their youngsters some help.

These are not terribly difficult practices. They're all things where one can sit down at a school site and figure out how to proceed. The sad fact, however, is that there aren't very many school where these practices are in place. There are not very many exceptions to the general patterns I mentioned earlier. Our own organization is engaged in an effort to try to change all of that. We've decided to focus on several strategies that you may wish to consider as well.

One is to help more principals to become the leaders that they need to be in order to bring about change. Our own vehicle for doing this is what we call "Principal-to-Principal," which is an institute with a faculty of 18 principals from high-achieving, predominantly minority schools that come to UCLA for a four-day period and teach other principals the steps to school improvement. They work together during the year to help each other with the problems schools encounter in the turnaround process. This is one way, but there are certainly others, of helping principals to undertake the very difficult task of taking a low-performing school and pushing, shoving, pulling it ahead. We need to provide more principals with that kind of help.

The second way that we've chosen is to help schools build leadership teams. For as critical as a determined principal may be, successful schools generally have a committed leadership team that involves other administrators and a number of teachers. All team members are committed to changing their schools, and all are knowledgeable about the school improvement process. This, of course, is the participatory decision making we hear so much about. I think all of us are well aware that not very much that could be labeled participatory decision making goes on in schools today. Schools tend to be little fiefdoms where teachers close the doors and teach, and administrators close their own doors and manage. That needs to be broken up. Teachers and administrators must see as *their* responsibility the need to improve achievement among minority and low-income kids. Our Teams Institute, which brings school teams to UCLA for four days, is making an effort to do just that.

A quick aside about categorical programs. One of the very sad outcomes of our extensive use of band-aid, add-on programs for providing assistance to minority and poor students is that in the minds of many so-called regular teachers and administrators, these kids are no longer their responsibility. We visited many schools, typically 60 or 70 percent ethnic minority, where we would ask the principal or vice-principal, "What are you doing to raise achievement among your minority and poor students?" And we would get in response either a blank stare, or a finger pointed to the trailer across the playground that housed the compensatory education reading lab, or another comment about the University of California coming on campus one day a week to talk to 13 kids about going on to college. What we didn't hear is, "This is our school plan. This is how we've retooled our curriculum, this is how we've retrained our teachers, these are the kinds of decisions we have collectively made about what kids belong in what kinds of classes."

This is a serious problem for all of us. We simply must help regular classroom teachers, regular administrators, to come once again to the notion that motivated many of them to come into the classroom: the belief that they can change things for kids who need their help. We need to rekindle that feeling, that sense of responsibility for change.

In my view, if those of us who are in higher education and other places can help more administrators and more teachers to regain that sense of responsibility—help them with assistance in the way of ideas, available research on what works and what doesn't, even a shoulder to cry on—we can help to bring about the flood of activity that will bring about the gains that we need for minority and poor young people in this country.

SIX

Effective Instructional Approaches to Bilingual Education

FRED TEMPES

Effective instructional approaches in schools need to be based on some rationale, but often they are not. Bilingual education programs are a good example. If you go into a school and ask about the bilingual program, you might be directed to a particular classroom where one teacher has been successful with bilingual students. But there may be another teacher in the same school who takes a different approach, yet has a good class too. The first-grade teacher may believe one thing, but the second-grade teacher doesn't, so he does something different. Nobody gets together to talk about why they are doing what they are doing and, as a result, kids go through a hiccup approach to education. Good, effective instructional approaches are based on some sort of rationale. This chapter will describe how we attempted to implement that idea in bilingual programs in California, specifically in five California elementary schools.

In 1970, 27 percent of the school-age population in California was made up of minority group members. In 1980 it increased to 42 percent. Coming up on 1990, we anticipate that it will be 48 percent, and by the year 2000, the minority will be the majority in our public schools.

Language minority students (students who have a home language other than English and who come from a home where another language is spoken) make up 25 percent of the student population in California—one in four. About 13 percent of the students in this state are officially identified as having limited English proficiency—one in eight. Our problem is what to do for these kids, and I think we may want to do something different. We need to look at the routines and practices that we are using in our schools and decide whether they are appropriate. In the elementary school project, we used a decision-making model in which outcomes are a response to instructional treatments or instructional treatment factors. Additionally, some outcomes occur because of the interaction between what is done in school and the kinds of kids who are coming to school.

We made mistakes in the past because we wanted the kids to be different than they were. They didn't speak English, but we pretended they did. We treated them as if they spoke English. Obviously, what kids bring to school is a reflection of their community. If they come from a non-English speaking community, they probably won't speak English. If they come with some excess cultural and psychological baggage, they are going to have certain attitudes about the school system. All of those factors need to go into the mix. The things we have available to us in terms of instructional statements are related to educational background factors. Some, such as how much money we have in the school, turn out to be relatively minor. Other things are more important, like the attitude of the superintendent, the principals, and the teachers, and also how well-informed our instructional decisions are.

When we started our program with the five schools, we asked the teachers what they wanted to have happen for their limited-English-proficient kids. They all came up with the following answers, and invariably, groups I talk to always do. "We think these kids should speak and understand English." This is always the first response. When I ask, "Is that all that you hope for these kids as a result of the instructional intervention you are talking about, that they can speak and understand English?" someone raises his hand and says, "We think they ought to do well in school, beyond grade level." There are a few gasps from the back of the room. "Well, maybe close to grade level." Their second concern is that students ought to adjust well to living in this multicultural society. Minority students should not feel that they have to reject some aspect of their backgrounds or reject participation in the majority culture.

Just knowing where you want to go, though, doesn't tell you how to get there. This is where we need to bring in some of the available information that often is not used to make instructional decisions. At the State Department of Education, we are neither researchers nor practitioners. We are in between, and that is a good place to be. Researchers can tell us what they are doing, and since most of us have been practitioners, we feel we can interpret some of their findings for school people.

We have tried to do that in bilingual education with a series of books that we have published over the last six or seven years. The first book, *Schooling and Language Students*, was followed up with *Studies on Emerging Education*, right at the peak of the English-only movement. Our most recent publication, *Beyond Language*, deals with nonlanguage-related factors in the education of limited English proficient students.

Publishing books is one thing, but really culling out the instructional approaches to it is another. We synthesized all this information and presented to the schools what we felt informed research was saying about the education of language-minority students in the United States. We boiled the information down into five principles: what the theory of bilingual threshold is, what language proficiency is, how language proficiency in one language relates to another language, how kids acquire a second language, and how nonlanguage factors influence the education of language-minority students.

The threshold hypothesis examines the theory that bilinguals are more, or less, intelligent because they are bilingual. Do they suffer or do they gain some kind of academic advantage? Research is contradictory, but there has been some work that looks at the type of bilingualism involved and has really cleared up the question. Basically, we posited three types of bilingualism.

The first, limited bilingualism, occurs when a student has less than native proficiency in two languages. This student comes to school speaking a language that everyone says is not important. He is told to forget that language and learn English, so he tries to pick up the second language. Then, one day in the third or fourth grade, he realizes, "Gee, I really can't speak English, or write English, or read English as well as everyone else, and I can't speak Spanish, or read Spanish, or write Spanish as well as everyone else, either." This is subtractive bilingualism. A kid loses proficiency in one language while he is trying to play catch up in another. These kids seem to suffer negative affects associated with their bilingualism.

The second type of bilingualism is partial bilingualism, which is often the result of typical foreign language programs. Students study a language for three years, and can order a meal in a French restaurant anywhere outside of Paris or get a beer in Encinada, but it doesn't really affect their academic achievement.

Proficient bilingualism, the third type, is much more interesting. The research supports the notion that people who are at equally high levels— native or nearly native—of proficiency in both languages seem to gain some academic and cognitive benefits that are associated with their bilingualism. In other words, they do better on certain tasks than do monolingual students of either language.

A more crucial issue for us in California, and the one we were concerned with when designing an instructional approach for limited English proficient kids, is the question of limited bilingualism. When kids come to school speaking Spanish and are convinced that they must drop Spanish and catch up in English, we find that they are two and three years below grade level by the sixth grade. We have to do something to prevent this loss of Spanish while students acquire English; students need to be able to do some tasks in Spanish at the same time. In order to get any kind of positive benefit from the instructional approach you choose, you must get beyond these thresholds.

The second principle concerns the dimension of language proficiency. Basically, language proficiency, in our view and based on the research, can be defined as the language ability necessary to complete a task found in one of four quadrants. The quadrants are defined by how difficult the task is, how cognitively demanding or undemanding the task is, and how much context there is for the task. I always give the following example about the first-grade student who has been in California only two weeks and speaks only Spanish.

The teachers says, "Boys and girls, I want you to put your math books away and line up for lunch," and this little kid is the first in line. The teacher turns and says, "See how fast Juanito is learning English. He's only been here two weeks, and he's learned a lot of English." What did Juanito hear? Those who have had this experience as young children know exactly what he heard. He heard a bunch of noise. But Juanito knows that it's 11:30 in the morning, he's starting to get hungry, and the math books have been out for a while. The teacher stands up and says something, and all the kids close their math books and line up for lunch. He knows he can excel at that last task, so he gets in line first. This is a context-embedded task.

A context-reduced task, at the other end of the continuum, occurs when the entire message is imbedded in language. Reading is an example. If a student picks up a journal article he's not familiar with and reads it without anyone giving him instruction, it is a context-reduced task. Everyone acquires the basic language proficiency to complete context-imbedded, cognitive-undemanding tasks in some language. This is not the problem. The problem accompanies the context-reduced task.

Not everybody develops the ability to complete cognitively demanding tasks in context-reduced situations to the same degree. This is true among native speakers of English. Give them the CTBS or MAT (Metropolitan Achievement Tests) at the end of the sixth grade and their scores will be all over the map. The same is true for language-minority students. We made a big mistake in California, and we are probably still making it in some places today: We assumed that when kids could complete context-embedded tasks in English, they were no longer in need of any specialized instructional programs. They could defend themselves on the playground, they could ask permission, they could take home a note from the teacher, have it signed, and return it to the teacher. Based on their ability to do these things, we predicted that they were ready to do context-reduced tasks.

This was not true. What the research showed was that it takes kids two to three years to learn how to do this type of task. It takes them five to seven years to approach grade-level norms in terms of cognitive academic proficiency. That presented a problem. We weren't sure we had the resources to go five or six or seven years, the time needed to increase proficiency. However, there was another bit of research that helped us out.

There are two views about the way bilinguals process information: The first asserts that there is a common underlying proficiency, the second asserts that there is a separate underlying proficiency. With the latter, the two languages are like two balloons in the brain, with the first language represented by L1 and the second language, English, by L2. If you want to develop English language proficiency, you must teach in English. You blow up the L2 balloon. If you spend time instructing in the first language, you inflate the L1 balloon, taking up space that kids could be using to process English. Teaching in a language other than English is a waste of time.

Most of the public believe that this is true. Letters to the *Los Angeles Times* say, "What is this about teaching kids in Spanish? If they want to succeed in the United States they need to know English. You need to teach them in English." All of these people believe that teaching in the first language has no eventual influence on English skills and only takes up valuable time.

The other view maintains that there is a common underlying proficiency. Academic skills learned in one language are readily expressed in a second language once a student has gained initial facility in the first. Once kids know how to read in Spanish, they will be able, by and large, to read in English. All they need, then, is to be able to speak English.

There is no research that supports the first view. Many research studies support the second, and this is what convinced the teachers with whom we work. Kids who do well in one language do well in a second language. Kids who do poorly in their first language do poorly in their second language. If we can help them to do better in their first language, they will eventually do better in English. Our research and our project studies support this.

The fourth point deals with second language acquisition. We looked at the research on second language acquisition and it seemed to be divided into two schools of thought. Proponents of one think language should be taught sequentially, based on the introduction of specific grammatical skills. Kids learn this language, then the next. Anyone who had a foreign language in high school was probably taught by this method. First you learned present tense forms. Next you learned personal pronouns, and you put the two together. The instruction was grammatically sequenced. After three years of putting the little blocks together you should have been able to speak that language. How many can speak that language now?

The other school of thought says that second language can be acquired the same way first languages are acquired. This research is based on the work of Steve Prashen, at the University of Southern California, and others. Prashen talks about comprehensible input and nongrammatically sequenced input—input that is meaningful and supported by lots of contextual clues. The research indicated that this second method was the way to go.

The fifth point relates to the status of kids. Kids who don't speak English in California are, for the most part, minority students. Minority students suffer from unequal status in the classroom. Teachers interact differently with minority and majority students. They interact differently with kids who have accents and kids who don't. The high-status kids get all the attention.

Teachers don't ask kids who don't speak English to answer questions because they don't want to embarrass them. There is a status ranking in class, and it is reflected by the peer group. Minority students pick up on that fairly soon, in kindergarten or first grade, and they may not talk in class for a number of years.

There are certain status characteristics in our society, including ethnicity, dress, age, and language. People tend to rank those things in a hierarchy based on their previous experiences and attitudes, and behave differently toward people as a result. When kids don't speak English, they don't ask as many questions. That behavior, in turn, influences outcomes that reinforce the status characteristics, and around and around we go.

We tried to break that pattern up in the schools we worked with and had some degree of success. Teachers were trained in cooperative learning. Tracking begins in elementary school, and we wanted to break that up. We placed perceived high-ability kids and perceived low-ability kids in the same group. The input of everybody is valued, so that helps to break up the status ranking. We also trained teachers to give Maria the same amount of time to answer as every other student, to give the low achievers the same amount of time as the high achievers, and to move around the room and talk to all of the kids. These teaching methods are inequitably distributed in most schools. Teachers don't do it consciously, but it has been documented over and over and over again.

We put all of these points into an instructional program. The end product, the instructional design, addressed kids in four phases of language instruction: non-English speaking students; limited English speaking kids who had been in the program a couple of years; kids who were more proficient but were still limited in English; and fluent English proficient students.

Non-English speaking kids learned all their subject area material in Spanish. Language arts were taught in Spanish; math was taught in Spanish; science, health, and social studies were taught in Spanish. A little bit of English as a second language was incorporated for these students, using a natural approach or an approach not based on grammar, as the research suggested. Then, we treated them as if they were native speakers of English in art, music, and physical education, because the context level in those areas is so high. This gave us a chance to integrate them with native speakers of English, which didn't usually happen in other classes.

As the kids gained more proficiency, we started to move some of those content-area classes into sheltered English. We taught math and science in English, but we taught it in a special way, with many contextual clues and a lot of teacher paraphrasing and built-in redundancy, using slower rates of speech. Often we didn't integrate the kids with native speakers; we kept them with nonnative speakers because English is a powerful tool. If ten nonnative speakers of English are put together with two native speakers, the teachers will teach to the native speakers. It is the register they are most familiar with. The other kids get lost.

In the third phase, we started to move more subjects into sheltered English and math and science into mainstream English. By the time students were in fourth grade, most of the kids were in phase four, and everything was being done in mainstream English. We also encouraged the schools to maintain some academic use of Spanish. These kids were already four or five years down the road to becoming proficient bilinguals, and if there are intellectual advantages to proficient bilingualism, as the threshold hypothesis suggests, why should students forget Spanish?

The results of this program, which will be reported in Chapter 14, were fairly encouraging. The five schools did very well. Some of them did exceptionally well, including the one in Los Angeles. Los Angeles has replicated this program in seven or eight schools. The last time we counted, there were about 25,000 students enrolled in spin-off programs from the model we developed for these five schools. The same kind of instructional design was used because it was based on sound research, the best research available at the time.

To conclude, there are some things I would do differently if we were to start this project again. I would have greater faith in the research that we synthesized and I would not move so rapidly from Spanish to English. We found that the more things we taught in Spanish and the higher our expectations were in Spanish, the better the students did in English. I also would make greater changes in the organizational structure of the schools. I think if we had changed the decision-making process, we would have started to address some of the many other issues that are related to the achievement of language-minority students.

Other than that, I think we are on the right track. When you design an effective instructional program for minority children or for underachieving children, it must be based on some rationale, and someone has to be able to make the rationale explicit. People don't necessarily have to agree with the underlying rationale, but they need to be informed by a principal who is an instructional leader, and who will say, "You are free to disagree, but you are not free to do something else in this school, because this is where we are going."

SECTION B

Reducing Dropouts

SEVEN

Systemic Approaches to Reducing Dropouts

MICHAEL TIMPANE

There are three points that will interweave through this chapter that strike me as overarching in talking about dropouts. One is that the act of dropping out is really a symptom or a symbol of shortcomings and failures in the social and economic and education systems. The second is that from the individual's point of view, and often from the school's point of view, dropping out is the anticlimactic conclusion of a long, visible, and painful process. There are few surprise actors in the tragedy of dropping out. The third is the point that Henry Levin made in Chapter 1—that is, for a series of profound and durable demographic and economic reasons, the issues represented by this symbol of dropping out are going to be with us for a very long time and, no doubt, in a more and more serious form. If we bear these three fundamentals in mind, we can have some chance to address the problems that dropping out stands for in our education system and in our society. If we do not, we may not have that chance.

In historical perspective, it is interesting to note that for the past 10 to 15 years, up until just a few years ago, the issue of dropouts had virtually disappeared as an issue in education policy. It had a certain currency in the late 1960s. There was a "Dropout Prevention" title in the Elementary and Secondary Education Act. A series of demonstration projects funded by the federal government and many manpower programs, such as the Job Corps and the Neighborhood Youth Corps, were aimed at the group of young people who were going to have trouble finishing school and making the transition to the rest of their lives. Attention to all of those problems and, indeed, to the problem itself waned greatly throughout the 1970s. It is not a strictly partisan phenomenon. I did not locate it at the beginning of the Reagan administration; it goes farther back. Why?

The most realistic analysis is that society, and especially the economy, could get along without the dropouts. To be sure, it was annoying that so many people were unqualified at the hiring desk, but at the bottom line, as employers are fond of saying, there was a labor surplus. One could "cream" the public schools, take the best of their graduates; one could recruit from private and parochial schools and take a great many of their graduates; and one could sit back and enjoy the influx for the first time of millions and millions of women returning to the labor market—and all this in the context of the baby boom passing through the entry years of the labor market. One could be worried about those whom the schools were failing, but not too worried—one's needs were satisfied.

This was always a shortsighted policy, because it ignored the economic costs of crime, welfare, unemployment, and the loss of productivity, not to mention the reduced earning power and quality of life of the individuals concerned. But it was nevertheless a pervasive policy. In the 1980s, though, perceptions began to change, and precisely because all of the trends mentioned above began to reverse themselves. The baby boom ended; the increasing rate at which women were reentering the labor market began to diminish. There were fewer young people, and the competition was greater. Institutions of higher education were, shall we say, adjusting their standards. The military was sustaining and expanding its appetite for young college graduates. All at once, potential labor shortages loomed. Employers began to conclude that from their self-interest (not altruism, not enlightened impulses toward social justice) they needed every single young person in our high schools to be well and adequately trained. Attention began to shift to those populations who are not being so well-trained, who are not so frequently completing high school with adequate skills, and who are overrepresented among dropouts. So the issue is hot now because, as is so often the case in education, society has needs. If education is swift and smart, education will respond to that need, because it is an appropriate and legitimate need, but in a way that builds and strengthens education itself. Education's objectives and society's objectives are coincident in a way that they have not been before. It is a time of great and sustained opportunity, a time when there is great political and economic concern and strength behind us in dealing with dropouts.

This was the latent message of the reports of the so-called excellence movement in the early 1980s. The message was latent, and it is only as persons like yourselves have reexamined and reflected upon those reports and the imperative call for educational improvement that we have come to understand that true excellence in our schools is and must be deeply and profoundly equitable. If more excellence is needed, for whom is that greater excellence needed more than for those groups that have had the least of that excellence so far—namely, the minorities and the disadvantaged? We should continue to worry that the excellence movement may become a threat to equity, but I would argue, nevertheless, that it is also an opportunity. Strangely enough, no one understands this better than the business community, which, indeed, understands it better than many other sectors of our society, including some sectors of education, which ought to know better.

The neglect of a decade or more leaves us in some ways poorly prepared to make progress, to take advantage of the opportunity. The issue was largely ignored in educational research, as well as in the policy area. When the *Teacher's College Record* published a volume on dropouts in 1986 (Natriello), it was, to my knowledge, the first collection of fresh articles on the issue in perhaps 15 years.[1] There had been an article here and an article there, but this was the first time that any community of scholars had come together to develop a more-or-less comprehensive perspective on the issue. The consequence of this extended dearth of new thinking is that as we talk about what we know and what is working, we speak about promise as much as about proof. We have many promising activities launched, but few have had time to be proven. There will be trial and error in what we do as a result of past neglect.

Second, the data base on dropouts is a hopeless mess. I tried to review it in preparing for this chapter, and I came away confused and discouraged. I thought I knew what the dropout rate was. I thought I knew what *a* dropout rate was! I do not know what *a* dropout rate is anymore, let alone what *the* dropout rate is. In New York City, the range of published opinion on the matter goes from 33 to 53 percent, and these researchers are using fairly similar methodologies of cohort analysis, differing only in the details. It appears that the dropout rate may be between 33 and 53 percent in many cities, and most cities do not know which figure is closer to the fact. There have been reports for 15 years that the dropout rate is about 25 percent in the nation and holding steady, but now Chester Finn and others analyzing the 1980 census data report that among people 25 to 29 years of age, only 14 percent say they have not finished high school.[2]

Locally, of course, the issue is more confused than at the national level. A recent survey of 21 cities found almost that many different methodologies for computing dropout rates.[3] As a result, there was nothing to compare among cities, no benchmark one might look at. Rules concerning age, grade level, counting period, frequency of attendance, extended absence, student transfers, and attendance in alternative systems differ wildly. How could this happen? My answer is political: mostly, because we did not care very much. If we had cared very much as a nation we would know what the dropout rate was much more accurately than we do. If it were a profoundly important political issue at the local level, we would know more than we do. But the accurate analysis of dropout patterns was obviously not as important as trying to avoid blame for having a high dropout rate or trying to preserve state aid based on attendance figures—both of which seem to me, in my brief review of the literature, to be far more important determinants of how dropouts are counted than any analysis of the etiology of the dropout problem.

What do we know with some fair confidence about the most common patterns of dropping out? The pattern begins very early. It is most often observed in poor and minority families, those who are least-well-prepared and have the lowest expectations and least support for the educational enterprise. It often includes a lack of early-childhood training, early school failure, sometimes culminating in holding back, and a pattern of falling farther and farther behind. It includes the development of low self-esteem and of a fatalistic outlook on the part of the student. Later, it includes truancy, absenteeism, in-school delinquency, and suspension. But one thing it does *not* include is lack of academic talent. I have never seen a dropout study that could find much difference in the range of academic talent between dropouts and any comparison group in the school and the community. That amounts to a double tragedy: we are producing incompetent people who could very well be highly competent.

As the point of dropping out approaches, the pattern seems to culminate for the student in active dislike for school, alienation from it, and rejection of it—all accompanied by "pushout," the significant collaboration of the school in the latter stages of the process. For some students who have been through this pattern, dropping out is the easiest thing they ever did in school. They are welcomed into that central office as they have never been welcomed before, on that day when they come in to say that they are not going to grace this school with their presence anymore. Finally, there is a decision to go to work or to the street, and, in the case of young women, there is very often pregnancy and motherhood.

During the past decade, the consequences of dropping out have been increasingly devastating, as it more and more conforms to the cycle of dependency for young families formed in this way, and as it becomes a more and more serious economic disaster for the young person who drops out. When Jerrold Bachman did one of the first modern studies of dropping out in 1971, he found many cases in which the dropouts, at least in the short run, did as well economically as similar young people who had stayed in school.[4] By and large, those days are gone forever. Dropping out is now an economic disaster for the person who drops out. The unemployment rate is astronomical even as compared to high school graduates, let alone people who might go on to college.

What can work against this pattern? There is much that is promising and has, in individual instances, worked to reduce dropouts. The litany would include:

- Good early childhood programs
- Smaller schools
- Alternative schools

- Summer programs
- Programs with a larger experiential base or component
- Bilingual programs
- Administrative steps that change the rules of reentry to make it easier for students to return to school
- Programs that focus on teenage mothers
- Programs that focus on extended intensive counseling
- Programs that focus on collaborative efforts drawing on the business community and social service and community organization

All these approaches can work, and there seem to be instances in the literature in which they all do. But, considering the process I described earlier, many of these start late in the game; and in aggregate, the situation does not seem to improve much. We seem to have the problem encountered so often in education in which we can find hundreds of programs that work, and yet what we accomplish is to stand still at best. We cannot today say to ourselves that we have begun to make substantial inroads into the dropout problems in our nation or in our urban schools.

There is, then, a giant step yet to be taken. We must look beyond all special programs and projects for dropouts and begin to correct how the system as a whole works. And that, with all of the shortcomings of the excellence movement, is the fundamental insight of the education reforms proposed in the last four to five years. Look at the system itself rather than concentrating on improving this, that, or the other program that might correct this, or that, or the other aspect of the system. In looking at the system itself, the prescriptions are going to be the prescriptions given in this volume. We must give value to these students and their culture, both as individuals and as we construct the curriculum; the assumptions that these children bring to school are often remarkably different from the assumptions of the inherited curriculum in that school, and we must examine that right at the outset. We must understand and attend to their individual needs and talents and strengths, which may not be packaged in the conventional categories upon which school success has been predicted. We must expect them to succeed academically. We must create a disciplined climate of encouragement and fairness in the schools—not authoritarian rules, but a disciplined environment that pushes and presses students toward achievement. We must design a system that gives individual schools and teaching professionals autonomy and resources to respond daringly to local needs; the difference of these local contexts cannot be underestimated in constructing appropriate educational responses. We must draw on the family and the community and business to work collaboratively with us. It is in the nature of the problem that no one institution is going to be able to solve it. And we must not track or shunt off the problem to our Chapter I program or to our vocational education program or to our special education program or to our dropout program or to our alternative setting. Not that all of those do not have a role in the solution, but we must confront the issue in every ordinary school and ordinary classroom and begin to surmount it there, or we will not succeed in conquering it elsewhere.

We need to be talking about programs that engage the whole school, a school that is open and reaching out to the community it serves, and drawing that community in rather than walling it off, a high-status place with high expectations. Only then will fewer students endure the extended agony and the dire consequences of dropping out.

NOTES

1. G. Natriello, ed., *School Dropouts: Patterns and Policies.* New York: Teachers College Press.

2. C. E. Finn, Jr., "The High School Dropout Puzzle," *The Public Interest*, Spring 1987.

3. F. M. Hammack, "Large School System's Dropout Reports: An Analysis of Definitions, Procedures, and Findings." *Teachers College Record,* 87(5), (1986), 324–41.

4. J. G. Bachman, *Dropping Out: Problem or Symptom?* (Ann Arbor: University of Michigan, Institute for Social Research, 1971).

EIGHT

Reducing Dropouts Through Community-Promoted Initiatives

Roger D. Mitchell

The issue of school dropouts is one that has been with us for a long time. It remains a subject of extensive research, debate, and handwringing among parents, teachers, local school administrators, and national policy makers. By engaging in an ERIC (Educational Resource Information Center) search, one can acquire an extensive bibliography on the subject composed of citations of position papers, project descriptions, and research reports. Despite this growing body of literature, the dropout problem remains as a grim, constant reminder of a major failure in our multibillion-dollar education industry. A very positive element surrounding this issue is the continuing search for promising practices on reducing dropouts. This chapter profiles two specific programs (in Rochester, New York, and Flint, Michigan) that indicate promise of contributing to the solution, while at the same time addressing much broader issues.

In 1985 the National Urban League launched a five-year Education Initiative in response to the growing list of blatant inequities existing in the educational system. For example:

- Black college enrollment has decreased 18 percent since its high point in 1976.
- Dropout rates from high school are two to three times greater for Black students than for White students.
- The average child from a bottom quarter income family receives four fewer years of education than the child from a top quarter income family.
- Only half of the almost 10 million eligible students actually receive Chapter I compensatory education services.

With the launching of the Education Initiative, the National Urban League continued and heightened its leadership in the effort to upgrade the quality of education for all students in general and for Black, poor, and minority students in particular. Educational equity and excellence are the standards by which progress is assessed. Equity as now defined holds that, in addition to access, the educational system must provide a learning environment in which Black and poor students are able to demonstrate results that are commensurate with those of White students. Equity of educational programs can be measured by outcomes, such as reduction in dropout and pushout rates, improved attendance, improved retention rates of minorities in the four-year higher education programs, proportionate representation in programs for the gifted, reduction in the disproportionate representation of minority males in disciplinary actions (such as suspensions and expulsions), and standardized test scores that more nearly approximate those of similar White populations.

A Nation at Risk asserts that "the twin goals of equity and high-quality schooling have profound and practical meaning for our economy and society, and we cannot permit one to yield to the other either in principle or in practice."[1] In pursuing these goals, 90 of the 111 Urban League affiliates have designed education projects for Black, minority, and poor students in their service areas, aimed at overcoming their educational disadvantage and providing access to higher education and employment.

ROCHESTER, NEW YORK, PROGRAM

Rochester has an extraordinary program in operation. The Rochester Urban League continues its community-wide initiative, begun in 1985, which now involves over 60 local organizations in school improvement. The nearly 600 persons involved have formed building-based projects implemented by numerous school action committees, each of which is a member of a citywide steering committee.

Joining forces with the Center for Educational Development, the Rochester Urban League developed a community task force on education whose educational theme focused on the need:

- to involve parents more fully in their children's education and to improve communication between home and school
- to involve pupils more fully in their own education
- to encourage the professionalization of teaching
- for prekindergarten education

The task force's goal was "to engage the entire community in this initiative." Every segment of the community has an important role.

1. School-readiness was to be encouraged by city school district and community organization programs in parenting education, school/home coordination, and funding.

2. Parents, as the child's first teachers and continuing guardians, have vital roles in student health and motivation, and in supporting school activity and monitoring student progress.

3. Teachers, as "professional partners of the education team," were urged toward further professionalization, while setting high-quality educational goals for their students and cooperating with parents to accomplish those ends.

4. Business community commitment was sought to implement the recommendations of the Chamber of Commerce/Industrial Management Task Force. These included commitment to: (a) provide job placement opportunities as incentives for student performance; (b) join in partnerships between individual businesses and schools at every school building in the district; (c) help market education, in order to raise community awareness and participation in schooling; and (d) provide opportunities to teachers and staff to help enhance teaching and school management skills.

5. Community groups were given three general recommendations: (a) make education a focus of all organizations, (b) provide reinforcement by community funding sources, and (c) provide volunteer support for education.

6. Human service agencies were called upon to: (a) be knowledgeable about public school achievement issues and concerns, (b) make improvement of education achievement a priority in their work with parents and students, and (c) communicate the availability of their supportive services to educators and potential service consumers.

7. Cultural organizations play vital roles in providing arts that enhance student understanding of the world around them and help to build student self-esteem and personal development. Therefore they were urged to: (a) establish collaborative educational plans for city school district students, and (b) enhance their services and make them known to this clientele.

8. Service organizations, including labor unions, veteran, fraternal, social, and other groups, also were urged to expand upon some of their current activities in support of education.

9. Religious institutions were asked to consider the many activities for youths, parents, and families that can help to ensure the background strengths on which the challenges of educational achievement rest.

10. Colleges and universities play a major role in the educational life of the community, beyond educating teachers and school administrators. Further staff development, curricular consultation, and student motivation and training were cited as examples.

11. Libraries are important complements to the educational system, through access to their collections and through programming that helps students to understand ways in which learning fits them for the world around them.

12. The Department of Recreation and Community Services, through its athletic and arts and crafts programs for children and youth, helps to reinforce values

that enhance school performance. Complementary relationships between these programs and the school offerings increase the effectiveness of both.

As a result of the task force's "Call to Action," a phenomenal number of school-community partnerships were formed in a relatively short period of time—13 months. A partial list includes:

- Deloitte, Haskins and Sells will be working with Monroe High School to introduce accounting as a viable career choice for minority students through speakers, field trips, and provision of materials.
- The Gift Center and Third Presbyterian Church are teaming up with School 6 to detail needs and develop complementary programs using volunteers and donations from the church.
- Monroe Community College's Educational Opportunity Program is working with a number of Monroe High School seniors who are at risk, in order to insure their graduation.
- NOBCCHE (National Organization for the Professional Development of Black Chemists and Chemical Engineers) is continuing its award-winning joint science curriculum enrichment with School 2.
- University of Rochester helps sponsor the Career Beginnings Program, in which high school seniors get summer jobs and meet with adult mentors during the school year.

School action committees across the city school district were formed last year by principals of the district's 45 schools and community volunteers, with support and organizational assistance from the Urban League of Rochester. The objectives of these groups were tailored to address the perceived needs of the various schools. They ranged from direct academic objectives such as improving reading and language skills, to providing tutoring, improving student attendance and reducing suspensions, improving school image and/or environment, and improving parent understanding and parent/community involvement and parent/school communication.

A unique aspect of the citywide education initiative is the effort being made to raise public awareness about the issues and the program. Hutchins/Young and Rubicam is the lead agency serving in partnership with the Education Task Force of the Advertising Council of Rochester in a communications campaign supporting quality education in Rochester. The focus of the communications effort is to reach students, parents, teachers and school administrators, community and business leaders, as well as the general public. As described by the campaign director:

- "First and foremost, there will be a common program identity.
- Second, there will be a theme for the general community and its segments that speaks to our shared responsibility to help kids learn.

- Third, we will establish a different theme for the kids that speaks their language, in terms they understand and will respond to.
- Fourth, all the messages will have a compelling emotional element to them.
- And finally, we will promote progress as it is made, to keep the momentum going."

It is clear that a major commitment has been made by all of the major segments of the Rochester community to effectuate change in support of quality education. This commitment has been translated into action by many groups. The change has begun. The Urban League contact person in Rochester is:

Ms. Betty Dwyer
Manager, Education Initiative
Urban League of Rochester
177 North Clinton Avenue
Rochester, New York 14604
(716) 325–6530

FLINT, MICHIGAN

The Flint Urban League has initiated a program to collaborate with local school districts and other educational institutions to improve academic achievement. The program, entitled Equal Results Educational Initiative, identified four components that address barriers to Black educational achievement in Flint. These were identified by the "Think Tank Committee," a volunteer community-based group of parents and educators who serve as an advisory board to the Educational Initiative. The components include:

1. *Parent Enrichment*: Focusing on assisting parents in becoming more effective advocates for their children by providing information on accessing the school system, preparing children to function equally and competitively with majority culture children, and providing parenting information on techniques that produce confident, disciplined, young people able to succeed in spite of barriers.

2. *Incentives for Success*: A long-term approach to providing comprehensive assistance to children out of school. Twenty high-risk seventh graders have been selected to participate in a six-year educational enrichment program that will focus on overcoming individual barriers to their educational success. Participants who complete this program and successfully graduate from high school will be awarded scholarships to fund their post-high school educations.

3. *Incentives for Black Scholars*: Seeks to encourage those Black high school honor graduates who have demonstrated academic excellence by honoring all Black high school graduates at a Black Scholars Awards Dinner. In addition, efforts will be made to increase the number of Black scholars by offering alternative guidance, support, and scholarships so that each Black scholar will be able to adequately finance post-high-school education.

4. *Conflict Resolution School Initiatives*: Focuses on reducing the number of Black students suspended from school for fighting, by training students to be volunteer conflict managers within the schools. This will be an effort whereby the Urban League will work with school officials and parents seeking to use this alternative method of identified Black reactive behavior that is hindering academic achievement.

Activities for all four program components were launched in January 1987. A number of program objectives have already been attained. In the Parent Enrichment component, parents of at-risk students entering middle school were chosen as the target population. A series of five workshop modules was developed for use with participating parents. The modules were designed to: highlight the complications involved in raising children today, point out the predominate influence parents have in the lives of their children, and suggest methods to help parents positively influence their children's lives. The five program modules were entitled: Overview: Challenges of Parenting in the 80's, Challenges of Early Adolescence, Nurturing Self Concept, Social Pressures of Early Adolescence, and Parent Involvement in Successful Academic Preparation. Outside speakers were engaged to make presentations to the parents at each session. The five workshops were run over a seven-week period, with 21 parents participating.

Most of the first five months' work on the Incentives for Success component was spent on planning and start-up activities. The Incentives for Success Advisory Committee hosted a banquet for the 20 parents and students at Bryant Middle School with whom the committee will be working.

The Advisory Committee developed an Incentives for Success Statement of Commitment stating the program's objectives and identifying the comprehensive support services to be provided to student participants. Those included:

• Tutorial Services
• Mentors
• Crisis Intervention
• Cultural Enrichment
• Career Awareness
• Self-Concept/Self-Esteem Development
• Peer Support
• Manners and Morals Development

To formally engage parent participation and support for this program, a Parent Commitment Pledge was also developed for the parents or guardians of student participants to sign. At the end of the school year the students, who are considered members of the Incentives for Success Club, and their parents and adult sponsors are special guests at the Flint Urban League's Salute to Black Scholars Banquet.

The stated goal of the third program component, Incentives for Black Scholars, is to recognize and support the academic achievements of Black graduating high school students throughout Genesee County, thereby encouraging them to continue to achieve and influence younger students to emulate them and strive to graduate as Black scholars. To attain this goal the program will:

- identify Black high school seniors in the Flint area with very good and excellent grades
- provide recognition for the achievement of those students earning cumulative 3.0 grade point averages by the third quarter of their senior year
- provide motivation and information to students eligible to be Black scholars; over the course of their senior year, to further promote academic achievement, post-secondary education and career planning
- track Black scholars as they move through their educational and occupational careers, for record keeping and to provide a resource pool for the Urban League of Flint and the community
- provide financial assistance for the continuing education of eligible Black high school seniors

In February, the Black Scholars Incentive Subcommittee hosted an Orientation Rally for newly identified scholars. Letters were mailed to 170 students identified by 11 school districts in the county as eligible to participate. Approximately 140 students and their parents attended the rally.

In May a Salute to Black Scholars Banquet was held honoring 114 students. Twenty organizations joined the Urban League in presenting scholarships to 73 students. Urban League-administered scholarships totaled more than $50,000. In addition, each Black scholar received a $50.00 U.S. Savings Bond.

A widely quoted statistic indicates that at high school levels, Black students are suspended three times as often as White students. The Conflict Resolution School Initiative seeks to see that conflict mediation techniques are used in resolving conflicts with students instead of standard disciplinary measures, thus reducing the incidence of school suspension.

This component is patterned after "Justice Without Walls," a program sponsored by the Flint Human Relations Commission, which calls for disputants to discuss their problems and solve their differences before a panel trained in conflict resolution. While this program is aimed at helping resolve conflicts in the community, the Urban League's Conflict Resolution School Initiative specifically targets high school students.

For those wishing to serve as mediators the training is free and voluntary. Each trainee receives 20 hours of training in conflict mediation techniques, using a special training manual, videotape, and role playing in which the students practice the different roles involved in a conflict.

In the period January–May 1987, a total of 32 persons successfully completed training. These included 13 students, 9 school staff, 6 community volunteers, and 4 who were unidentified as to group. There is a growing waiting list for the next round of training. In addition to the local training effort, the Flint Board of Education sent one of its staff persons to be trained as a trainer by Community Boards in Washington, D.C. This person will assist the Urban League effort in training Flint Community School's students and staff during the summer.

Commenting on the Conflict Resolution Program, the superintendent of the Beecher School District stated that the district is adopting the program because it will give students an alternative route to solve conflicts. He also said the program will definitely reduce suspensions, and he hopes students will use it in their lives. The Urban League contact person in Flint is

> Ms. Marcia Johnson
> Director of Educational Service
> Urban League of Flint
> 202 East Boulevard Drive
> Flint, Michigan 48503
> (313) 239–5111

The two programs described above highlight the key elements of educational equity and excellence for the communities and students being served. The Rochester program is unique in the scope of activities being conducted, in the broad base of community organization support and participation, and in the relatively short period of time it took to attain the current level of program activity. Likewise, the Flint program has quickly rallied community support and participation for its more focused agenda on parent and student support services.

Since both programs have been operating for less than a year, they have not had time to fully mature, or to generate sufficient data to be able to claim success in realizing educational change and significant positive outcomes for disadvantaged students in their respective communities. What can be confidently stated is that these two programs, like a number of others being run by Urban League affiliates, represent promising practices that will not only impact on the dropout problem, but on the broader issue of educational equity and excellence.

NOTE

1. National Commission on Excellence in Education, *A Nation at Risk: The Imperative for Educational Reform. A Report to the Nation and the Secretary of Education* (Washington: D.C.: U.S. Department of Education, 1983), p. 13.

NINE

Making Education Work for Hispanic-Americans: Some Promising Community-Based Practices

Lori S. Orum

INTRODUCTION

The American educational system is often portrayed as a pipeline, success-fully transporting individuals from childhood to college or full participation in the world of work. However, it has become increasingly clear that this pipeline more closely resembles a sieve where Hispanic children, youth, and adults are concerned. National and state data and local experience doc-ument that Hispanics slip out of this pipeline at disproportionate rates. From kindergarten through college, proportionately fewer Hispanics than either Blacks or Whites are enrolled in schools, and those who are enrolled are often prepared for very different futures than non-Hispanic children.

Only recently have the public and the schools begun to confront the fact that student demographics are changing rapidly. The schools are being called upon to serve a growing proportion of ethnic- and language-minority-group children—the very children they have historically served least well. While business and labor leaders, commissions, and study groups continue to warn about the inability of dropouts and students without post-high-school edu-cation and training to find productive work in our changing economy, dropout rates remain high, and the majority of minority-group students continue to be found in non-college-bound tracks. In fact, some of the measures adopted

This chapter is copyrighted by The National Council of La Raza, © 1987, and is used with the permission of The National Council of La Raza.

in the past five years in the name of "school reform" may actually push these figures higher.[1]

The National Council of La Raza believes that fundamental changes in the philosophy, structure, and practices of schooling are necessary if the public schools are to do a better job of educating Hispanic and other minority group students. Equity and excellence in education must be viewed as twin and inseparable goals. However, given the resistance to change inherent in most bureaucratic systems, systematic restructuring of the schools must realistically be viewed as a critical but long-term agenda. The Council's Innovative Education Project was launched in 1984 both as a means of contributing experiences and input from the community level to the school reform process, and as a means of addressing some of the short-term needs of students who are currently enrolled in school systems unresponsive to their needs.

This chapter provides an overview of the National Council of La Raza's Innovative Education Project, an effort to demonstrate and evaluate effective models for use by Hispanic community-based organizations to improve educational outcomes for Hispanic students. Based on a review of the research literature, data on educational outcomes for Hispanics, and extensive interviews with Hispanic community-based organizations, the council developed five program models that can be used by community-based organizations to improve the educational attainment of Hispanic students.

Three of the five models are designed to address the school-age groups and special populations that both national research and local community experience indicate are among the most educationally "at-risk." The remaining two projects address the needs to parents and teachers, whose informed assistance is essential to improve children's educational outcomes.

The project is currently working with local Hispanic community-based organizations, formally affiliated with the council, to demonstrate and evaluate these models. Since such demonstrations in most cases require new sources of funding, all models are not currently operational in all sites. Five projects in four sites have been fully funded and are operational; 15 other agencies are developing local variations of the models, seeking funding and training staff.

At this point in our project, there are no evaluation results to present our definitive assertions about "what works" with Hispanic students in community-based programs. This chapter reports on the progress of the project to date, provides information on the models themselves and the information that led to their development, and offers some general impressions gathered during the process of demonstrating and evaluating these programs.

The approach of working with Hispanic community-based organizations reflects the council's belief that these institutions are critical components of the Hispanic community and centers for leadership development and for change within communities. The project also reflects the belief that parents and communities have both a strong interest in and a responsibility for helping to improve the quality of education available to their children and youth.

The models for community-based educational programs developed by the council's Innovative Education Project are based on an examination of the educational status of Hispanics, promising practices, and the specific concerns raised by local communities. An overview of that information is provided below.

THE EDUCATIONAL STATUS OF HISPANICS

Of the 41.4 million children attending public schools in the United States in the fall of 1984, 8.8 percent, or approximately 3.6 million, were Hispanic. While Hispanics were enrolled in elementary school at about the same rates as Blacks and Whites (99.2 percent), only 90.3 percent of Hispanics of high school age were enrolled in high school, and only 60.0 percent of Hispanics aged 18 to 24 were high school graduates. Thus national data indicate that approximately four in ten Hispanics ages 18 to 24 were high school dropouts.[2]

Signs of educational risk appear early for Hispanic children, as indicated by enrollment below expected grade level. Data from the 1984 Current Population Survey indicate that almost one-third (28 percent) of Hispanic children in grades one through four are enrolled below grade level, compared to 25 percent of Black students and 20 percent of White students. By middle school years, this enrollment below grade level has increased so that nearly four in ten (39.5 percent) Hispanic students in grades five to eight are at least one year below model grade, compared to 37.3 percent of Blacks and 24.9 percent of Whites. That figure increases to 43.1 percent in the early high school years, then drops to 34.8 percent in grades eleven and twelve, when many of these below-grade-level students are old enough and discouraged enough to withdraw from school.

Additionally, recent research suggests that grade-level retention as an educational strategy is of questionable benefit, since children who are underachieving but who are promoted with their peer group seem to make greater gains than children who are retained to repeat the grade. According to Wheelock "retained pupils fall behind during the year they are retained and spend the rest of their academic careers in a vain attempt to catch up."[3] In a review of the literature on retention, Wheelock concludes: "being held back once increases chances of dropping out by 90%."[4] Since below-grade-level enrollment occurs frequently among Hispanic youth, school delay must be seen as an important risk factor in the education of Hispanics.

Regarding the type of curriculum and classes taken, Hispanic students are less likely to be placed in programs for gifted and talented children than are White or Black children. Hispanics are similarly underrepresented in high school honors classes; in fact, of all racial/ethnic groups, Hispanic high school seniors were the least likely to participate in honors mathematics and English courses, according to the High School and Beyond study.

Hispanics are also disproportionately represented in remedial courses and low-level curriculum tracks. High School and Beyond reported that nearly four in ten Hispanic high school students were enrolled in remedial mathematics and English classes.[5] By their senior year in high school, High School and Beyond data indicate, nearly three-fourths of Hispanic students had been placed in nonacademic curricular tracks. Some 40 percent were in "general" curricular tracks, designed for students who do not expect to continue their education beyond high school; and 35 percent were in vocational programs, with the majority enrolled in business and occupations courses. As well documented in the William T. Grant Foundation Commission on Work, Family and Citizenship's recently released report, "The Forgotten Half: Non-College Youth in America," a high school diploma does not open many doors in today's labor market. The commission found that "where high school graduates could once seek steady, good paying jobs in manufacturing, agriculture, and transportation, they find these positions are disappearing by the millions."[6] These youth are being prepared to participate in a labor market that no longer exists and, in the words of the commission, "face a questionable future."

Data from John Goodlad's "A Study of Schooling" as reported by Jeannie Oakes in *Keeping Track: How Schools Structure Inequality* and various journal articles, point out clearly that children in lower level tracks (which are disproportionately composed of Hispanic and Black students) are taught with very different methods and aims than students in higher level tracks. Teacher expectations—a powerful influence on student outcomes—are lower, higher-order thinking skills are not developed, and students are taught mainly by drill and repetition. Oakes further reports that high-level tracks teach "high status content," which she defines as "literature, expository and thematic writing, library research, and mathematical ideas." In contrast, she found that students in low-level courses were not expected to learn these skills, but spent most time practicing language mechanics and computation.[7] With such different curricular content and teaching styles, assignment to lower level tracks usually operates as a dead-end placement, with the students being prepared throughout their school experiences for a significantly limited future. Thus, even those who graduate from high school finish their education at a competitive disadvantage.

Hispanic students graduating from high school in 1980 had completed fewer Carnegie Units than White students in almost every type of academic subject. Hispanic high school graduates were also less likely than White high school graduates to have received As in school and were almost twice as likely to have received grades of D or F. Compared to other minority students, grade point averages of Hispanic graduates were slightly higher than those of Black students and dramatically lower than those of Asian and

Pacific Islander students. Hispanics were also most likely to report failing or below-average grades in core academic subjects: mathematics (35.3 percent), natural sciences (34.6 percent), social sciences (34.2 percent), and English (31.4 percent). Over one-third of Hispanic high school graduates in 1980 earned a D or F average in core academic subjects. Thus, as measured by both type of courses taken and grades received, Hispanic high school graduates have had a high school experience quite different from that of most White students, an experience that does not prepare them well for the future.

Almost half of Puerto Rican and Mexican-American students do not stay in school long enough to earn diplomas from any track; they drop out, some 40 percent departing before the second semester of their sophomore year. Some of these youth reenroll in adult education or community-based employment and training programs and secure General Educational Development (GED) certificates, or return to school. A recent study by the General Accounting Office estimates that 50 percent may return, but other studies indicate that Hispanic students return less frequently than White students.[8] Regardless of the number of students who eventually reenroll, the fact remains that something important was missing in their initial public school experience.

There are a variety of reasons why students leave high school without receiving a diploma. Some are personal characteristics or factors; some are characteristics of the schools that they attend. While many laundry lists are offered of personal factors that purportedly identify potential Hispanic dropouts, the factors most consistently linked to dropping out have to do with family socioeconomic status (SES) and other aspects of family background. However, caution should be taken in assessing the relationship between student behaviors and choices (e.g., marriage, pregnancy, working) and the decision to drop out. While a relationship is indicated, the direction of causation is unclear.[9]

The characteristics of the schools that dropouts attend are more important factors in why students leave school. Schools may not be able to change the social or economic backgrounds of the students they serve, but they do control the decisions made on how to educate those students.[10] Among the factors within the schools' control are attendance, discipline and promotion policies, resource allocation, hiring practices, the availability of special instruction to meet special needs, inservice training for teachers and counselors, and provisions made to ensure parental involvement. Certainly the lack of Hispanic role models among teachers and other school staff, the limited attention counselors report giving to Hispanic students, work-study and cooperative education programs that underserve Hispanics, the lack of appropriate programs to meet language needs and involve parents, and the fact that many Hispanics attend schools in districts with low per-pupil expenditures, high pupil/teacher ratios, and limited resources all affect the quality of education provided to Hispanics and contribute to decisions to leave school.

The 1982 Follow-up to the High School and Beyond Study asked Hispanic youth who had been sophomore participants in the 1980 study and subsequently dropped out of school about their reasons for leaving school. Early marriage and/or pregnancy were listed as contributing reasons by Hispanic girls, with 33 percent reporting leaving because of marriage or plans to marry, and 25 percent listing pregnancy as a reason for dropping out. Some 26 percent of male dropouts indicated that they left because they had been offered a job and chose to work, and 17 percent indicated that they had been expelled or suspended. Again, the caution about the lack of clarity in the direction of causation in the relationship of these factors should be noted.

The largest group of Hispanic students (34 percent of males and 32 percent of females) reported leaving school because of poor grades. Other national data on Hispanic educational attainment support the youths' contention that they dropped out in large part due to poor grades and low attainment that led them to conclude that school was simply not for them. In fact, Michelle Fine's work in New York City high schools revealed that so convinced are these students that they have failed and that they are simply not able to be learners in the school setting, that they may actually experience—in the short term—higher self-esteem after they drop out than do non-college-bound students who stay in school.[11]

Teachers and parents, two groups with immense influence on student achievement, are often not effectively and positively involved in the education of Hispanic students. Many parents face educational barriers to effective participation. The average Hispanic adult 25 years and over has completed only 11.5 years of schooling, and 13.5 percent of Hispanics in this age group have less than a fifth-grade education. Further, some studies have suggested that some 56 percent of Hispanic adults can be considered functionally illiterate in English. Parents with low educational levels, high rates of English illiteracy, and previously unsuccessful experiences with school often have a difficult time knowing how to help their children succeed in school. Further, when the language of the parent is Spanish and the language of the school, its teachers, office workers, counselors, and principals is English, communication becomes a formidable barrier. While studies indicate that Hispanic parents have high—sometimes unrealistically high—aspirations for their children, many lack the skills and confidence to provide their children with the academic benefits associated with active parent involvement.

Regarding teachers, there are few Hispanics in the nation's teaching force (only 2.6 percent of elementary school teachers and 1.7 percent of secondary school teachers) and a similarly small proportion among administrators (2.5 percent of central office staff and 2.0 percent of principals) and guidance counselors (2.7 percent). Thus there are few role models among school personnel, and few persons who are intimately familiar with the Spanish language and the cultures of Hispanic children.

While there are non-Hispanic teachers who speak Spanish and are familiar with the cultures of their students, those teachers are often assigned to work in bilingual education and other language-assistance programs, which serve only a small proportion of Hispanic children. These teachers are also in short supply in almost every district. Consequently, Hispanic students who do not need language assistance rarely encounter such teachers, and so short is the supply of bilingual teachers with cross-cultural skills that Hispanic students who are in such programs often do not encounter such teachers either. Most are taught by teachers who know little about Hispanics, and were never trained to provide instruction to language-minority students.

November 1983 data from the Survey of Teacher Demand and Shortage conducted by the National Center for Education Statistics indicated that there were 3,590 uncertified teachers teaching in bilingual education programs, accounting for 12 percent of all uncertified teachers in the schools. The same survey found that bilingual education had the greatest proportional shortages of any field of education, and that the fewest special recruitment and training incentives were offered by public schools to attract teachers in that field. At the same time, traditional education and teacher training programs have not prepared teachers or administrators to be effective educators of minority group students who may have different language needs and cultures different from those of "mainstream" students, and many school personnel feel unequipped and frustrated.

Unfortunately, some have translated this frustration, along with their inability to understand or effectively teach Hispanic students, into low expectations for those students. Several studies have found that Hispanic students report feeling that their teachers and counselors hold low expectations for them. A Colorado study found that dropouts cited "problems with school officials" and "negative attitudes of teachers" as two of the principal reasons why minority students left school. Some 46 percent of minority dropouts interviewed for that study also reported that a school official had encouraged them to drop out, and more than 50 percent said they would have stayed in school if someone had encouraged them to do so.[12] The minority dropouts were also more likely than others to report perceiving racism and prejudice in society and school and related these perceptions about school strongly to teachers' expectations and school policies on suspension and expulsion.

DESCRIPTION OF THE MODEL PROJECTS

While some school districts, or—more commonly—individual schools, are highly effective in meeting the needs of Hispanic students, the majority can be more fairly described as "underachieving" schools. These are the schools that most Hispanic students attend. Either through lack of will, training, or resources (or some combination thereof), these schools have not succeeded well in providing an equitable and excellent education for their Hispanic students.

Even when commitment is high, sufficient resources are available, and teachers and administrators are willing to tinker with the structure of the school, the schools face a formidable challenge in effectively serving Hispanic students and their families. Bilingual personnel are in notoriously short supply in most schools, and the shortage of bilingual counselors, psychologists, health personnel, and parent outreach workers is even more pronounced.

The segmented nature of public education also makes it difficult for schools to plan for or coordinate familywide learning programs. Few elementary and secondary schools are able to offer education or training to parents either to help them become partners in their children's education or to upgrade their own skills. Adult education programs are generally not connected to programs serving children, and most concentrate on the basic educational skills necessary for parents to learn English or secure GED certificates, rather than the skills that might help them help their children with school. Those parent programs that are run through elementary and secondary schools are too often viewed as a "frill," and when budgets must be cut, are usually among the first casualties.

Few schools have the resources to address the nonacademic needs of students and their families, although those needs can frequently interfere with a student's ability to be an effective learner. Lack of affordable safe housing, unemployment, emergency cash needs for food and heat, lack of affordable health care, needs for counseling or assistance in times of crisis can cause formidable barriers to education for low-income Hispanic families. In recent years, several approaches have been developed to try to pull together community resources to meet these needs for students, including Cities in Schools nationally, and Focus on Youth in Los Angeles.

However, few schools have discovered or utilized a natural resource in many Hispanic communities or Hispanic community-based organizations (CBOs). These CBOs have several advantages in reaching Hispanic families, especially low-income, non-English speaking families. They are located in the community, are staffed by bilingual personnel, and generally offer a variety of services that are used by low-income, limited English proficient parents. Many of these agencies provide services that reach families in crisis situations—emergency food, clothing, or fuel assistance; neighborhood health clinics; teen pregnancy programs; substance abuse or family counseling programs. Others assist undocumented families in legalizing their immigration status; provide low-cost child care for preschoolers, latchkey services for school-age children, and dropout recovery programs; and offer employment and training programs for unemployed or underemployed adults. Some Hispanic CBOs offer English as a Second Language (ESL) and GED programs. These organizations are designed to serve the very people whom the schools have often had the most difficulty reaching—the poor, the non-English speaking, the recent immigrant, and families in crisis.

Hispanic CBOs are also some of the few Hispanic-controlled community institutions to provide leadership development, programs, and advocacy for the Hispanic community. There is no network of historically Hispanic colleges and universities, Hispanic sororities and fraternities, or Hispanic churches comparable to those institutions in the Black community. In many Hispanic communities, Hispanic community-based organizations, therefore, play a key role in providing services to Hispanic families, informing and involving parents and developing leadership.

In 1984, the La Raza council conducted a survey of its affiliated Hispanic community-based organizations to determine what kinds of services were being provided relating to education. The survey indicated that many organizations had developed preschool and early childhood programs, but then did little with school-age children or their families. Educational programming resumed only in working with youth who had dropped out of school, become delinquent, developed alcohol or drug dependency problems, and with adults who were working to obtain a GED in conjunction with an employment and training program. These groups had become expert at operating "recovery" programs, helping youth and adults pick up the pieces of their lives after unsuccessful adolescence and schooling.

This approach was dictated in part by the fact that funders have traditionally viewed the provision of educational services to school-age children as the exclusive domain of the schools, and in part by limited staff expertise in education. However, the same survey noted universal concern with the state of schooling for Hispanic students in local communities, and the desire to be able to prevent some of the educational damage to Hispanic children. The Council's Innovative Education Project was designed to help Hispanic CBOs become effective partners with the schools, and use their unique ability to combine social service approaches with educational programming for students and families that the schools have traditionally had difficulty serving well.

Using the results of the above-mentioned survey, extensive interviews with affiliated CBOs, and a synthesis of the previously cited research, the La Raza council developed five models that Hispanic CBOs could use to contribute to improving education for Hispanic students and their families in their communities. These models were designed to be relatively low cost, bring together a variety of community resources and volunteers, involve whole families, and utilize innovative and effective educational techniques. While the programs are run by the CBOs, they are designed to cooperate with the schools, provide information and feedback to teachers and local administrators, and share their insights and experiences with the schools.

This process led the council and its affiliates to define the following as critical needs to be addressed by community-based interventions:

- Reducing grade-level retention in the early school years.
- Increasing the number of Hispanic youth who enroll and succeed in college-preparatory tracks in high school (recognizing that those decisions are most commonly made based on junior high school grades and experiences).
- Helping youth who have already dropped out to reenroll in an educational program and complete a course of study that will lead to either higher education or stable employment.
- Improving the ability of Hispanic parents to help their children become successful learners in school.
- Raising the expectations that teachers hold for Hispanic students and improving their skills in working with Hispanic children.

Five program models were designed in response to these concerns. The models and their essential components are described below.

THE MODELS

Academia del Pueblo

The Academia del Pueblo addresses the problems of early academic failure and grade retention faced by many Hispanic children in elementary school, by establishing after-school and summer "academies" to provide reinforcement and supplemental educational assistance to help children meet and exceed grade promotion requirements in elementary school. During the school year, the program can be offered from two to five afternoons per week, depending on local resources and needs.

Children may be recommended for the Academia by either parents or teachers, and teacher assessments of the areas in which a child needs additional skills are solicited. While the programs typically charge a very minimal fee for participation (which may be waived based on income), the real "cost" to the parent is time for parental involvement. A parent contract is required for each child, stipulating that the parent will attend at least 50 percent of the monthly parent education activities, read with the child at home for a contracted amount of time (or, in the case of parents with limited reading skills, have the child read aloud to the parent), establish and enforce rules for homework and school attendance, review and sign the child's homework, and ensure that the child has a library card.

Instruction for the child centers around language arts and reading (ESL where necessary), mathematics and problem solving skills, and enrichment activities such as computer education and Spanish. Instruction is provided by a group of teachers (the head teacher must be certificated and experienced in working with Hispanic children) and cross-age tutors. Hispanic high school honors students have been used very successfully in the first Academia demonstration. Instructors are encouraged to use cooperative learning techniques wherever possible, and the belief that all children can learn given the appropriate instruction is the credo of the program.

While local variations occur depending upon specific needs and resources, the council has defined the following as essential components of the Academia, and insists that each local demonstration:

1. Primarily serve children in kindergarten through fourth grade who are experiencing difficulty in school as indicated by low reading ability, limited proficiency in English, above-average rates of absenteeism or disciplinary problems, low test scores, or previous incidence of retention.

2. Give highest priority for admission to students who are in immediate danger of being retained to repeat a grade level.

3. Have improvement of reading skills as a central program component.

4. Contain a component designed to assist the parents of children enrolled in the program. Such a program must seek to increase the parents' ability to help their children learn, confidence and skills in interacting with the school systems, and their expectations and aspirations for their children.

5. Base instructional programs on an individualized assessment of need.

6. Secure a cooperative agreement with the schools referring children to the project and establish a regular means of communication between the Academia and the schools.

7. Be based on the philosophy that all children can succeed in school given proper assistance and instruction.

8. Have on its instructional staff at least one certified teacher experienced in working with limited English proficient and Hispanic students.

9. Make some use (on either a volunteer or staff basis) of student tutors to provide positive role models for younger children and allow for cross-age tutoring.

10. Provide students with instruction through the language in which they are most proficient. Thus, limited English proficient students are to receive content instruction in Spanish and also receive assistance with English language development.

11. Comply with the evaluation design and collect and report data to the council evaluator on a timely basis.

Other components that are desirable, but not required, include providing enrichment activities to gifted children or children meeting or exceeding grade requirements. Such children may be served in a separate group or on a special day, or a restricted number of slots may be allocated for these children to participate in the general Academia program. Programs are also encouraged to use an enrichment rather than a remedial approach for all children (low and high achievers) participating in the program. Instruction in Spanish as a second language and instruction with and about computers is also encouraged where possible.

The Academia del Pueblo is currently completing its second demonstration year in Kansas City, Missouri. The program is being operated by the Council-affiliated Guadalupe Center, a multiservice Hispanic community-based organization, and has spurred the development of several additional educational programs at the agency. The Kansas City Academia services neighborhood Hispanic children in kindergarten through sixth grade from both public and parochial schools. Currently 48 children are served in this after-school and summer program. Preliminary evaluation results give the program high marks from students, parents, and the local school principals and teachers. This model will also be demonstrated in Milwaukee, Wisconsin, by council affiliate Centro de la Comunidad later in 1987.

Project Success

Project Success is designed primarily to serve Hispanic youth in middle or junior high schools to increase their high school completion and college entrance rates by providing them with academic enrichment, career and academic counseling, and other special opportunities. In most cases, the project is specifically concerned with equipping youth with the skills and interest to enroll and succeed in college-preparatory curriculum tracks when they reach high school. It is designed to operate from two to five days per week after school and in the summer, depending on local resources. Project Success offers academic instruction, career awareness, and personal development activities, since youth need to be not only encouraged but also enabled.

While the research literature and all the communities included in the project to date have identified middle school/junior high school as a critical point for intervention, the model does not have to be used exclusively for that age group. Project Success may also be used with younger or older at-risk students if the aim is to increase academic success, reduce tracking, lead to higher rates of high school graduation, and increase the possibility of postsecondary education and/or training. Since an important goal of the project is to avoid low-level tracking, a project in Rochester, New York, discovered that critical tracking decisions in that school system were being made in fifth grade and, therefore, designed a Project Success to work with fourth- and fifth-grade students. A Project Success demonstration just beginning in Chicago will work with fifth- through eighth-grade students, and a project under development in northern New Mexico plans to work with youth enrolled below grade level and in high school. However, the majority of Project Success demonstrations will involve early adolescents.

As in the Academia, referral may come from parents or teachers and participation requires both a signed parent contract and a teacher assessment. However, given the much higher level of choice available to adolescents—who typically vote with their feet—the programs must also be reflective of student-perceived needs and design activities that meet the interests of the young people. Program practitioners working with middle and junior high school students are asked to draw on the research of the Center for Early Adolescence in planning programs to ensure that activities are developmentally appropriate for young teens.

Because many of the students participating in Project Success will be the products of low-level ability tracks, the projects are to pay particular attention to the development of higher order thinking and analytic skills, and problem-solving skills in math rather than simply computation skills. They are also asked to employ cooperative learning techniques wherever possible. Curricula available through the council reflect these needs.

Through a partnership with Time, Inc. and the Xerox Corporation, four local sites are using the "Time to Read" program as a part of their reading improvement efforts. The program uses high-interest materials (*Time, Sports Illustrated,* and *People* magazines), features small "study group" style instruction, involves adults from local businesses who also serve as role models and sources of information about the world of work, and provides students with their own subscriptions to magazines—ensuring that high-interest reading materials are available at home. This curriculum has been used for one year in four sites (three with young teens and one with adults) and has been very warmly received by students and tutors alike.

The council also makes available training in and curriculum for Law Related Education as a vehicle for improving students' oral language, analytic, and reasoning skills. Through a partnership with the Constitutional Rights Foundation, a special set of materials is being developed for use in Innovative Education Projects. Evidence that Law Related Education also has a positive influence on delinquency reduction also makes the program popular with communities that have identified delinquency, drugs, and gang activity as a major concern for youth of this age.

Finally, a relationship with the American Association for the Advancement of Science (AAAS) Opportunities in Science program has made available training and curriculum for teaching problem solving in math and science. Groups are also encouraged to form relationships with local science and technology centers and museums to provide students with hands-on experiences with science and math, and recruit individuals who can tell youth about careers requiring math and science proficiency.

Career education is to be addressed by involving as many volunteers in the program as possible—either as subject-matter tutors, guest speakers, or mentors for students interested in specific fields. At least one lead teacher and a counselor are required and each student is to have an individually developed "success plan." To provide essential components, each local Project Success is expected to:

1. Primarily serve students who are at risk of being tracked into nonacademic programs (or already are in such programs). Students enrolled in or achieving below grade level are primary candidates for participation in Project Success.
2. Involve parents and other significant family members.
3. Include both academic services and career awareness activities so students are encouraged and provided with needed information and skills.
4. Provide real opportunities for students who are below grade level to "catch up" with peers by offering tutoring, special classes, or seminars. Projects should also investigate the possibility of arranging for mastery exams through the school district.
5. Have some type of cooperating relationship with the schools and provide for communication with the students' school counselors.
6. Provide opportunities for students to learn about a variety of professional and technical careers, and include opportunities for youth to interact with and learn from adults working in careers of interest.
7. Provide youth with the opportunity to form supportive relationships with knowledgeable and caring adults who are neither family members nor regular school teachers.
8. Include bilingual personnel.
9. Collect data, document project progress, and follow the Innovative Education Project's evaluation design.
10. Design project activities that reflect the developmental needs of early adolescents, of the age group of the target population.

Project Second Chance

Project Second Chance was designed in recognition of the needs of the large proportion of Hispanic youth who have already left school without diplomas. The program may operate in a variety of different ways because funding sources for these types of endeavors vary tremendously. Local programs may be full- or part-time, and with or without job training and placement. However, the basic aim of the project is to provide educational services and counseling so that youth can either gain a high school equivalency certificate or diploma and continue on with some type of education—traditional postsecondary or specialized training.

As with Project Success, Project Second Chance programs must deal with the fact that most students will be products of low-level tracks and consequently need assistance in developing higher order thinking and reading skills and problem-solving abilities. The programs utilize the curricular materials and approaches outlined for Project Success, plus whatever other materials and subjects are required by local accrediting agencies. Several computer-assisted instructional curricula are also being evaluated for possible use by these programs as one facet of the program.

As with the models previously described, instructional programs are individualized, parent involvement is required, cooperative learning techniques are used, and counseling and career education are part of the program. A Project Second Chance is currently being demonstrated in Houston, Texas, by the Association for the Advancement of Mexican Americans, an Hispanic community-based organization that has had its educational program accredited by the State of Texas and can grant Texas high school diplomas. Other variations are being developed by organizations that do not have such status, but plan to concentrate on preparation for the GED certificate. This project, perhaps more than any other, will vary substantially by local site; still, each site shall:

1. Recruit and enroll youth or young adults who have dropped out or been excluded from school.
2. Involve parents, spouses, and other significant family members.
3. Provide an academic program that will allow participants to acquire a strong foundation in reading and writing and all other required subjects and earn either a high school diploma or GED certificate.
4. Provide career awareness activities that expose students to information about a variety of professional and technical careers (especially nontraditional careers or fields where Hispanics have been underrepresented), and provide opportunities for youth to interact with adults working in careers of interest.
5. Provide students with personal development activities such as goal setting, planning, study skills, conflict resolution, family living, job success skills, and other "maturity" skills.
6. Have some type of cooperative relationship with the schools from which the students have dropped out, where possible, in order to gain access to students' records and to determine the possibility of the student's reenrolling in school.
7. Provide youth with the opportunity to form supportive relationships with knowledgeable and caring adults who are neither family members nor regular school teachers.
8. Include bilingual personnel.
9. Collect data, document project progress, and follow the Innovative Education Project's evaluation design.

Parents as Partners

The Parents as Partners model recognizes that Hispanic parents are their children's most important teachers but often lack the necessary skills to help their children progress successfully through school. It provides training and assistance to parents so they can become active partners in their children's education. The program is a required component of the Academia, Project Success, and Project Second Chance, but may also be operated as a free-standing program by organizations that do not operate educational programs for children or youth, but are interested in parent leadership development.

The program is designed to offer a variety of educational seminars to parents, with topics ranging from activities parents can use at home in everyday life to help their children, to developing skills to help parents understand test scores and report cards, school budgets, and policy-making procedures, and the structure of the other entities that influence the quality of life in the community. The model has been operational for two years in Kansas City, Missouri, and the council is collaborating with this site to develop a comprehensive parent training curriculum that will be available to all parent programs.

Because of the need to involve parents in helping children improve math abilities, training has also been provided to demonstration sites on the use of the Family Math approach developed by the Lawrence Hall of Science at the University of California at Berkeley. This approach is being used in several sites, including Chicago, Phoenix, and Kansas City. The council has requested that each Parents as Partners Project:

1. Provide for training and follow-up assistance to help parents create a home environment that reinforces and expands children's learning. These seminars or minicourses might include sessions on: child development and learning theory, language acquisition, effective parenting skills, effective discipline, communication and dispute resolution skills, and activities to reinforce reading or math skills at home.

2. Provide training to help parents monitor their children's educational progress, become more effective participants on school advisory committees and better advocates for their children's educational rights. Specific training priorities must be established by local communities based on needs assessments, but in most communities, training will be needed in understanding the structure and functions of advisory committees, school governance and finance, understanding school budgets, legal rights of children, and effective advocacy strategies.

3. Provide leadership development activities that could support the organization of a local task force on Hispanic education to provide a continuing forum for assessment and cooperative projects to improve educational opportunities in local schools. Leadership development activities should also be designed to enable parents to improve other aspects of life in their communities and participate more widely in civic affairs.

4. Be staffed by a bilingual Parent Coordinator.

5. Establish a cooperative relationship with a school or schools serving children or youth in other projects operated by the agency.

6. Establish an advisory group that works with project staff to set training priorities.

Such a group must include parents, school personnel, representatives of business and industry, community agency leaders, and other community members.

7. Conduct training seminars and activities at such times and in such manner so that they are accessible to working and single parents and other relatives (grandparents, older siblings, etc.) who may have caretaker responsibilities. Wherever possible, activities should be designed to involve both mothers and fathers.

8. Collect data, document project progress, and follow the Innovative Education Project's evaluation design.

The Teacher Support Network

The Teacher Support Network is designed to bring together community resources to provide training and assistance to Hispanic teachers and other teachers working with Hispanic children to provide them with community support and additional skills and resources in serving Hispanic students. The aim of this project is to increase the expectations that these teachers hold for Hispanic students and the positive linkages between the teachers and Hispanic communities, and make them more effective teachers of Hispanic children.

The projects may use a variety of approaches to achieve these aims, including providing workshops for teachers, helping to recruit classroom volunteers, initiating special minigrant programs for teacher-generated enrichment programs, and providing recognition for teachers making outstanding efforts. The project is currently being demonstrated by Association House in Chicago. As essential components, the council has determined that each project shall:

1. Recruit as participants and provide assistance to Hispanic and non-Hispanic classroom teachers serving Hispanic children.

2. Include both educational and motivational activities since teachers need to be both motivated and enabled to better serve their Hispanic pupils.

3. Provide opportunities for participating teachers to form cooperative relationships with other teachers and community members, and provide teachers with the opportunity to share successful strategies and programs with each other.

4. Offer activities and services that encourage the continuing professional development of participating members.

5. Seek the cooperation and participation of local school officials (principals, bilingual supervisors, staff development specialists, etc.).

6. Include an assessment of teacher-perceived needs and attitudes early in the project planning phase.

7. Assess parent and community perceptions of teacher attitudes, expectations, and needs to determine possible topics for workshops and parent/teacher activities.

8. Include a formal or informal advisory committee.

9. Collect data, document project progress, and follow the Innovative Education
   Project's evaluation design.

National Council of La Raza Role

Each of these projects is designed to be implemented by Hispanic community-based organizations, in cooperation with parents, schools, members
of the business and corporate communities, and other local organizations.
The National Council of La Raza assists demonstration sites in securing
resources to demonstrate the selected model projects, provides demonstration sites with the necessary training and technical assistance to implement
the models, and monitors and evaluates the projects. Other assistance provided by the council to local sites includes facilitating the transfer of information among demonstration projects, so that the various projects can learn
from each other's successes and errors.

The project has been tremendously enriched by a relationship with the
UCLA Center for the Study of Evaluation, which is working with staff to
develop evaluation models that can be used throughout the project. The
assistance of staff from the center in reviewing evaluation designs and data
collection instruments has been invaluable.

CONCLUSION

Educational outcomes for Hispanics are well below those for other major
U.S. subgroups, and current levels of local, state, and federal resources
devoted to improving the situation are inadequate. In addition, efforts that
are solely remedial and not preventive do not improve the education provided for the thousands of Hispanic children entering school each year. While
the council continues to work at the national level to advocate systemic
reforms and adequate funding for teacher training, parent and adult education, effective school practices and programs, and appropriate programs
for at-risk children, La Raza also believes that much change can be effectively
initiated through community-generated local projects that can supplement
school offerings and work with parents and teachers to increase their ability
to help Hispanic children succeed in school.

The council's Innovative Education Project is designed to demonstrate
and evaluate low-cost models that communities can use to help improve
educational outcomes for Hispanics. When the models have been evaluated
and refined, the project will disseminate the evaluation findings so that
education policy makers can incorporate effective approaches into public and
parochial school programs. The project also plans to produce implementation
guides and curriculum materials to facilitate the replication of effective
models by additional community-based organizations. In this way, the council hopes to continue to contribute to the restructuring and reform of public

and private school policies and to increase the level of Hispanic community involvement in providing high-quality educational services to Hispanic students, their families and teachers.

NOTES

An earlier version of this chapter, entitled "Making Schools Work for Underachieving Minorities: Some Promising Practices," was delivered at the American Educational Research Association (AERA) 1988 annual meeting in New Orleans, Louisiana, as part of a panel presentation on "Making Schools Work for Underachieving Minorities." The title was changed in this version to more closely indicate the content of the chapter, which describes the work of the National Council of La Raza with Hispanic community-based organizations to improve education for Hispanic students and their families. The deletion of the term "underachieving minorities" also reflects the council's belief that schools are underachieving as often as are students where minority and low-income students are concerned. Appreciation is expressed to Emily McKay, Executive Vice-President, and Arturo Vargas, Senior Education Policy Analyst, of the National Council of La Raza's Washington, D.C. office, and Maryann Reyes, Education Policy Fellow in the Council's Los Angeles Program Office, for their review of the chapter, and their comments and suggestions.

1. E. McDill, G. Natriello, and A. Pallas, "Raising Standards and Retaining Students: The Impact of the Reform Recommendations on Potential Dropouts," *Review of Educational Research*, 55(4) (Winter 1985).

2. Unless otherwise cited, the educational data in this section are taken from Lori S. Orum, *The Education of Hispanics: Status and Implications* (Washington, DC: National Council of La Raza, 1986).

3. A. Wheelock, "Dropping Out: What the Research Says," *Equity and Choice*, 3(1) (Fall 1986).

4. Ibid.

5. C. Acher, "Raising Hispanic Achievement," in *Make Something Happen: Hispanics and Urban High School Reform, ERIC/CUE Digest*, 26 (April 1985).

6. William T. Grant Foundation, Commission on Work, Family, and Citizenship, "The Forgotten Half: Non-College Youth in America" (Washington, DC, January 1988).

7. J. Oakes, "Tracking, Inequality and the Rhetoric of Reform: Why Schools Don't Change," *Boston University Journal of Education*, 168(1) (1986).

8. U.S. General Accounting Office, "School Dropouts: The Extent and Nature of the Problem" (Washington, DC, June 1986).

9. S. M. Barro, "Who Drops Out of High School?: Findings from High School and Beyond" (Washington, DC: National Center for Education Statistics, 1987).

10. Wheelock, "Dropping Out."

11. Ibid.

12. R. Martinez, "Minority Youth Dropouts: Personal, Social, and Institutional Reasons for Leaving School" (Colorado Springs: University of Colorado, Center for Community Development and Design, Summer 1986).

Preparing Students for Success at the Secondary and Postsecondary Levels

TEN

Teaching and Learning: Nonnegotiable Components at the Secondary Level

SHIRLEY THORNTON

This chapter is about effective secondary schools, particularly emphasizing the implementation process from my perspective as a high school principal at Balboa High School in San Francisco.

It is impossible to run a school that stays in compliance with the many federal, state, and local rules and regulations and also make a difference with the kids. Many of us who are maverick principals ended up having success and being seen as stars because we were given schools that were meant to be failures. When we were given these schools it was with the understanding that we would not succeed. Instead, things began to happen, we began to have success, and no one could touch us. Our success was an aberration; it was not supposed to happen. A high school of color, a school filled with graffiti and all the other indicators of failure, is not supposed to be successful. All of a sudden, when the school begins to turn around, people start to wonder how it happened.

I don't know what I learned about administration in college; I don't know what I learned about administration by taking on the job at Balboa. I did learn that if you use your resources, treat your staff people as humans, set high expectations for students and staff that are nonnegotiable, and then leave everything else open, it works. Being successful was a nonnegotiable goal. There was never a need to discuss that. Being successful was a matter of teachers and administrators together setting up the process to reach that goal.

As a high school principal in San Francisco, setting the process was very simple. First we looked at the data. Balboa was a school with 2,100 kids. The average grade point average was 1.6. There was a 70–80 percent transiency rate, and the school was filled with gangs, graffiti, smoking, and fighting. You name it and it was there. People would say, "That used to be a good school." Twenty years ago it was a good school. I attended that school; it was an Italian, Irish, Catholic school. Teachers who had taught during that time and were still teaching were waiting for San Francisco, and the school, to return to that mode. Many inner city teachers talk about the "good old days." What does that mean? Those teachers are really talking about and yearning for a different student population; they are passive bystanders, escaping responsibility, not active, responsible educators. Our teachers were not looking at the fact that they were not giving homework and were not setting high expectations for kids. They were going into the classroom and telling the kids, "When you are ready to learn, we are ready to teach you." How do you focus a staff that believes that kids can't learn?

First, the belief that all kids can learn and that all teachers can and must teach had to be adopted. Anything that got in the way of that understanding was not dealt with in a nice manner. Next we had to determine where, in a city like San Francisco, kids could go after they graduate, so we could pinpoint relevant goals. We looked at the labor market and types of available jobs in the city. We set that profile in place and then reviewed our school philosophy and goals to see if they were in sync with the world that these kids would be a part of if and when they graduated. We realized, of course, that they were not. Most of the kids who left our high schools went into unemployment. We took a look at data from the California Postsecondary Education Commission study, which said that Black and Brown kids in California are not making it to our colleges and universities. Less than 10 percent of these students are eligible for the University of California and California State University. Balboa students fit that profile. Our minority students weren't going to college, and the system we were using to try to assure the quality of their education wasn't working.

Students had to pass a minimum proficiency exam to get a high school diploma. A kid would first take the exam in the ninth grade and then could take it twice a year for the following four years. We didn't have levels A and B, or forms A and B; the test did not change. By his senior year, because he had taken the exact same test so many times, that kid had it more or less memorized. He could even try the test one more time on graduation day. When a student passed the test, what was he passing? A test an eighth grader could pass. The fact that we had minimum proficiency standards really didn't say anything—nor did it do anything for educational quality.

When we sat down with the teachers, we asked them what they thought it would take for students to be successful in San Francisco, or anyplace else. We heard the usual: they must be able to speak, they must be able to think, they must be able to read. Then we asked: Where in the course of the school day were these things operationalized? What do we do every day that assures that when a kid graduates, he will have the prerequisite skills to be successful?

To determine a course of action, we took our department chairs and our parent liaison workers, the critical mass of the school, to FarWest Lab for a week, and we brought in representatives from the California State Department of Education. We looked at our curriculum in relation to a nonnegotiable set of skills, the skills that are required on the Scholastic Aptitude Test (SAT) of the College Board entrance exams and the American College Testing program (ACT). Students who don't master these skills will not be successful. Everything we do as teachers is based on curriculum, so we looked at our curriculum in relationship to these skills. We saw that a discrepancy definitely existed.

We decided together that our goal for our students was that they go on to productive postsecondary experiences. We helped the teachers look at what had to happen at Balboa to make that happen for the students; we looked at the core skills that they needed to master. We decided what the indicators of achievement were—number of credits, required classes, what the student had to take at each grade level, whether a student passed the proficiencies—and agreed that these things would have to be followed for each student for four years before actually looking at what was going on with student achievement. The process enabled us to come up with a common vocabulary, and branching off from that, we were able to really understand what the nonnegotiable skills should be.

We discussed what we had to do to make necessary changes. We talked about conducting departmental reviews, and the department chairs said, "We cannot evaluate staff." Our response was, "We are not asking you to evaluate staff. We are asking you to evaluate the program." Others would say that collective bargaining would not allow teacher evaluation, but it does allow you to look at the program. It does allow you to figure out how to evaluate and critique your program.

Once we determined what we wanted to do and where we wanted to go, we could see what we needed to do to pull back into a common core. We looked at all of the research on effective schools and started applying those principles in our school. We set up a five-year plan. Teachers understood that we were not going to change everything at once.

What did it do for Balboa? In 1980, less than 7 percent of our kids went on to college, or a technical school, and few got jobs. Of the first class we started working with as ninth graders, 75 percent either went to college or went to a trade school.

How did we do that? We collaborated with San Francisco City College on their campus, and we brought in a bridging program from San Francisco State. We sent staff to schools where positive things were happening. The people who had been saying "It can't happen here" came back saying "Why isn't it happening here?" We showed our staff how the programs made a difference.

As an administrator, it is my job to get consultants if they are needed. If the school needs more support from downtown, it is my job to get that. However, even if we need those things, we will not lower our level of expectancy because we don't have them. We will not expect less; we figure out how to expect more.

As educators, we have to look at what we are doing to get kids to think. Gifted students go one place, bilingual kids go someplace else, and special ed kids go yet another place. The classroom teacher says, "I'll teach whoever is left, I'll teach the regular students," and she doesn't have to deal with any of the special students. So we don't end up with the model we want, a model where there is only one way to academic success. Algebra is algebra. Algebra is the first in the series of math courses for kids. Don't give them remedial math or business math or survival math. They need algebra. These programs are supposed to be the "how," the practical application. Instead, we make them separate courses, and separate the students.

It is not surprising that at-risk kids are labeled defective. They are pulled out of the mainstream, and then all the data show that they can't learn. Here is an analogy: Put your arm in a cast for five years. Take it out of the cast and try to catch a ball. That arm is not going to work. It's atrophied, the joint is probably frozen. There was nothing wrong with that arm when it was put in the cast. We are allowing our kids to be placed in categorical programs, and then we are not demanding that these programs do what they are supposed to do. They are supposed to teach the same principles; the categorical program is supposed to be the "how," not the end. As principals, as central office staff, as support staff, the only thing we have to do is to make sure that all students are getting what they need to learn.

ELEVEN

Educational Pathways That Promote Student Success at the Postsecondary Level

LESTER W. JONES

This chapter will describe a program established at Xavier University (New Orleans) in association with the high schools in the area. We believe that if there is to be any increase in the number of blacks in the professions—in math, science, medicine, and so on—there has to be a significant increase in the number of Blacks excelling in academics. The best approach for increasing the number of Blacks in the professions is to view the process as improving the educational pathway. In our view, undergraduate colleges form a crucial link in this pathway. They must help students move along that pathway, and, in my view, they don't seem to be doing that.

Xavier University is small, liberal arts, 90 percent Black, and Catholic, with a strong Catholic heritage. Xavier has an arts and science college, a pharmacy college, and a graduate school of education (master's degrees only). Most of the White students are enrolled in the College of Pharmacy, since it is the only one in Southern Louisiana.

Xavier has a core curriculum of 56 hours, including English, literature, and foreign language requirements. We are very successful and we are very proud of it. We are number one in the nation in placing Black Americans in pharmacy schools. We are number two in the nation in placing Blacks in the medical and dental schools. (36 placed in the spring of 1987, and that was more than all the other colleges in the state of Louisiana combined).

One of the reasons we have done such a good job is because we have worked hard with the secondary schools on several ongoing projects. We sponsor a math/science olympiad that promotes excellence in the sciences, and we foster competitions in biology, chemistry, mathematics, and physics. About 1,200 junior and senior high students take part in these competitions. We are the only school in New Orleans that bothers to do that sort of thing.

Why? Look at the publicity for any high school or college. All you hear about are the athletic stars. You seldom hear about the students who excel at mathematics or chemistry. We don't put up posters for those students. If you are a Black student growing up in the ghetto of New Orleans, or even if you are a White student and you aren't growing up in the ghetto, you don't get your name in the paper if you are an excellent math student. You're just patted on the head by your teacher. The math/science olympiad is one way to help those students get some recognition.

We also have a summer science academy, with programs called Math Star, Bio Star, Chem Star, and Project Soar. In Math Star we work with pre-ninth graders. We take good Black students who will be taking algebra in the ninth grade, and we try to make stars out of them. We should probably work with every Black student who is going to be taking algebra, but we can't. Our arms can reach just so far, so we take good students and try to make stars out of them. It is the stars who are going to become the medical doctors and the Ph.D.s in mathematics. Bio Star is a four-week program for pre-tenth graders. Chem Star and Project Soar are for upper level high school students.

Project Soar stresses analytical reasoning and has several components: biology, chemistry, physics, and math. It is a learning-by-doing activity that features verbal quantitative problems and vocabulary building. We have group competitions to motivate the students and help them to develop a peer support group, which is very necessary in college. Black students who have done well in the past succeeded because they were loners. They had to separate themselves from their society to become stars. Students need to learn that when they get into an environment like a college, they need to work with their peers. In our competitions, they cheer their groups on just like they would cheer a basketball team.

To develop these programs, we spend a lot of time working with schools. We work with the teachers and the teachers help us develop programs. These teachers have been very beneficial, telling us things that we never would have known because we haven't had their experiences. These programs were not developed by mathematicians and chemists existing in a vacuum.

These summer programs lead into other academic-year spinoffs. Two of them, developed jointly, are in engineering and biostatistics, and we are working with the local graduate and professional schools on a program in the computer science area. We also offer Medical College Admissions Test and Graduate Record Exam prep courses. Our Xavier faculty take these tests periodically, so we know what they contain.

On our campus we have a philosophy that we call "standards with sympathy." It is simply a coupling of high academic expectations with mechanisms that help our students succeed. To solve our problems in education, we have a common approach in our department, and it reaches across departmental lines. Our curriculum is standardized. The core courses for arts and sciences are precalculus, calculus, general chemistry, general biology, general physics, and organic chemistry. In those courses content is determined by each department, not by the individual instructor. Handbooks in these subjects force the instructors to teach what they are supposed to teach.

Objectives are written in math-teacher language, not education-teacher language. They don't go according to Bloom's taxonomy, but are written in words that my faculty can understand and that I can understand. They tell the teachers exactly what they are supposed to cover in a given week. We don't leave it up to the faculty members to pick out the problems they are going to work on in class. For example, when they teach objective No. 1, they turn to page 257 and work problems 5, 8, 11, and 13. We meet weekly and talk about how to present those problems, so we all agree on the same methods of working them. We do that because it helps us when the students get together. They don't argue with each other about the correct method.

In addition, we realized when we started this program in 1983 that our students had to improve their vocabularies, which are weak, and this is one of the primary reasons for the trouble they have reading textbooks. Students in the basic sciences courses take a five-minute quiz once a week on general, not scientific, vocabulary. The science faculty wrote 5,000 questions for a vocabulary question bank. Critical reading exercises have also been integrated into the science courses.

At Xavier we focus on exit criteria. We focus on where we want our students to be when they leave precalculus, where we want them to be when they leave calculus, where we want them to be when they leave the university—not just where they are at any particular time, or how much they can possibly do in six weeks. The exit criteria we choose for our program are the entrance criteria for graduate and professional schools. We must set our curriculum standards at those entrance levels or we short-change our students. We cannot ask the Harvard Medical School to take a student because he is a good kid, even though he doesn't satisfy their entrance criteria.

We have been working on this program for ten years. Its standardization has evolved; it didn't start out this way. The faculty have found that there are advantages in standardizing courses. It gives them a common foundation for upper level courses. The faculty who teach organic chemistry know every detail of what those students cover in general chemistry. It gives direction to new and part-time faculty; it makes their jobs easier. It makes our jobs as supervisory faculty easier, and it makes the departmental support system possible. The tutors we hire can tutor no matter what section of precalculus a student comes from.

To keep up, our biology, chemistry, math, and physics faculty formed a support group—the science education research group—that meets weekly to discuss problems and develop programs. This nucleus is what keeps us going, and what has kept our programs going for ten years.

TWELVE

Dividends Derived from Structured Intervention at the Postsecondary Level

Ed C. Apodaca

For generations public schools have represented America's investment in the future. Education has traditionally served as the primary route for social and economic advancement, providing vitality, opportunities, and strength to our society. When offered in an academic environment that combines quality and diversity, education can contribute greatly to individuals' intellectual, personal, and financial betterment and can develop greater understanding and cohesiveness among the different segments of our society.

CURRENT OPPORTUNITIES FOR MINORITY STUDENTS

For a variety of reasons, our educational structure is not currently providing these advantages to large segments of our population. Almost half of the American Indian, Black, and Hispanic students fail to receive a high school diploma, and of those who graduate from high school, many are poorly prepared and have limited educational or employment choices. In today's competitive, high technology world, the need for a good education is greater than ever. In order to remain competitive in the world market, our society must raise the level of educational achievement of all our young people.

Dropout rates are at an all-time high, and minority children and children from low-income families are leaving schools in alarming numbers. As of 1980, three times as many high-school-age youth in California from families earning under $10,000 a year were not attending school as were those from families earning $50,000 or more. As is true in most states, in California, Blacks and Hispanics make up a disproportionately large percentage of the poor and of the dropouts.

Harold L. Hodgkinson, a senior fellow of the American Council on Education, described this educational problem as follows:

High school drop-outs have a rather typical profile. They are usually from low-income or poverty settings, often from a minority group (although not often Asian-American), have very low basic academic skills, especially reading and math, have parents who are not high school graduates and who are generally uninterested in the child's progress in school and do not provide a support system for academic progress. English is often not the major language spoken in the home, and many are children of single parents (p. 11).[1]

Not only do unprepared students result in a great loss of human potential, but their underachievement will also have serious negative consequences for the future of the economy and for the overall well-being of the state. California's minority population is increasing rapidly. Current projections indicate that by the year 2000, ethnic minorities will account for over half of the state population. Furthermore, in California the school-age minority population is growing at a faster rate than the general population, because of higher birth rates and greater immigration into California of young minority families. Of the approximately 4 million students now attending California's schools, more than 44 percent are ethnic minorities. In 1981, 26 percent of K–12 enrollments were Hispanic, 10 percent were Black, 5.5 percent were Asian, and 0.8 percent were American Indian.

INCREASING MINORITY ENROLLMENT

For years, the University of California has maintained structured efforts to increase the enrollment of minority and low-income students. The university values the intellectual and cultural contributions of a diverse student population and has allocated special resources for programs designed to identify, prepare, and recruit underrepresented students. Significant gains have been made over the last 20 years in the enrollment of women and ethnic minority students. While some ethnic groups still remain underrepresented, existing efforts appear to be working and annual enrollment increases are being reported. The ethnic groups currently identified as underrepresented at the University of California are Blacks, Chicanos, Latinos, and American Indians. As a basis for determining "underrepresentation," the university uses California high school graduates as a comparison group.

The University of California admissions procedures are designed to select for each of its campuses the best qualified yet diverse student body possible. The extent to which it achieves this goal affects every student enrolled in the university, for diversity of students and faculty is essential in shaping the quality of an educational experience. Those admitted to the university undergraduate programs are chosen, as mandated by the Master Plan for Higher Education, from among students in the top one-eighth of the state's graduating class. Beyond the basic standard of academic excellence, the university strives to select individuals whose special qualities and experiences contribute to the educational environment of the campuses. Students applying for admission as freshmen must have completed a minimum of 16 units in specified academic/college preparatory courses with at least a 3.3 grade point average (students with 2.77–3.3 GPA can become eligible if they achieve specified composite test scores). The courses required by the university include four years of college preparatory English, three years of advanced mathematics, two years of foreign language, one year of U.S. history, one year of laboratory science, and four years of college preparatory electives.

A study by the university of barriers that affect enrollment and academic success of underrepresented students isolated three major problems in the academic preparation of junior and senior high school students:

1. Many students had difficulty with the algebra/geometry series required for admission to the university as well as with preparatory courses necessary to enroll in these classes.

2. Students had insufficient preparation for science and English course work and lacked the academic background required to undertake college preparatory courses in these disciplines.

3. There was also a need for increased parental and student awareness regarding the nature of and the opportunities available for education. Taken together, these factors contributed greatly to the disproportionately low rates of college eligibility for minority students.

A California Postsecondary Education Commission (CPEC) eligibility study of 1983 high school graduates found that a primary barrier to participation of minority students in postsecondary education is the disproportionately low rate at which these students attain University of California and California State University eligibility. The average eligibility rates of California public high school graduates was 13.2 percent and by major ethnic groups was: Asians, 26.9 percent; Blacks, 3.6 percent; Hispanics, 4.9 percent; and Whites, 15.5 percent. In 1983, there were 23,288 Black and 46,081 Hispanic high school graduates in California, of which only 3,096 (838 Black and 2,258 Hispanic) graduates were eligible to attend the University of California. They represented 2.5 and 6.7 percent, respectively, of the total eligible pool, while Asians represented 12.4 percent and Whites 75.3 percent.

In addition, the study indicated that a large number of minority students who were eligible to attend the university (approximately 60 percent) did not take the aptitude and achievement tests required by the university and most other four-year educational institutions. This brought into question the assumption that most qualified Black, Hispanic, and American Indian students were highly recruited and were attending prestigious four-year institutions. A new eligibility study is being conducted of 1986 high school graduates, and efforts will be made to survey students who met eligibility requirements but did not report taking the prerequisite college placement tests necessary for admission.

UNIVERSITY OF CALIFORNIA'S EARLY OUTREACH PROGRAM

The initial efforts of the Early Outreach Program (see below) focused primarily on identification and recruitment of minority youth. It quickly became apparent, however, that the success of this strategy was limited by the high dropout rate of minorities and the low rate at which minority high school graduates were achieving academic eligibility for the university.

After a thorough study of the attributes of students who achieved eligibility, the university determined that a strong program of academic and motivational intervention was needed, beginning at the junior high level. With funding from the state legislature, the university initiated the Early Outreach Program, which consists of junior high school and senior high school components. The former commenced in 1976 and the latter in 1978. These programs provide a pipeline to the recruitment and admissions programs of the University of California, the California State University, and California independent postsecondary institutions.

The Early Outreach Program is designed to address the problem of eligibility by assisting students to prepare for college-level work. The program helps students to achieve a level of academic preparation that will increase their options for enrollment in any postsecondary institution—including the University of California. The Early Outreach Program addresses the above problems by focusing its activities on five critical factors that affect student attitudes and achievement: (1) aspirations toward higher education, (2) information necessary to prepare for postsecondary studies, (3) instructional and tutorial assistance in required college preparatory course work, (4) motivation to achieve the required level of performance in the course work, and (5) academic and nonacademic support from parents, school personnel, and peers necessary to pursue and successfully complete college preparatory course work.

To bring about the desired changes in student attitudes and achievements, the Early Outreach Program provides a wide range of educational services, including the following:

1. *Academic Advising.* These sessions provide participants with information on: (a) what classes and performance levels will help them to meet the eligibility re-

quirements of the University of California and of other postsecondary institutions; (b) the appropriate sequence in which they should take their courses; and (c) how to prepare for college admissions tests. The focus of these sessions is academic program planning, related high school work, and entrance examinations.

2. *Tutorial and Learning Skills Services.* These services furnish students with tutorial assistance necessary to master the concepts in their college preparatory courses, especially those in mathematics, science, and English. Frequently these services entail learning skills modules designed to improve a student's proficiency in note-taking, asking questions, reading, studying, test-taking, and other skills.

3. *College and Career Counseling.* This service gives participants information on college admissions procedures and examinations, career choices, financial aid and scholarship programs, housing, postsecondary institutions of interest, college life, and the benefits of higher education. Vocational testing and seminars on specific career fields are also provided.

4. *Parent Meetings.* These gatherings introduce students and their parents to a wide array of information vital to college preparation and career planning. Meetings with parents are conveniently scheduled in familiar community settings.

5. *Campus Tours.* Such outings enable participants and their parents to tour local college or university campuses of interest. Frequently they include: (a) a campus tour of specific academic programs, services, and physical facilities; (b) department presentations; and (c) lectures on the history, traditions, and goals of the visited campus.

6. *Summer Programs.* These are designed to place students in an academic setting where they may obtain: (a) instruction that sharpens those reading, writing, mathematics, and study skills needed for academic success at the host campus; (b) social transition into college: (c) orientation to campus resources; (d) proper incentives for using academic support services throughout their freshman year; (e) assistance in identifying a support system on which they can rely while they negotiate the complexities of university life; and (f) a realistic expectation of the academic requirements of their career choices and of the university. Depending on the host campus, participants are provided room and board. Frequently, they are also provided with work experience for which they are paid a stipend.

At the junior high school level, the goal of the Early Outreach Program is to increase the number of minority and low-income students who aspire to attend postsecondary educational institutions. At the senior high level, the goals are to encourage minority and low-income students to enroll in and successfully complete a college preparatory program, and to increase the number of participants who become eligible for admission to the University of California. The senior high school component of Early Outreach assists students who were junior high school participants and other underrepresented and low-income students who attend targeted schools.

RESULTS OF EARLY OUTREACH PROGRAMS

The Early Outreach Program served 34,764 students in 505 junior and senior schools during the 1985–86 year. In 1986, high school graduates who

Figure 12.1
Comparison Between 1983 California Postsecondary Education Commission
Eligibility Study and 1986 Eligibility Rates for University of California Early
Outreach Graduates

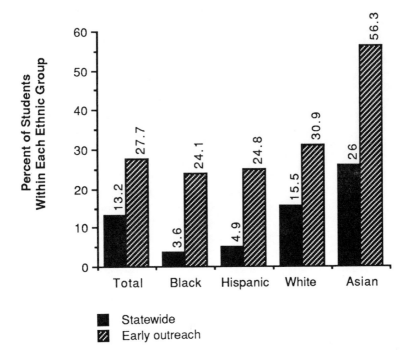

■ Statewide
▨ Early outreach

participated in the Early Outreach Program achieved University of California eligibility at a rate of 27.7 percent, compared with 13.2 percent general statewide eligibility rate. Each group of Early Outreach participants, when designated by ethnicity, achieved eligibility at a considerably higher rate than their counterparts statewide (see Figure 12.1).

Each of the University of California campuses has an Early Outreach Program that serves the junior and senior high schools in their surrounding communities. Universitywide, 2,187 (84 percent) of the Early Outreach graduates in 1986 enrolled in a college or university. Almost half (45 percent) of the graduating class enrolled in the University of California or in the California State University system. An additional 11.3 percent enrolled in other four-year institutions. This is much greater than the general statewide college-going rate (16.6 percent) reported by the CPEC for students enrolling in the University of California and California State University.

EARLY OUTREACH PROGRAM MODEL

The partnership among the school sites, the student participants, and the Early Outreach Program includes a formal service agreement that details the responsibilities and requirements for participation as well as the services to be delivered.

Services Provided

The selected schools receive services from the University of California campuses with emphasis on identifying and assisting students who show interest and potential to succeed in higher education. The following services form the foundation upon which additional services can be added: academic advising, role model presentations, college and university visits, dissemination of information, and parent involvement.

Selection of Sites

Target schools within each region are drawn from schools that have large representation of minority students and that in the past had not been successful in sending minority students to the university. The type of services offered to each school varies according to its needs. The number of schools served within a region was determined by geographic distances from university campuses and availability of resources to perform essential services. Selection of the target schools was based on: (1) willingness of school officials to participate, (2) number of targeted students enrolled (schools that serve targeted students "bused in" as part of an integration program were included), (3) need for services offered, and (4) availability of resources.

Selection of Participants

The Early Outreach model is based on the belief that services in the seventh grade should be offered to as many students as possible. Thus, selection of seventh-grade students is relatively unrestricted; within the participating schools, all underrepresented minority and low-income students are invited to participate. Beginning with the eighth grade, there are certain expectations of participants, including taking college preparatory courses.

Faculty and Parental Involvement

Faculty input and participation are sought in the development and implementation of the Early Outreach regional efforts. Linkages with existing student preparation efforts such as the California Writing Project, the California Mathematics Project, and the University of California at Irvine's Project STEP have been maintained and strengthened. The amount and types of services provided vary by area and are determined by the needs of the region and the resources available. Advisory boards, with faculty and community involvement, are established to reflect the cooperative nature of the effort. They provide direction regarding the type of services to be offered in their regional area.

In order for the advisory boards to make knowledgeable decisions, evaluation of program methods and accomplishments are available at regular intervals. Since the regional efforts also involve new school sites, baseline data have been gathered to assess the effects of the program.

Intersegmental and Related Program Involvement

Of equal importance to effective coordination and to the cooperative efforts with the junior and senior high schools is the ability of the program to work well with other college outreach efforts. By sharing the mission of preparing underrepresented minority and low-income students for postsecondary educational opportunities, services can be more comprehensive and complementary.

The university has begun collaboration efforts with representatives from the California State University, the California Community College, the State Department of Education, MESA, Cal SOAP, Upward Bound, and the California Academic Partnership Program. Both the University of California and the California State University are funded to support early outreach efforts and have programs that coordinate efforts.

In light of the many junior high and senior high schools that are currently not served, the segments work together in order to expand their efforts and to avoid duplication of services when working the same schools. Periodic meetings among the segments are held to share information, ideas, and resources needed for college nights, field trips, parent visits, and dissemination of information.

During the 1985–86 academic year, the Early Outreach Program served 273 high schools and 185 junior high schools located in 25 counties. In fall 1986 the program expanded, providing new or additional services to 48 high schools and 66 junior highs. The 1985–86 ethnic composition of Early Outreach schools is provided in Figure 12.2. The proportion of underrepresented ethnic minority students in schools serviced by the program is significantly greater than the statewide averages and of schools that traditionally send students to the university. While 32.4 percent of California's public high school students are underrepresented ethnic minorities (Asians are not included as underrepresented), they comprise 48.5 percent of the students enrolled in Early Outreach public high schools. Similarly, while underrepresented ethnic minorities constitute 38.0 percent of the junior high school students, their proportion in schools serviced by the Early Outreach Programs is 64.5 percent.

For purposes of comparison, selected ranges of the Scholastic Aptitude Test mathematics (SATM) and verbal (SATV) scores for fall 1985 University of California freshmen were reviewed alongside those of students enrolled

Figure 12.2
Ethnic Distribution of Schools in Early Outreach (Existing and Expansion Programs) and California
Public Schools, 1985–86

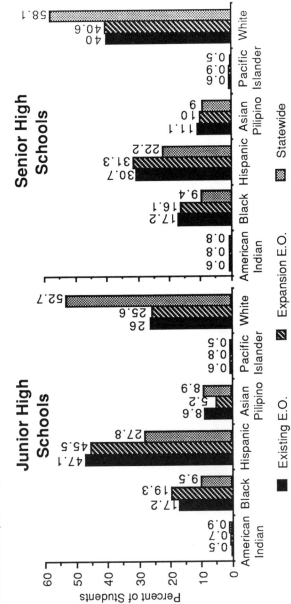

in Early Outreach high schools. A comparative analysis indicates that the average SATM score is 20.2 percent (114 points) and the average SATV score 21.2 percent (106 points) below that of entering University of California freshmen.

EXPANSION OF EARLY OUTREACH EFFORTS

The Early Outreach Program, as well as similar efforts conducted by the California State University, have been highly successful. However, the number of schools involved has been relatively few. Recognizing the magnitude of the eligibility problem for underrepresented minority students, the university has expanded its efforts to reach increased numbers of these students. With much of the Black and Hispanic population concentrated in urban areas of the state, regional centers were established in the Los Angeles, San Francisco Bay, and San Diego areas. The Los Angeles area will be the focus of concentration, as more than 51 percent of the Black and 43 percent of the Hispanic high school graduates in the state reside in this county.

The expansion of the Early Outreach Program into the three regions allows the university to work with schools that are presently unserved or underserved. With this expansion, 48 high schools and 66 junior high schools have been added to the program and the number of participants is expected to increase by at least 16 percent. Each region will be serviced by more than one campus, which should add to the overall support and success of Early Outreach efforts.

Since its inception in 1976, the Early Outreach Program has undergone a number of changes. Initially the emphasis of Early Outreach was on enrolling underrepresented ethnic minority students in postsecondary institutions. Later, the goals were changed to include low-income students to prepare for and apply to four-year institutions. This change was important, given the fact that 85 percent of the Black and Hispanic students attending college were enrolled at two-year institutions and were not transferring into baccalaureate programs. In 1986–87 the following goals were established:

1. at least 75 percent of the program participants are to be from underrepresented ethnic groups,

2. at least 70 percent of all students served by the program are to be enrolled in at least four A-F courses per semester beginning in the tenth grade,

3. at least 50 percent of all students participating are to have cumulative GPAs of at least 2.5 in grades 7–9 and of at least 2.7 in grades 10–12,

4. at least 35 percent of the program graduates are to be eligible, and

5. at least 55 percent of the program graduates are to attend four-year colleges.

Figure 12.3
University of California Enrollment Data, First-Time Freshmen, California
Resident Minority Groups, Fall Terms, 1978 through 1986

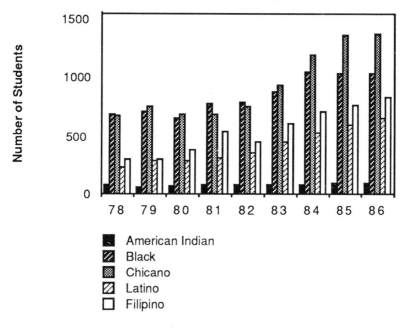

CONCLUSION

Within the scope of the programs, the University of California Early Outreach efforts have been successful. As a result of structured student affirmative action efforts, such as those provided by the Early Outreach Program, the number of *eligible* entering underrepresented students has increased annually (see Figure 12.3).

Expansion of efforts such as the Early Outreach Program are needed to serve the broader population of underachieving students. It is apparent that the educational, occupational, and social problems confronting minority and low-income youths will continue to increase if not corrected. Given the current lack of adequate resources and the growing as well as changing population mix, those problems that are common to such an environment will continue to be reflected in the schools and will directly affect their ability to educate students. It is extremely important that affirmative steps be taken to address existing problems and to put in place an educational system that is sensitive and effective in responding to a changing environment. The full participation of all students within the educational system is essential for assuring a better future. Cultural pluralism in schools is not only of educational value but is also important in developing a better understanding of ourselves and our society and encouraging greater tolerance of each other.

NOTE

1. Harold L. Hodgkinson, *All One System: Demographics of Education, Kindergarten through Graduate School* (Washington, DC: Institute for Educational Leadership, 1985).

SECTION D

Helping Limited English Proficient Students Succeed

THIRTEEN

Enhancing Academic Literacy for Language Minority Students

Kris Gutierrez

The issue of teaching English effectively to diverse student populations is not new. Sessions, workshops, and seminars discussing ways to improve language instruction to linguistic and culturally diverse student populations have been visible at national and local conferences for the past two decades. During that time period, the educational underachievement of linguistic and cultural minority students has been well documented and, by now, has become a commonplace notion in educational research. This underachievement has been measured by tests, chronicled by national assessment data over the past 15 years, and supported by a variety of educational measures including dropout and graduation data and patterns of placement in special education and remedial programs. More specifically, the National Assessment of Educational Progress writing assessment data continue to reveal findings about the poor writing performance of Black and Hispanic students. Consider some of these findings: At the grade levels assessed (fourth, eighth, and eleventh), Black and Hispanic students performed at significantly lower levels than Whites. At eleventh grade, the average writing achievement for minority students did not equal the achievement demonstrated by eighth-grade White students. In spite of some marked improvements over the past decade, the average reading ability of Black and Hispanic 17 year olds was only slightly higher than that of White 13 year olds (NAEP, 1986).

In light of the rapidly changing demographics of school populations in this country, understanding the reasons for poor academic achievement and, in particular, the underachievement in reading and writing of disproportionate numbers of ethnic minority students, should be an immediate concern to us. The demographic data predict that by the year 2010, one out of three Americans will be Black, Hispanic, or Asian-American. These population dynamics can already be seen in the public schools. Today, 27 percent of all public school students come from ethnic minority backgrounds, 2–4 million for whom the schooling language, English, is not the native language. Twenty-four of our largest city school systems have "minority majorities" (Hodgkinson, 1986).

Nevertheless, as we approach the beginning of another decade, we are still struggling with what to do with culturally and linguistically diverse students. In fact, as a profession, we have not demonstrated that we understand much more about this student population than we did 25 years ago. We face, in short, a significant increase in numbers of ethnic minority students and a continuing problem of academic underachievement for this student population. So what does all this mean for educators? Given this dismal portrait of underachievement, what can be done? What do we know about linguistically and culturally diverse and underprepared students and about the teaching of writing/reading to these students?

A number of hypotheses emerging from traditional research paradigms have been posited in an attempt to explain the underachievement in writing/ reading of large numbers of these students. Many of the explanations emerging from these studies are grounded in deficit model perspectives that presume a lack of fluency in language—that is, reading and writing—is the result of a deficiency or deficiencies in the students' educational, linguistic, cognitive, and cultural and social backgrounds. These deficit-model theories can be organized into several major categories: (1) those that present sociocultural environmental explanations of academic underachievement; (2) those that attribute academic disparities to genetic differences; and (3) those studies that cite linguistic deficiencies as explanations of academic underachievement.

Newer theories in psychology, sociopsychology, sociolinguistics, and anthropology, however, have challenged these hypotheses and have examined the sociocultural contexts of learning in general and learning to write in particular. Researchers such as Cummins (1986), Heath (1981; 1986), Scribner & Cole (1981), Ogbu & Matute-Bianchi (1986), Trueba (1987), and Moll & Diaz (1982; 1983), for example, have proposed that the schooling vulnerability of minority students must be understood within the broader contexts of this society's treatment of minorities in and out of schools. These researchers have attended to the importance of social and cultural continuities between minority students' home, community, and school experiences and their relationship to educational and literacy achievement. This more comprehensive view of the schooling of minority students includes an understanding of the relationship between home and school, the sociocultural incongruities between the two, and the resulting effects on learning and achievement.

More recently, our understanding of the importance of the sociocultural contexts of schooling has been greatly expanded by the work of researchers who, over a 20–year period, were involved in the Kamehameha Early Education Program (KEEP) research and demonstration project (Tharp & Gallimore, 1988; Gallimore & Howard, 1968; Gallimore, Boggs & Jordan, 1974). Their studies of a culturally compatible language arts program for primary-grade Hawaiian students have suggested that attributing academic vulnerability primarily to broad school/home discontinuities cannot sufficiently account for explanations of underachievement. Instead, these researchers have proposed that understanding ethnic minority students' developmental paths to school competence must necessarily include an assessment of how student, home, school, and teacher variables influence academic performance.

Using an ecocultural theoretical model for research and practice, Weisner and Gallimore (1985) have provided us with a powerful research paradigm with which to assess home/school discontinuity and continuity, and the complementarity of home- and school-based learning activities. Specifically, this research model has been used to examine the relationship between parents' educational values and beliefs, parents' role in the child's learning process, home literacy practices, and literacy achievement. By using the "activity settings" in the home and school as the units of analyses, this research has produced rich data that challenge earlier theories about the role of culture in the acquisition of literacy. For example, preliminary findings from a research project on the home literacy practices of Latinos in an urban community in the Southwest (Goldenberg, 1984; Goldenberg & Gallimore, 1987) suggest that low-achieving Latino children are indeed motivated to learn and, specifically, to learn to read; that the values and motives of poor Latino families are more similar to those of the school than they are different; and that the parents' noninvolvement or minimal involvement in the child's educational experience is more appropriately attributed to their lack of information and lack of access to information about how children learn and acquire literacy. These findings (Tharp & Gallimore, 1988; Goldenberg & Gallimore, 1987) have profound implications for reenvisioning the role that culture plays in the learning and achievement of language minority children.

Such conclusions drawn from the Kamehameha studies (Tharp & Gallimore, 1988; Weisner, Gallimore & Jordan, 1988; Gallimore, Boggs & Jordan, 1974) should help educators revise assumptions about the ways in which culture constrains learning for culturally and linguistically diverse students. These researchers have proposed an alternative explanation to those theories that look to deficits in the learner or to cultural discontinuities as explanations of the academic underachievement of minority students. Instead, Gallimore and his colleagues suggest that educational researchers must develop comprehensive and more precise understandings of the sociocultural contexts in which the learner resides in order to "identify the necessary and sufficient features of culture to which teaching and schooling must be accommodated and to discover those aspects of natal activity settings that can be adapted for use in the classroom" (Weisner et al., 1988, 346). This theoretical perspective allows for the accommodation of cultural differences and the acquisition of new school-based content knowledge in classroom instructional arrangements that are both culturally compatible and new to the student (Tharp, 1989).

Recent emergent literacy research also underscores the importance of understanding the sociocultural contexts of literacy acquisition. The acquisition and development of language are described as profoundly social phenomena. Goodman (1980), for example, suggests that literacy development cannot be understood without recognizing the significance of literacy in culture—that is, the culture of both the larger society and the specific eco-cultural niche of which the child is a part. According to Goodman, then, becoming literate is a sociocultural process that is influenced by cultural factors before formal literacy instruction occurs. From this perspective, speakers and writers do not simply acquire a language like English, or Spanish; rather they acquire their community's version of that language. This notion of multiple literacies, however, is one that the schools have failed to incorporate successfully into their language instructional programs and, consequently, have left untapped the linguistic knowledge that children do have—knowledge that could be used to help students acquire academic literacy.

Researchers of second language acquisition have also examined the importance of building on the language skills students already have when they enter school and have argued that facility in the acquisition of the second language is highly correlated with the level of proficiency attained in the first language (Cummins, 1984). Cummins (1981) and Hakuta (1986), for example, propose that skills learned in one language transfer to the second language and further suggest that a well-developed framework in the native language provides "scaffolding" for the acquisition of new knowledge in the second language. It follows, then, that children most at risk of failing in school especially need language, literacy, and conceptual development in their first language (Gutierrez & Garcia, in press). The implications of these new understandings of learning and language for the teaching of bilingual students are significant when we consider that much of the language instruction provided to language minority students is designed to replace students' linguistic knowledge rather than to build on it. Ironically, the schools have compounded the problem of language instruction to language minority children by providing language instruction that very closely resembles the impoverished language practices that educators have long attributed to minority students' homes literacy practices (Tharp & Gallimore, 1988; Tough, 1982). If a child's specific sociocultural environment is a significant influence on the development of literacy (Hall, 1987), then schools must capitalize on the linguistic and content knowledge children bring to the learning situation while providing abundant opportunities for students to appropriate new linguistic forms and knowledge in instructional contexts in which language learning is meaningful and purposeful. Learning, then, is significantly enhanced when it occurs in contexts that are both socioculturally and linguistically meaningful for the second language learner (Vygotsky, 1962, 1978; Scribner & Cole, 1981; Diaz, Moll & Mehan, 1986; Heath, 1986; Trueba & Delgado-Gaitan, 1988).

This sociocultural perspective of language learning is one that recognizes that learning must take place in the context of the student's experiences, background knowledge, and existing schemata (Tharp, 1989). While studies have revealed that lack of access to meaningful language instruction cuts across racial and ethnic lines, it makes sense that this lack of opportunity would have even more serious effects on language minority students whose academic vulnerability is compounded by other home/school discontinuities and whose familiarity with the schooling language is limited. Applebee, Langer and Mullis (1986), for example, report that in spite of a major shift in the nature of the teaching of composition over the last ten years, writing instruction has not significantly changed for high school students in general and for larger numbers of minority students in particular. Duran (1986) reports that significant numbers of Black, Hispanic, and Native-American students are still routinely assigned to high school English courses in which no writing is assigned and drill and exercise work is emphasized, and to remedial college English courses in which the generation of text to make meaning is not the central focus. My own observations of language instruction to second language learners in the elementary school in the Southwest reveal that students have limited opportunities to engage in and produce authentic and elaborated discourse, to integrate and build on their own linguistic knowledge, and to participate in instructional activities for which the making of meaning and the learning of content knowledge are primary learning goals. Such instructional practices have particularly deleterious effects on language minority students whose homes may not provide opportunities to learn "school-relevant skills" (Tharp, 1989) and whose acquisition of academic literacy is highly dependent on the schools to provide contextualized language instruction and regular opportunities to hear and generate authentic and purposeful language.

Instead, their educational experiences are often characterized by instructional practices that systematically exclude the students' histories, language, experiences, and values from classroom curricula and activities (Giroux & McLaren, 1986; Walsh, 1987); by limited access to academic courses and learning environments that do not foster academic development and socialization and perception of self as a competent learner and language user (Applebee et al., 1986; Duran, 1986; Eder, 1982); and by limited opportunities to engage in student-centered learning activities that are developmentally and culturally appropriate (Garcia, 1987; Morine-Dirshimer, 1985; DiPardo & Freedman, 1987; Bruffee, 1982).

The schooling of language minority children need not be characterized as hopeless or ineffective. The work of Tharp and Gallimore (1988) with Hawaiian children in the Kamehameha project should be considered a prototype of effective instructional programs for culturally and linguistically diverse students. Moreover, recent studies of effective schools for language minority students (Garcia & August, 1988) have informed us that learning and literacy acquisition can be enhanced by the following:

1. The utilization of small group instructional strategies and classroom arrangements in which cooperative modes of learning are emphasized.
2. Instructional practices that emphasize the importance of context and the social nature of written and oral communication in the language learning process.
3. Classrooms in which generating, reading, and responding to written texts are functions of the greater social and cognitive dynamic of the learning activity.
4. Classrooms that define students as communities of learners in which speakers, readers, and writers come together to define and redefine the meaning of texts.
5. Classrooms that respect and integrate the students' background knowledge, values, beliefs, histories, and experiences and that recognize the active role that students must play in the learning process.
6. Instructional activities that help expand students' knowledge beyond their own immediate experiences while using those experiences as a solid foundation for appropriate new knowledge.

These findings support the development of a new pedagogy for teaching language and for helping all students become academically literate. This "responsible pedagogy" necessarily recognizes the developmental nature of learning academic literacy and provides abundant and diverse opportunities for speaking, listening, reading, and writing, along with the necessary scaffolding to help guide students through the learning process. Finally, the research summarized above suggests that an effective program for language development and the acquisition of content knowledge for second language learners should include classrooms in which

- the student is an active participant, the key participant, in the literacy activity and in the learning process
- the goal/purpose of the literacy event is to make meaning
- the learning of content knowledge, not the learning of isolated language skills, is central
- students generate texts, read their own texts, as well as those of their peers
- students read real texts
- the teacher assists students through the learning process
- discourse is authentic/real and elaborated, not contrived or fabricated
- the literacy event includes reading, writing, speaking, and listening

- the learning of reading and writing skills is taught in the context of the students' own reading and writing
- peer and teacher feedback is purposeful, meaningful, timely, and appropriate to the task
- learning activities include opportunities for students to incorporate prior knowledge and experiences and opportunities to appropriate new understandings and information
- students write a variety of texts for authentic audiences and purposes
- classroom organization and activities capture and build on the sociocultural nature of learning and, in particular, language learning
- the classroom climate is one that encourages experimentation and risk taking
- assessment and evaluation are compatible with classroom learning goals and instruction

Finally, developing an effective pedagogy for teaching language requires that teachers become self-conscious about their own teaching practices and assumptions and about those factors that both enhance and constrain learning and achievement. An important part of that process would require teachers to do the following:

1. Assess their understanding of language acquisition and, in particular, their understanding of the acquisition of literacy.
2. Assess their understanding of how students learn and the contexts which enhance learning.
3. Reexamine pedagogies for teaching reading and writing and the curriculum implemented in the classrooms, especially in light of new research and understandings of literacy and learning.
4. Reexamine current beliefs about the learning processes and of the knowledge and experiences that all students bring into the classroom.
5. Develop culturally compatible instructional activities for those cultural features that must be accommodated in the learning process.
6. Provide students with the assistance needed to move beyond their own current skills and understandings of language and content.

I believe that this reassessment will not only better prepare us to teach diverse student populations but also will enhance our teaching of literacy to all students.

REFERENCES

Applebee, A., Langer, J. A., & Mullis, I.V.S. (1986). *The writing report card: Writing achievement in the American schools*. Princeton, NJ: Educational Testing Service.

Bruffee, K. A. (1982). Liberal education and the social justification of belief. *Liberal Education, 68*, 95–114.

Cummins, J. (1981). The role of primary language development in promoting educational success for language minority students. In *Schooling and language minority students: A theoretical framework*. Los Angeles: California State University, Evaluation, Dissemination, and Assessment Center.

———. (1984). *Bilingualism and special education*. San Diego: College Hill Press.

———. (1986). Empowering minority students: A framework for intervention. *Harvard Educational Review, 56*(1), 18–35.

Diaz, S., Moll, L., & Mehan, H. (1986). Sociocultural resources in instruction: A context-specific approach. In *Beyond language: Social and cultural factors in schooling language minority students*. Sacramento: Bilingual Education Office, California State Department of Education, pp. 197–230.

DiPardo, A. & Freedman, S. W. (1987). *Historical overview: Groups in the writing classroom* (Tech. Rep. No. 4). Berkeley: Center for the Study of Writing.

Duran, R. (1986). Improving Hispanics' educational outcomes: Learning and instruction. Unpublished manuscript, University of California, Graduate School of Education, Santa Barbara.

Eder, D. (1982). Differences in communicative styles across ability groups. In L. C. Wilkinson, ed., *Communicating in the classroom*. Orlando, FL: Academic Press.

Gallimore, R., Boggs, J. W., & Jordan, C. (1974). *Culture, behavior, and education: A study of Hawaiian-Americans*. Beverly Hills, CA: Sage Publications.

Gallimore, R. & Howard, A. (1968). Hawaiian life style. In R. Gallimore & A. Howard, eds., *Studies in a Hawaiian community: Na Makamaka O Nanakuli* (pp. 10–16). Pacific Anthropological Records, No. 1. Honolulu: Department of Anthropology, Princess Bernice Pauahi Bishop Museum.

Garcia, E. (1987). Instructional discourse in effective bilingual classrooms. Working paper No. 3, Bilingual/Bicultural Education Center, Arizona State University.

Garcia, E. & August, D. (1988). *Language minority education in the U.S.: Research, policy and practice*. Chicago: Thomas Publishing Company.

Giroux, H. A. & McLaren, P. (1986). Teacher education and the politics of engagement: The case for democratic schooling. *Harvard Educational Review, 56*, 213–38.

Goldenberg, C. (1984). Roads to reading: Studies of Hispanic first graders at risk for reading failure. Unpublished doctoral dissertation, Graduate School of Education, University of California, Los Angeles.

Goldenberg, C. & Gallimore, R. (1987). The social context of emergent home literacy among Hispanic children. Paper presented at the Institute on Literacy and Learning, Linguistic Minority Project, University of California, Santa Barbara.

Goodman, Y. (1980). The roots of literacy. In M. P. Douglass, ed., *Reading: A humanizing experience*. Claremont, CA: Claremont Graduate School.

Gutierrez, K. & Garcia, E. (In press). Academic literacy in linguistic minority children: The connections between language, cognition, and culture. In O. Saracho, ed., *Cognitive styles in early childhood*. London: Gordon & Breach Science Publishers.

Hakuta, K. (1986). *Mirror of language: The debate on bilingualism*. New York: Basic Books.

Hall, N. (1987). *The emergence of literacy.* Portsmouth, NH: Heinemann Educational Books.

Heath, S. B. (1981). Toward an ethnohistory of writing in American education. In M. Farr-Whitman, ed., *Variation in writing: Functional and linguistic-cultural differences.* Vol. 1 of *Writing: The nature, development, and teaching of written communication* (pp. 225–46). 2 vols. Hillsdale, NJ: Lawrence Erlbaum.

———. (1986). Sociocultural contexts of language development. In *Beyond language: Social and cultural factors in schooling language minority children.* Sacramento: Bilingual Education Office, California State Department of Education, pp. 143–86.

Hodgkinson, H. (1986). *Higher education: Diversity is our middle name.* Washington, DC: National Institute of Independent Colleges and Universities.

Moll, L. C. & Diaz, E. (1982). *Bilingual communications in classroom text.* Final report. Washington, DC: National Institute of Education.

———. (1983). Toward an interactional pedagogical psychology: A bilingual case study. San Diego: Center for the Study of Human Information Processing, University of California.

Morine-Dirshimer, G. (1985). *Talking, listening and learning in elementary classrooms.* New York: Longman.

National Assessment of Educational Progress. (1986). *The writing report card: Writing achievement in American schools.* Princeton, NJ: Educational Testing Service.

Ogbu, J. & Matute-Bianchi, M. E. (1986). Understanding sociocultural factors: Knowledge, identity, and school adjustment. In California State Department of Education, ed., *Beyond language: Social and cultural factors in schooling language minority students* (pp. 73–142). Los Angeles: California State University, Evaluation, Dissemination, and Assessment Center.

Scribner, S. & Cole, M. (1981). Unpackaging literacy. In M. Farr Whiteman, ed., *Variation in writing: Functional and linguistic cultural differences.* Vol. 1 of *Writing: The nature, development, and teaching of written communications* (pp. 71–88). 2 vols. Hillsdale, NJ: Lawrence Erlbaum.

Tharp, R. (1989). Psychocultural variables and constants: Effects on teaching and learning in schools. *American Psychologist,* 44(2), 1–11.

Tharp, R. & Gallimore, R. (1988). *Rousing minds to life: Teaching, learning and schooling in social context.* Cambridge: Cambridge University Press.

Tough, J. (1982). Language, poverty, and disadvantage in school. In L. Feagans & D. C. Farran, eds., *The Language of children reared in poverty* (pp. 3–18). New York: Academic Press.

Trueba, H. (1987). *Success or failure? Learning and the language minority student.* Cambridge, MA: Newbury House.

Trueba, H. & Delgado-Gaitan, C. (1988). *School and society: Learning content through culture.* New York: Praeger Publishers.

Vygotsky, L. S. (1962). *Thought and language.* Cambridge, MA: MIT Press.

———. (1978). *Mind in Society.* Cambridge, MA: Harvard University Press.

Walsh, C. (1987). Language, meaning, and voice: Puerto Rican students' struggle for a speaking consciousness. *Language Arts Journal,* 64, 196–206.

Weisner, T. & Gallimore, R. (1985). The convergence of ecocultural and activity theory. Paper read at the annual meeting of the American Anthropological Association, Washington, DC.

Weisner, T., Gallimore, R., & Jordan C. (1988). Unpackaging cultural effects on classroom learning: Native Hawaiian peer assistance and child-generated activity. *Anthropology and Education Quarterly, 19,* 327–53.

FOURTEEN

The Eastman Success Story for Helping Limited English Proficient Students Succeed

BONNIE RUBIO

This chapter will describe the Eastman Curriculum Design Project. In 1981, five case-study schools were funded under the California Department of Education. I will share a little bit about what is now going on in the Los Angeles Unified School District as a result of that initial project.

The basic philosophy of bilingual education was put together by the state Department of Education. A curriculum design was set up that reflected all the latest information, research, and theory. The purpose of the case-study schools was to take theory and put it into practice with real live children and in all kinds of varying conditions. Eastman Elementary, where I was principal from 1980 to 1985, has 1,800 students, is located in the heart of Los Angeles, and was identified as one of those case-study schools.

In 1985 I was reassigned by the Los Angeles Unified School District as an administrator and was put in charge of replicating the changes that occurred at Eastman Elementary in seven other schools. The Los Angeles school district, which has been very supportive and is currently supportive of bilingual education, funded my position and those of several consultants to change the world in these seven schools. We are now in the process of implementing change for about 10,000 students in Los Angeles Unified. The schools are located throughout the district.

Our philosophy centers on language separation. Traditionally there has been a concurrent approach to instruction in bilingual education that requires on-going translation. We are implementing language separation because we feel it is much more effective. It is an effective use of the resources as well as a more effective use of time during the school day. There is no translation. Subject material is taught either in English or in Spanish. English is either sheltered English, a version that is modified to make it more understandable, or mainstream English. All training is directed by that approach, as is the transfer of skills, so that the higher level skills transfer and are consistent throughout the design.

One of the main goals of the project is high-level oral fluency in English. Academic achievement is another target area, self-image another. Obviously, if a student does not feel good about himself in school, he is not going to do too well, and that affects the academic achievement.

As we structured and began to implement the theory and the curriculum design, we found that we were able to put together a program that was good for all the children in the school, not just the limited English proficient (LEP) children. Over a five-year period, those efforts resulted in most students graduating from elementary school at grade level, at the 50th percentile, although 80–90 percent of the students who had entered school had started kindergarten as Spanish-speaking. These achievement results began to be noticed throughout the East Los Angeles community. The change was gradual; it was not magic. The achievement was the result of teacher training and good-quality, consistency programs.

Sometimes people are not sure what causes positive change; I feel there are a few key components. One is the school organization. As you begin to implement any project or any program, there needs to be a consistent, schoolwide organization so teachers will know what the program is, and so the articulation between grade levels is clear. The teachers need to know what is expected of them and they need to get the training to support the program that will be implemented in the classroom.

Our goal was to have a quality program and an equal educational opportunity for both English and Spanish classes. We ended up with English classrooms, Spanish classrooms, and a portion of the day when students were mixed together and all were taught in English. The teachers were teamed and departmentalized so the monolingual teachers could teach a classroom in English, bilingual teachers could teach in Spanish, and both had responsibility for limited English and English-only during art, music, and physical education. Another important concern was the issue of oral language development for all of the students, not just the LEP students. All of the students, including the English-only students, needed that opportunity to address the development of better oral English skills.

Scheduling was another key area. People have a tendency to focus on the basics. We wanted children to have the opportunity to apply skills. We didn't want them to learn to read and then never get a chance to use their skills. Our interest was in providing a fully balanced curriculum regardless of the language. This occurs only when time is budgeted and each subject area is identified. Teachers, in some cases, had been teaching two hours of reading, maybe a little bit of ESL, some math, and some other things, but it was often inconsistent. We worked with them, implementing a pool for a balanced curriculum, and we were able to develop a good-quality training process to help teachers understand how to deliver a balanced curriculum. Many teachers had not taught music for a long time, or perhaps had skipped science because it was not an area of strength. So we did a great deal of teacher training to shore up skills in subject areas.

One of the important things that happened in the organization of this program was that we were able to take the credentialed bilingual teachers and concentrate them with the limited English students, rather than using the traditional approach of one-third, two-thirds. Separating the languages required organization in a different manner. It ended up being a much more effective use of resources. We also took a look at the resources in the schools and how they were being utilized. When we first started we found there was a very inconsistent use of resources in the existing programs of the seven replication schools. Sometimes teachers weren't even sure what support was available; sometimes it was unrelated to the basic program. Often the texts in use did not reflect the composition of the school. We found a school where children were learning to read in Spanish, and that was all they had to read. We went into a library in a school that had 1,000 LEP students, but only two shelves of Spanish library books. Those are the things you have to begin to look at.

The project's design places the limited English child—usually Spanish-speaking in California—in a program where the four academic subjects are taught in the primary language, and art, music, and phys ed are taught in English, using the natural approach. We go into a strong, consistent ESL program. Gradually we move into the sheltered English approach, shifting math first. The goal, obviously, is to move the entire curriculum into English, but we do not do it at the expense of academic development. We are not in a hurry, and that seems to pay off. Children who had gone through the program were actively involved in academic learning on grade level, not just sitting in the back of the room trying to figure out what was going on or trying to copy from somebody else. We also incorporated into the curriculum design a place for the native English speaking child. All children in the school were assessed in English fluency. Monolingual teachers also became part of the total package. The structure proved to be quite effective, and the training the teachers received also proved to be effective.

Courses in the school were based on the student's primary language, his English-language fluency, and reading levels. Children were transitioning from primary language to sheltered English to mainstream English, over a period of years, at grade level. Often children transition at a preverbal level in English basal series because the criteria for transition are so low. As a result, students don't develop high-level skills. They are cut off at the pass. This was happening to us in 1981, and the State Department helped us realize that some of the criteria we were using were too low.

In terms of replication, there were a number of programs that people are attempting that are based on the work that was done initially by the case study program. These schools are involving huge numbers of children, and the existing principals are getting the kind of training that it takes to be effective school leaders. After working two years with the seven schools in the replication attempt, we noticed a spread that was directly related to the quality of the instructional leadership of the principal on site. Most of us know that feeling when you walk into a school or onto a campus, when you know if there is a philosophy, you know if there is consistency, you know if teachers have high expectations. When we first walked into some of these schools, we could not find ESL. They said they had it, but it was very difficult to find.

The district has also funded an extensive evaluation design. We are taking a look at the factors that effect quality programs, such as teacher training, leadership expertise, teacher attitude, and administrative attitude. We are using parent and student surveys, and we are taking a look at the academic progress over time. We are finding in the original data that some of the teachers who were most satisfied with the old program of one-third, two-thirds structure and concurrent instruction were monolingual teachers, and that was surprising. Why would monolingual teachers be satisfied with having a bilingual class? We began to wonder if they were satisfied because they were not really responsible for those children. Perhaps the aides were doing the teaching; things like that happen in the classroom.

We have worked very closely with the seven replication schools. They are all operational, and the organization of their programs is based on what happened in the original Eastman design, the original program. We have worked very carefully to help the teachers change their attitudes, to raise their expectations, to get the administrators involved in instruction, to get them involved in the training, and to have teachers involved in curriculum committees. We believe student achievement has to go up because the quality of teaching is going up, and because the materials provided are going to reflect what is needed in the schools.

There is a great deal to be learned from the Eastman replication and its evaluation. We hope to create seven models that other schools in the district will be able to replicate as well. Los Angeles is currently interested in further expansion, and I am trying to convince them that one of the best ways to go is through administrative training. If we can really define these seven schools and use them as key models, we can then take them to those administrators who have the interest and the desire to improve the quality of their schools. We also offer administrative leaders the opportunity to do some training.

FIFTEEN

Integrated Content Language Approach

JOSE GALVAN

In this chapter I will discuss the rationale for integrating content and language instruction, with particular reference to the school. It is my assumption that an integrated approach is desirable, regardless of whether the educational programming emphasis is on the teaching of language or on the teaching of a specific subject content such as math or physical science. I feel that LEP students who are at the intermediate level or beyond will benefit from these programs because their transitional progress will have the added advantage of a strong affective element. Interest in the language being used will likely rise dramatically, and, additionally, their progress in the subject matter of the course can continue even as their language is developing.

Let me begin by describing what I see as the changing nature of education for the LEP student in the United States. The advent of bilingual education in the late 1960s brought with it a national movement to address the specific needs of the non-English speaking student and other previously disenfranchised language minorities. This effort was an extension of the attempt to fix the educational inequities that were pervasive before the Civil Rights Act of 1968, and a result of the "separate but equal" mentality that had prevailed previous to its passage. The major focus of the movement was the development of both first and second languages, seeking to address the needs of linguistic minority youngsters. The few programs that attempted to provide Black children access to standard English were based on a similar rationale.

The majority of bilingual education programs were supported by funds outside of the local school district. This locus of support suggests that educational planners viewed the needs of the students for whom these programs were patterned as outside the basic core curriculum. And, indeed, language instruction was handled as a remediation problem. Thus the needs of the non-English speaking student were not immediately institutionalized. Further, there was also minimal communication between the language specialist, the teacher responsible for English literacy training, and the content teacher.

Things are very different in the 1980s. While educational equity for language-minority youngsters is very much a national priority, the manner of addressing these needs has shifted from an educational policy based on an affirmation of a pluralistic language-diverse American populace, to one focused on mainstream education and driven by a push toward assimilation.

The 1980s have seen a movement toward increased state and local autonomy in education. The federal Department of Education relinquished to the states and local school systems its responsibility for addressing the needs of language-minority students, a direct reflection of the priorities of the executive branch. The Congress and the judicial branch have also acted in favor of less federal direction in addressing language-minority issues. There is an increased emphasis on basic skills and literacy for teachers and students. As we are well aware, several states have invoked minimum competency tests in these areas for both teachers and high school graduates. Mathematics and language arts skills are periodically assessed at designated grade levels on a statewide basis in many parts of the country, which is a move toward greater accountability. Concordant with this back-to-basics movement is the push toward quicker mainstreaming of language-minority children.

Traditional mainstream content instruction, however, will be hard pressed to meet the needs of language-minority children. Although there is a trend toward process teaching that makes use of hands-on activities and a greater awareness of the student's cognitive functioning and development, in most cases traditional content instruction is still delivered in a teacher-centered lecture format. Here the emphasis is on the textbook as a primary source of content and on summative evaluation through paper and pencil tests. These features of the traditional mainstream content classroom assume a student population that is fully proficient in the language of instruction. They assume that the students are at or close to grade level in basic literacy skills and that they have mastered a full range of requisite concepts and vocabulary, including items normally associated with the informal registers of the home and playground.

Under the best of circumstances, a second language speaking student cannot be expected to possess the same linguistic competence as students who have had continuous English language development from birth. In fact, this disjunct between the language and literacy assumptions of the mainstream programs and the actual reality for language-minority students is evident in several ways.

First, other than the language itself, the typical academic lecture provides a minimum of clues to help the student derive meaning and, therefore, understand the content. Second, language-minority students can be expected to achieve various degrees of literacy in English. In most cases, these students are not able to read on or near their grade level, rendering it unlikely that they will be able to extract the main points of the subject matter. Finally, because the ability to write cogent and lucid interpretations of content material is one of the principal educational objectives in school, the evaluation techniques that prematurely place an emphasis on writing skills may not fully enable the language-minority students to demonstrate their knowledge of content material.

The convergence of research from second language acquisition and education supports and integrated acquisition theory have facilitated an understanding of the processes involved in second language acquisition. We now understand, more clearly than ever, that language is acquired through meaningful communication in a variety of naturalistic settings. We know that in both first and second language acquisition, a key appears to be how well the linguistic input is received. Thus language development is dependent, to a large degree, on the extent to which the linguistic input results in a genuine exchange of information and on the extent to which the input corresponds to the learner's developing linguistic abilities. Researchers in Canada and the United States have demonstrated that a second language can be acquired successfully simply by making content instruction meaningful for nonnative speakers of the language. Subject matter teaching, when it is comprehensible, is language teaching.

Even though the trend in U.S. public schools appears to be toward a focus on student achievement in the cognitively demanding subject areas, the challenge for American schools is to provide access to higher level subject matter for our ever-increasing number of students with special needs. These students include newly arrived immigrants and our already linguistically diverse student population, both of whom exhibit a lack of language and literacy in English.

Why have we become so concerned with this issue at this point in time? There are at least two answers to that question. The first is that we in California have come to realize that some dramatic shifts in demographics are just around the corner. For the past couple of decades, we have noted that steadily increasing numbers of language-minority students are entering the educational setting. That pattern is predicted to continue in the foreseeable future. Another pattern is a trend toward more heterogeneous student populations in our schools. While there are many population areas in our state that continue to reflect a clustering of ethnically and linguistically homogeneous people, the demographic trends indicate that we can expect more integration in our student populations. Furthermore, we can expect more newly arrived immigrants that represent diverse language groups, but they will not necessarily be arriving in large enough numbers to warrant separate special programs. Finally, the immigration pattern suggests that the language-minority students will begin to exhibit a wider range of backgrounds in education and socioeconomic status. In fact, there is already ample evidence of these trends in our schools.

When you consider that in the twenty-first century in California some 80–90 percent of the language-minority student population will be either Latin American or Asian, it is clear that it is only a matter of time before they begin to wield an increasing political power. We will also see a broader range of mobility expectations than has ever been evident before. All of these factors present a strong image of change.

We now feel that we are able to make a significant difference in the education of these populations. Educational planners must be concerned with the fact that traditional approaches to providing academic content may be inappropriate for increasing segments of the school population. In fact, in some urban settings, the traditional instruction may be less than optimal for a majority of the students. Thus content instruction will have to be modified to meet the linguistic and academic needs of these new students.

SECTION E

Improving Teacher Effectiveness

SIXTEEN

Improving the Quality of Teachers for Minority Students

ANA MARIA SCHUHMANN

In spite of two decades of efforts, educational equity has not been achieved in the United States. The issue of equity in education has the potential of becoming a time bomb, given the profound demographic changes this country is experiencing. Can improving the quality of teachers help close the existing achievement gap between majority and minority students? I believe that it can, but making schools work for Black and Hispanic children will take much more than improving the quality of teachers: it will take a concerted effort of national and state agencies, parents and communities, public schools, colleges and universities, and the private sector.

The first issue affecting the quality of teachers for minority students is one of numbers. Teaching has traditionally been a profession of both choice and necessity for minorities—*choice* because many students were committed to uplifting their once profoundly undereducated population group, and *necessity* because access to other professions was historically limited by discrimination and restricted admissions (Wilson & Melendez, 1985). However, the number of minorities who enter teacher preparation programs and who actually become teachers is declining rapidly. In 1970 Black professionals made up 12 percent of all teachers at the elementary and secondary levels, while today they constitute about 8 percent of that pool (NCES, 1983). Black colleges and universities historically have produced more than 50 percent of the nation's Black teachers (Wright, 1980). Since 1978 the number of new teachers produced annually by 45 predominantly Black colleges has declined 47 percent (American Association of Colleges of Teacher Education [AACTE], 1983).

Even though the percentage of Hispanics in the teaching profession has increased slightly since 1975, they are even more seriously underrepresented than Blacks in the teaching force (Garcia, 1985). While Hispanics comprise almost 7 percent of the total U.S. population, they constitute only a little over 2 percent of all teachers. The slight increase in the number of Hispanic teachers can be attributed to the fact that the U.S. Hispanic population began a rapid rise around 1965 (from 10 million to the current 17 million).

Currently, only 11 percent of all teachers and 8 percent of all newly hired full-time teachers are members of a minority group. Minorities, however, constitute 21 percent of the total population and 27 percent of the school-aged population. Projections indicate that, if trends continue, minorities may comprise as little as 5 percent of the teaching force by 1990, while the minority student population will be about 33 percent of all students.

Smith (1984b) states that if the minority teaching force is reduced to 5 percent and if schools become uniformly integrated, the typical school child, who has about 40 teachers during his or her school years, can expect only two of those teachers to be from any minority group. The absence of a representative number of minority teachers and administrators in a pluralistic society distorts social reality for children and is detrimental to all students, White as well as minority (Witty, 1982).

Among many factors contributing to the declining numbers of minority teachers, the ones cited most often are (1) the general decline in college enrollment and college completion among minority youths, (2) expanded career choices for women and minorities, (3) dissatisfaction with the teaching profession, and (4) the impact of competency testing (Baratz, 1986; Rodman, 1985; Witty, 1982; Webb, 1986).

The reform movement in education and public concern over the quality of instruction in American schools have led to an increased emphasis on teacher competency testing. According to Anrig (1986), teacher testing is one of the fastest-moving changes in this period of educational reform. In as little as five years, state-required testing for aspiring teachers to enter preparation and/or to become certified has become a nationwide trend involving 38 states, with 7 additional states currently considering a teacher testing requirement. In 1984 alone, 9 states enacted teacher training laws or regulations. An AACTE survey completed in June 1986 shows that 21 states currently require tests for entry into teacher training programs, while 37 states require tests for exist and certification. Anrig (1986) reports that 21 states currently use one of the Educational Testing Service's National Teachers' Examination tests, but that states also use the SAT, ACT, California Achievement Test, and state-developed tests (Alabama, Arizona, California, Connecticut, Florida, Georgia, and Oklahoma).

The single most important issue regarding teacher certification tests involves the high failure rates among minorities (Galambos, 1986). Widely published statistics show that failure rates for Blacks and other minorities are two to ten times higher than those of Whites. It is too early to know if competency testing will improve the quality of teachers for minority students. We do know, however, that using tests intended to improve teacher quality has resulted in reducing the minority representation in the profession (Witty, 1982; Smith, 1984 a, b; Mercer, 1984; Garcia, 1985; Cooper, 1986; Baratz, 1986).

Other than competency testing, what are practices that can improve the quality of teachers for Blacks and Hispanics? Effective instructors of minority students, whether they are members of the same ethnic group as their pupils or not, display similar behaviors to those of all successful teachers:

1. Effective teachers of minority students, like all effective teachers, exhibit "active teaching" behaviors that have been found to be related to increased student performance on academic tests of achievement in reading and mathematics.

a. Teachers communicate clearly when giving directions, specifying tasks and presenting new information, using appropriate strategies like explaining, outlining, and demonstrating.

b. They engage students in instructional tasks by maintaining task focus, pacing instruction appropriately, promoting involvement, and communicating their expectations for students' success in completing tasks.

c. They monitor students' progress and provide immediate feedback (Tikunoff, 1983).

2. Effective teachers of minority students, like effective teachers in general, communicate high expectations for student learning. Research on teacher and school effectiveness has established the existence of a relationship between teacher expectations and student achievement. Students

for whom low expectations for academic success are held are taught less effectively than those for whom teachers hold high expectations. In general, students who are not expected to make significant progress experience limited opportunities to engage actively in learning activities. Teachers are less likely to plan for or direct instruction toward this group. These students, most of whom are minorities, come under fewer demands for academic performance and increasingly greater demands for conformance in terms of behavior (Brown, 1986, p. 32). We must train and hire teachers for minority youngsters who display proven characteristics of effective teaching. In addition to the features exhibited by successful instructors in general, there are additional behaviors teachers of minority children must possess. These practices apply whether the teachers of Black and Hispanic students are members of these groups or not.

3. Effective teachers of minorities have a knowledge and appreciation of their pupils' culture and use this knowledge for instructional purposes. Tikunoff (1983) found that effective teachers of limited English proficient students make use of their understanding of LEP students' home cultures to promote engagement in educational tasks. Teachers' use of cultural information takes form in three ways: (a) responding to or using L1 (native lan-

guage) cultural references to enhance instruction, (b) organizing instructional activities to build upon ways in which LEP students naturally participate in discourse in their own home cultures, and (c) recognizing and honoring the values and norms of LEP students' home cultures while teaching those of the majority culture.

4. Effective teachers of minority students recognize the legitimacy of the language variety of the students and utilize the students' language or language variety in developing English or a standard variety of English. According to Brown (1986, p. 38), "it is important for all of us, particularly those who have the responsibility for guiding the learning experiences of inner-city children, to recognize the legitimacy of the many dialects of American English and to utilize those dialects in establishing access routes to more effective communication." Brown adds that

children whose basic speech patterns are comprised of dialectical variants are often reluctant to offer oral contributions to classroom activities. This is particularly true if they have good reason to believe that those contributions will be judged for their conformance with accepted language conventions rather than content. Reticence on the part of these students elicits teacher interactions that serve to exacerbate further an already dehumanizing experience. The students soon succumb to feelings of not belonging and withdraw completely from all learning activities. This may be thought of as the point of no return. Regardless of teacher efforts to get these children actively involved, the forces operating against meaningful interaction are too firmly entrenched. Predictably, the outcomes of these actions and reactions are the same. Another group of minority students continues to make only marginal progress over the course of the school year (p. 38).

In the significant Bilingual Instructional Features study, Tikunoff (1983) found that successful teachers of LEP students mediate effective instruction by using both L1 and L2 (second language, in this instance English) effectively for instruction, alternating between the two languages whenever necessary to ensure clarity of instruction. Successful teachers of LEP students mediate effective instruction in a second way by integrating English-language development with academic skills development, focusing on LEP students acquiring English terms for concepts and lesson content even when L1 is used for a portion of the instruction.

There is widespread agreement in the field of bilingual education that a teacher of LEP students should possess a thorough knowledge of both languages of instruction, plus the ability to teach through those languages. The need for bilingual competency is supported by a number of investigations. Rodriguez (1980) studied 20 elementary bilingual teachers in an effort to determine the competencies need for effective bilingual teaching. She found that one of the characteristics most cited as synonymous with effective bilingual teaching was knowledge of the student's language. It was determined that effective bilingual teachers teach subject matter in the students' first language while giving this language and English equal status. In addition, effective bilingual teachers encourage their students to accept and use their native tongue.

A teacher of LEP students has the dual task of communicating information through one or two languages while at the same time developing the students' skills in a new language. In the assignment of teachers in bilingual education programs, weight should be accorded to their degrees of proficiency in the two languages of instruction. Administrators of programs should match the teachers' proficiencies with the instructional goals of the program and/or with the objectives of a particular grade level. In a program whose goal is the rapid transition of students to monolingual English classes, a teacher who is more proficient in the language of the students than in English would be better placed in the very early "port-of-entry" grades. A strong English as a Second Language component taught by ESL specialists with native or near-native proficiency should be an important part of the curriculum for those students. In that same program, an instructor with a higher proficiency in English would be best assigned to a grade where students are being prepared to enter an all-English curriculum. An administrator must also consider the language proficiencies of the students when assigning bilingual teachers. Studies show a very strong parallel between teacher language use and student language use.

A teacher who is much more proficient in English than in the language of the students would not be an effective bilingual education teacher for students who are monolingual in their language. Wong-Filmore (1983) has stated that the language used for instructional purposes in bilingual class-rooms must serve a dual function; it has to serve as a linguistic input for language learning purposes, but just as important, it must also communicate information and skills associated with the subject matter being taught. Assigning teachers with degrees of language proficiency that are congruent with the goals of the program and the proficiency of the students is easier if the children are grouped by linguistic ability.

In summary, improving the quality of teachers for minority students necessitates

1. increasing the number of minority teachers to provide role models for all students, and

2. training and hiring teachers who, in addition to exhibiting behaviors characteristic of effective teaching in general, are (a) culturally proficient and use their students' culture for instructional purposes, and (b) are linguistically proficient and utilize the students' language or language variety for the purposes of instruction.

REFERENCES

American Association of Colleges of Teacher Education. (1983). *AACTE Briefs*. May. Washington, DC.

————. (1986). *AACTE Briefs*. June. Washington, DC.

Anrig, G. R. (1986). Teacher education and teacher testing: the rush to mandate. In S. Packard, ed., *The leading edge*. (pp. 79–91). Washington, DC: American Association of Colleges of Teacher Education.

Baratz, J. C. (1986). Black participation in the teacher pool. Paper for the Carnegie Forum's Task Force on Teaching as a Profession.

Brown, T. J. (1986) *Teaching minorities more effectively*. Lanham, MD.: University Press of America.

Cooper, C. C. (1986). Strategies to assure certification and retention of black teachers. *Journal of Negro Education*. 55(1), 46–55.

Galambos, E. C. (1986). Testing teachers for certification and recertification. In T. J. Laskey, ed., *Issues in teacher education, Volume II: Background papers from the National Commission for Excellence in Teacher Education* (pp. 153–62). Washington, DC: American Association of Colleges of Teacher Education.

Garcia, P. A. (1985). *A study on teacher competency testing and test validity with implications for minorities and the results and implications of the use of the Pre-Professional Skills Test (PPST) as a screening device for entrance into teacher education programs in Texas*. Washington, DC: The National Institute of Education.

Mercer, W. (1984). Teacher education admission requirements: Alternatives for black prospective teachers and other minorities. *Journal of Teacher Education*, 35(1), 26–29.

National Center for Education Statistics. (1983). *The condition of education, 1983 edition: A statistical report*. Washington, DC: U.S. Department of Education, Center for Education Statistics.

Rodman, B. (1985). Teaching's 'endangered' species. *Educational Week*, 5(3) (November), 1, 11–13.

Rodriguez, A. M. (1980). Empirically defining competencies for effective bilingual teachers: A preliminary study. In R. V. Padilla, ed., *Theory in bilingual education* (pp. 372–87). Ypsilanti: Eastern Michigan University.

Smith, G. P. (1984a). The critical issue of excellence and equity in competency testing. *Journal of Teacher Education*, 35(2), 6–9.

————. (1984b). Minority teaching force dwindles with states' use of standard tests. *AACTE Briefs*, 5(9) (November), 12–14.

Tikunoff, W. J. (1983). Effective instruction for limited English proficient students. Paper presented at the 12th Annual Conference of the National Association for Bilingual Education, February, Washington, DC.

Webb, M. B. (1986). Increasing minority participation in the teaching profession. *ERIC/CUE Digest*, No. 31 (April).

Wilson, R. and Melendez, S. (1985). *Minorities in higher education: Fourth Annual Status Report*. Washington, DC: Office of Minority Concerns, American Council on Education.

Witty, E. P. (1982). *Prospects for black teachers: Preparation, certification, employment*. Washington, DC: ERIC Clearinghouse on Teacher Education, ED 213 659.

Wong-Filmore, L. (1983). Effective instruction of LEP students. Paper presented at the 12th Annual Conference of the National Association for Bilingual Education, February, Washington, DC.

Wright, S. J. (1980). The survival of black public school teachers: A challenge for black colleges and universities. In E. Witty, *Proceedings of the national invitational conference on problems, issues, plans, and strategies related to the preparation and survival of black public school teachers.* Norfolk, VA: Norfolk State University School of Education. ED 212 565.

SEVENTEEN

Improving Teacher Effectiveness

Twyla Stewart

The UCLA Center for Academic Interinstitutional Programs (CAIP) was established in 1981 with the express purpose of developing programs that would improve the quality of preparation of students at UCLA. The focus of those programs was not on students, it was on working specifically with teachers to improve the quality of their knowledge, to update their skills, and to provide them with opportunities for collaboration. As this model has evolved it has taught us some very interesting things about how a teacher's role is conceived, and how that conception needs to change to allow for the kinds of improvement that not only minority children, but all children, need in order to learn well in school settings.

This model also says some things about the kinds of changes that need to take place structurally within school organizations. CAIP emphasizes several basic principles. First of all, we focus on helping teachers address the issues of content and concept as opposed to those dealing merely with technique and strategy. These ideas focus on the issues of critical thinking, investigative inquiry, and direct confrontation with ideas in various subject matters. We help teachers to be facilitators of discovery when working with their students, to use hands-on techniques in science, to use writing processes like revision, editing, dialogue, and feedback, and to use discovery of meaning in literature.

We also believe strongly in the principle of teachers being the best teachers of other teachers, so we rely heavily on collaborative organization in our projects. In these collaborations, once teachers have gone through our intensive in-service training, they become instructional leaders in their school environments, working with us as professional consultants. That model has served us very well.

We have started to look at university and school collaborations to see what kinds of things are working, to see how we can more effectively employ researchers and our faculty to improve the caliber of teachers as well as the quality of learning and the environment of the school. We have discovered that there are various models that are working in the schools, and they work with varying degrees of effectiveness. We place these models into three categories. Most school-university collaborations involving school teachers and university faculty are considered alliance models—situations in which there is some sort of intellectual dialogue. This exchange can be in the form of a seminar, a limited conference, or a regular quarterly, monthly, or annual meeting where the primary emphasis is on developing collegiality, opening channels of communication, and exchanging ideas. Sometimes the dialogue evolves into faculty pontificating to practitioners because they see themselves in a superior role, but these types of relationships tend to have minor impact on what happens in the classroom. They don't deal directly with the problems that confront teachers and students and don't address the kinds of changes that have been described in this book.

The alliance model is a loose affiliation model. Its opposite, the cooperative research model, deals more with hard-core research. Our university faculty are the primary driving force on this model, because, as we all know, promotion and tenure depend on research projects and publishing articles. These articles may relate to what is going on in practice, but they may not benefit teachers and practitioners. This is the model that I think we are all too familiar with. This model means business as usual from the university perspective and often frustration from the practitioner's perspective.

The third model, the one that I think dominates CAIP's activities, is what we call a continuing education model, or an ongoing professional growth model. In this model teachers and administrators are encouraged to participate in programs, institutes, and seminars that provide them with an opportunity to update their knowledge, become familiar with what has been going on in research, and mull over findings on such things as effective schools and new approaches to dealing with science—experimentation and demonstrations—and all the things that are constantly being cranked out of research institutions. This gives educators a chance to think critically about how the research applies to their own situation and, more importantly, to have an opportunity to collaborate with one another and to collaborate as peers with university faculty. They are able to discuss their experiences in the school setting, modify materials and strategies, and share the things that they know, either from a gut-level feeling or, based on their own experience, have worked in the situations in which they find themselves. Opportunity for real change is present in this kind of supportive environment that is collaborative and that respects the expertise of both the practitioner and the faculty researcher.

What we have seen in this model is that those teachers who receive respect for their experience and are allowed to combine that experience with some new perspectives from research are able to go out and begin refining the benefits of that research in real school settings. They test it and bring the findings back to us, and together we fine tune the results. We publish these results—written by the teachers in many cases—and share them with other teachers. We make this the driving force of ongoing workshops, conferences, and professional development programs that are tailored to the needs of individual teachers.

This model for extending and expanding the role of the teacher as instructional leader, as professional developer, as mentor, and as a clinical consultant with university researchers is one I hope will be seriously considered for improving teacher effectiveness. This model feeds in two directions. It feeds into the loose affiliations that result from the more informal dialogue of casual gatherings, seminars, and conferences. It also feeds into additional research that benefits not only university faculty, but teachers/practitioners as well, because the teachers/practitioners become the driving forces behind that research.

Last year we began our first effort with the Teacher Researcher Project. We sent out a call to teachers who had been through some of our previous programs but wanted more; who wanted to test hypotheses and theories that they had discovered while going through one of our intensive summer institutes in writing, science, or math; and who wanted to develop a research plan they could implement in their classrooms during the school year. We became the sponsors for their research, giving them a small stipend and helping them define their problems and work on a research design. This project was implemented over the fall and spring semesters, and the teachers now have started to document their research in an anthology of articles that will be distributed through CAIP.[1]

This model for improving teacher effectiveness has been evolving since 1981. We are very excited about it simply because the people who have been working with us are now consultants with the state Department of Education, or consultants within their own schools and districts. They are called on by county offices to run workshops and develop curriculum, and to utilize that talent they already had but had not been able to nurture while working in an isolated classroom situation. We have learned in the course of these evolving programs that teachers are hungry for the opportunity to collaborate and question one another about what is working in their classrooms. They are eager to share what is going on in their immediate environments. Yet the school day is not structured in ways to make that possible. We all know that. Although we work with teachers, building up their expectations about what is possible, we also recognize that we must work with enlightened administrators and encourage them to restructure the school day so that teachers can come together, be supportive of one another, and exchange ideas. Teachers need time to discuss the things they observe happening with their students, the things they are aware of in the larger community, and the things they discover while reading research and professional literature.

The CAIP model is the beginning of a different concept of what the classroom teacher is and can be. We have seen teachers flourish and blossom when ways have been found to teach them. But it requires the support of the administrator. Our center has been a facilitator and has also provided a safe haven when school districts are hostile or principals don't have any understanding of what is going on. This model is what we need to create in school settings on a massive scale so we won't lose the best and the brightest and the most experienced teachers in our districts. Some of our teachers have come to us just on the verge of leaving the profession. Some we were not able to turn around. For those who are still teaching and are still willing to grapple with the problems, CAIP provides hope, it provides support, it provides constant intellectual engagement that nurtures these teachers. It also provides new options for their students, because the teachers take what they learn back into the classroom. This model is only one possibility among many that focus on the teacher's role, but we are extremely encouraged by what we have seen. We touch about 2,000 teachers a year. Considering what needs to be done, this is only a drop in the bucket, but it is a beginning.

NOTE

1. F. Peitzman, *The power of context* (Los Angeles: UCLA Center for Academic Interinstitutional Programs, in press).

EIGHTEEN

Teacher Effectiveness

CHARLES MOODY

Teacher effectiveness is only one of several things I would like to cover in this chapter. My belief is that it is futile to look at teacher effectiveness in isolation, as if we can make instruction more effective simply by divulging some mechanics. We have to understand the context of the problem if we are going to understand why teachers and schools are ineffective.

I think American public education is very successful. It is not a failure. American public education has been able to carry out two diametrically opposed missions at the same time without failure, without flaw. It has been able to educate some students to assume the high-status roles that have been ascribed to them by society and, at the same time, educate other students to assume their ascribed low-status roles. You don't need to be a researcher or a genius to know which roles have been ascribed to whom. Education has been used to legitimize adult economic inequality. When we start talking about making teachers more effective, I think we are really talking about a change in the mission of education. Teachers and schools have been very effective in doing what they were set up to do. That was to salt and sift.

We must make two basic assumptions if we are to have truly effective teaching for all students. First, we must accept the premise on which the late Ron Edmonds based his Effective Schools movement: all students can learn. That is a hard concept for some people to deal with, and they rationalize their bias by saying that Blacks are genetically inferior. These people believe Blacks can't learn because something is wrong with our genes, we come from one-parent homes, or we didn't have breakfast.

The second assumption we must make is that we know all we need to know to educate all students. Whether we do depends ultimately on how we feel about the fact that, so far, we haven't educated all students equitably. When we start talking about closing the achievement gap, we have to ask ourselves if that is really within our value system. Do we really mean that? Do we really want to close the gap? Do we really want minority kids to learn? If we do, then we must change the current mission of education.

When I was teaching in Chicago, I would go into the lounge and I would hear teachers say, "You know, we're doing all right, the kids are only two years behind," or, "They're only one year below grade level." I would reply, "If you were teaching somewhere else you wouldn't let them get fifteen seconds behind, because someone's head would roll." It is not all right for kids to be two years behind, or even six months behind. When we talk about improving teacher effectiveness, we first have to understand that we have to change the motives of education. We have to change the corporate structures within the schools and the school system.

When educators talk about improvements in school and teacher effectiveness they get caught in a game of "either/or." They say, "What are we going to have? Are we going to have equity, or are we going to have excellence?" The big reports on U.S. education, like A Nation At Risk, said we don't have excellence in our schools because so much time was spent in the 1960s and 1970s on equity, as if excellence and equity become an either/or proposition. If teachers, administrators, and other folks believe that these are two competing interests, our schools can't be effective. Educators can always say, "Now look here, I didn't choose to deal with equity."

Educators must understand that equity and excellence do not compete with each other. I recently did some research on excellence and equity. I talked to all 127 school superintendents (out of 16,000) who were Black. I also sampled non-Black superintendents who had a lot of minority students in their schools. Over 85 percent of those superintendents said that you should not try to have excellence without equity. They are compatible; both are necessary.

If we can get people to stop thinking about equity and excellence as competing issues, we might get some effectiveness. Ron Edmonds defined equity as a public agenda that will benefit the least advantaged member of society. Equity asks the same thing of schools serving children of poor families that any parent of any child might ask of schools. How can an agenda that gives the same thing to every kid who comes to school and establishes a high standard of performance contain competing elements? We can have excellence in any walk of life and in any thing we do. We can expect excellence.

I recently read an article about minority students entering universities. Within that article, I could not find one positive word about what minority students bring into the educational process when they enter college. Everything was negative. They didn't have good preparation in secondary school, they didn't have good study habits, and so on. If we are going to have effective education, it must be understood that all people have some strengths that they bring to school. They bring talents; they bring skills. We cannot expect to achieve effective, equitable teaching unless the correct motives of education are clearly defined, articulated, and understood. Then we can really get down to improving practices.

One model we have used to help define effective educational practices is a four-dimensional concept of an equity-based education. The first dimension concerns access to schools, classes, and programs for all students. Effective instruction is blocked by people who don't want some folks in their classes. It's what I call the "it-wasn't-like-this-before-they-came" syndrome. Even when the minority kids are in the classroom, that kind of thinking often doesn't change. We must change the mentality that says that schools would be better if minorities weren't present.

The second dimension focuses on process. How are people treated once they get in the school? Are they treated with dignity and fairness? Teachers call more frequently on students whom they perceive as being high achievers, they wait longer for them to answer, they give them prompts, they give them clues, they get closer to them, they give them feedback. Most teachers do not realize that they do this to kids. It does happen, however, and these teacher expectations directly affect student performance.

The third dimension is that of achievement, which is reflected by grades, test scores, graduation, and dropout rates; minority representation in multicultural curriculum; recognitions and awards; and the mastery of basic and advanced skills. Even when achievement shows that instruction is effective, others may not accept the results. In one instance in New York, kids in a reading program were doing well, and they were given the usual test in the spring. The kids achieved so highly that the State of New York sent some people out to investigate, because they were sure the kids had been cheating. The New York State Department of Education tested them again and got the same result, but they still wouldn't accept the fact that the kids were doing well.

The last dimension is transfer. If students get access to school and classes, and they are treated properly in the process, they achieve well. The next question to ask is: Are they able to transfer those achievements into additional educational opportunities and eventually into jobs that will provide them with equal pay, power, privilege, and prestige? The worst thing we can do is to tell minority kids that all they need do is to be competent and to achieve, and everything will be all right. These kids understand that folks at home with alphabets behind their name are unemployed or underemployed. Each generation doesn't have to start from scratch, we can help each other. We need to teach kids how to network.

There are some things we can do directly to improve teacher effectiveness. We can look at the school climate, we can look at teacher expectations, we can look at the notion of effective teaching strategies. Teachers often don't tell students what their objectives are; they just tell them to learn it and someday it will be useful. Teachers might try teaching to an objective. They use a lot of activities that are related to their objective but are not relevant. In addition, we shouldn't worry about not being able to use Bloom's taxonomy when kids happen to be in a minority or the kids happen to be in special ed. All kids can learn the next thing beyond what they already know.

We must be careful not to kill motivation. No kid comes to kindergarten wanting to be a failure. They come to school motivated, ready to learn. Unfortunately, some teachers don't know how to deal with a kid who is motivated and shows that by asking questions. In the school where I worked in Evanston, Illinois, most of the kids were from two minority groups, Blacks and Jews. The teachers were all White and gentile. They would describe the actions and reactions of the Jewish kids by saying, "They are really curious; they ask questions; they really push you." That was described as intellectual curiosity. When they described the same behavior in Black kids it was disrespect and insubordination. We have to look at how people respond and react to the same behavior from different kids.

The cultural congruence between student population and instruction is another educational aspect to consider. What kind of self-esteem would a White kid have if during his sixteen years in school, everyone he encountered was Black? What would he think if the only thing he read about Whites was that some guy named Columbus got lost in 1942? In most minority education, there is no cultural congruence, there is nothing that is relevant to minority experiences.

Finally, we must have administrators who know what good instruction is and can recognize it in the classroom. Administrators who, when they walk into a classroom, aren't looking at the shades to see if they're even, the seats to check if they're lined up, or the kids to make sure they are quiet. Some activities require movement, talking, and noise. Principals should also let teachers work with each other and do some peer coaching.

The basic point is: Do people *want* minority kids to learn? As soon as we close the gap and minority students are achieving, people will no longer have an excuse not to hire minorities. The fastest growing jobs are in the service industry. Some folks say, "You really don't need a degree for a service job." Maybe you've heard them say, "Now look here, we don't have to teach them, because we can give them service jobs for the minimum wage." The folks that are ascribed the high-status roles are the folks who need higher education.

The best way to see this difference is in Chapter I schools, which have as many computers as some schools in the suburbs. The difference is in what the students are taught about the computers. Kids at the Chapter I schools use their computers for drill and practice, drill and practice. In the other schools, computers are used to expand student thinking and capabilities; these kids learn how to program and how to manipulate the computer. Some teachers are not using dittos anymore for drill and practice, they are using computers for drill and practice.

We have been trying to instill some of these ideas into practice through our School Improvement Project, a teacher training program at the University of Michigan. One goal of this project is to increase teacher knowledge of research that deals with effective school correlates, successful implementation plans, effective teaching practices, time-on-task, curriculum development, and knowledge of effects on student achievement.

We also provide staff with development activities that will facilitate strategic planning, identify effective teaching practices, and improve the instructional leadership of supervisory personnel. We want to help schools create a more cohesive staff that feels they have a stake in improving instruction, and help develop mechanisms to increase community support and involvement. Staff development activities can facilitate an understanding of the impact of culture on schools.

Our third goal is to gather data that will give direction for planning, help in the evaluation of program effectiveness, and provide a basis for longitudinal studies.

The full model includes a model for Institutional Skills for Effective Training (ISET), which is used in conjunction with the School Improvement Project. This model has three cycles. The first deals with theory. Teachers and administrators attend workshops that focus on selecting an objective at the correct level of difficulty, monitoring learning and adjusting instruction, and using principles of learning to cause students to increase their rate of learning, retain more of what is learned, and transfer learning to new situations.

The second cycle is an instructional conferencing model. Teachers and administrators practice teaching, using feedback through discussion and videotaping to evaluate and improve instruction.

In the third cycle, educators make a commitment to become trainers. Intensive work on the elements of instruction and instructional conferencing are the major components. Additional workshops are provided on leadership, presentation skills, and effective workshop techniques.

Our school improvement efforts are based on the four-dimensional model of equity-based education. The ISET model provides a structure for communicating equity change to school staff. We chose this model because research has indicated that staff development is the most effective means of communicating these changes.

If we want to improve teaching, people must buy the premise that all kids can learn. We must not use education to legitimize adult inequality; we must not use the schools to promote salt and sift labor. That will improve effectiveness. I think all of the things presented in this chapter are part of effective teaching, but the most important aspect is the belief that kids can learn.

PART III

The Role of Testing and Evaluation in Improving Education for Underachieving Minority Students

SECTION A

Issues in Promoting a More Productive Role

NINETEEN

The Potential and the Reality: The Role of Evaluation in Improving Opportunity

Joan L. Herman

At CRESST we believe that testing and evaluation hold significant potential for helping to improve the quality of education for underachieving students. Their potential lies in their potency as tools that can help educators, policy makers, parents, and the general public better understand the quality and effects of what goes on in schools, help them to analyze the reasons underlying current performance, and stimulate them to improvement-oriented action. Several of the guiding premises of CRESST's R&D mission speak to these issues directly:

We believe that testing, evaluation, and standard setting can contribute importantly to the educational quality. Tests—when they are well conceived, validly constructed, sensibly analyzed and appropriately used—can provide valuable insights into how and what individuals, classrooms, schools, and systems of students are learning. These insights can help guide teaching, administration and policymaking with our educational institutions. Evaluations of programs—when they are sensitive to context, and especially when they are seen as improvement oriented, locally useful, and iterative—can help to guide the reallocation of resources, the modification and improvements of activities, and the retraining of personnel. Standards—when they are set with due attention both to what is desirable to what is feasible at the state and local levels—can help to focus attention and promote accountability for educational improvement.

We believe that testing and evaluation are important tools for promoting educational equity. Tests—when they are sensitive to individual differences and preferences in learning styles—provide a powerful means for diagnosing students' unique needs and providing effective instruction for all students. Furthermore, tests—when they match classroom instruction—can provide fair and equitable measures of student progress, measures which focus on learning accomplishments rather than background characteristics. Sensitive and meaningful measures of achievement, combined with measures of educational process and community context, can help to identify areas where the needs of particular groups are being met and areas where more attention is needed, facilitating more effective programs for all.

We believe that testing, evaluation, and standard setting are endeavors which are partly technical, partly political, and partly social. Technical expertise is essential in test development and analysis to ensure the valid, reliable, and meaningful use of test and evaluation results; social and political understanding are essential to ensure sensitivity to context, utility, and fairness (adapted from Baker & Herman, 1985).

While we are optimistic about the potential of testing and evaluation, we are well aware of the problems in current practice. Instances of productive and beneficial impact, in fact, have been overshadowed by instances of the reverse, particularly when the subject is underachieving minority students.

Rather than being a productive tool, a bridge to change, testing has more often been a barrier to mobility. Examples abound. Charges of bias in test content and of the unfair advantage tests give to students from the majority culture are long-standing (Williams, 1974; Oakland, 1977, Phillips, 1973). Because they do not adequately represent the culture and life experiences of minority students, results from such tests have functioned to limit students' opportunities. According to national studies of schooling, for instance, testing has contributed to the rigid tracking of students into vocational or academic programs, reducing the prospects for individual growth and satisfaction for those who do not score well (National Commission, 1983). Test results have been used to justify the placement of children from different language backgrounds or with different developmental histories into dead-end tracks with little opportunity for change and advancement. A similar story has been told at the postsecondary level, where college entrance exams (SAT, ACT) have been soundly criticized as detrimental to the interests of minority students (Nairn and Associates, 1980; Williams, 1974; Jenifer, 1984).

Some of the reasons for the current testing and evaluation's track record are clearly sociopolitical. Our models have been insensitive and tied to official program perspectives. Ernesto Bernal's Chapter 21 in this volume reminds us of some of these political issues and posits some alternative visions. He advocates the development of new, unbiased tests that might truly capture students' "thinking, learning, expressive styles, and bicultural survival competencies." He also recommends evaluation strategies that get inside program operations to document "what is really going on . . . [and] how these events are perceived by different actors."

Beyond significant, enduring social and political issues, shortcomings in technical practice also have limited the potential utility of testing and evaluation in improving education. The reality of current evaluation practice simply has not supported meaningful change. Among the problems is a reliance on standardized tests that at best (assuming we can remove bias) assess only a very narrow slice of the curriculum, emphasizing basic skills to the near exclusion of higher order thinking skills and ignoring the variety of important outcomes to which schooling is to contribute (e.g., attitudes toward school and self, citizenship, work skills). Accountability stressing such limited measures may well constrict rather than enhance the learning process in schools, a constriction that may particularly afflict schools serving poor, minority students. Consider a finding from a national study of testing practices conducted at UCLA (Dorr-Bremme & Herman, 1986). It found that teachers in schools serving disadvantaged students felt that the emphasis on test scores in their schools limited the breadth of curriculum they were able to teach to students. Beyond the obvious implications of limited breadth for long-term intellectual growth, one must wonder also about the short- and long-term affective consequences for students—such as what might be the effects on students' attitudes toward school, their attitudes toward learning, their motivation, of school programs that predominantly feature drill and practice on lower level, rote skills? Eric Cooper's presentation in Chapter 20 discusses how testing and evaluation practice can play a more productive and positive role in promoting effective schools. He emphasizes the importance of systematic monitoring of *significant* learning in effective schools, the need to look beyond multiple-choice measures of lower level skills, and the necessity for a variety of indicators of school effectiveness and equity. Ramsey Selden's Chapter 22 also attends to the variety of indicators that will be useful in formulating sound policies at the state and national levels.

Selden's comments also raise another issue: the importance of getting beyond the "outcomes only" orientation that has dominated much evaluation practice. Summary test scores alone do not carry sufficient information to justify judgments about school quality. We all know that students' performance on tests is the product of many factors, yet we report test results as though only schools were responsible for them. By ignoring contextual variables, such as community context, student demographics, and the like, we have created a system where schools serving advantaged students get too much credit. Not only does such a system disadvantage those schools serving poor students, but it also masks valid answers to questions such as "Who are the schools best serving?" and "Is there equity in educational process and outcomes." Cooper's chapter draws attention to this point as well, arguing that we adopt Ron Edmonds' empirical view of what constitutes an effective school.

We need to get beyond an "outcomes only" vision for another reason as well. Eliot Eisner (1985, pp. 5–6) states it succinctly: If we want to understand why we get what we get from our schools we need to pay attention not simply to the scores, but to the ways in which the game is played."

Test scores give us some inkling of effect, but they give virtually no information about the reasons for or causes of that effect. In contrast, we need good information about school and instructional processes if evaluation is going to be useful in school improvement. Dan Levine's Chapter 23 expands on these issues, providing a strong rationale for sound implementation data.

Against this backdrop of problems in current evaluation practice, we can also point to telling examples of success. One of the subthemes of this volume is that we have much to gain from the working knowledge of the field. In Chapter 24 Todd Endo tells of the trials, tribulations, and, yes, more than glimmers of success from Fairfax County, Virginia's efforts to improve education for underachieving minority students. Endo's reflections stress the importance of a strong leadership vision, a committed planning process, and a host of interpersonal and organizational factors. Walter Hathaway in Chapter 25 shares Portland, Oregon's accomplishments in creating a strong, curriculum-based, multipurpose assessment system that is helping educators to reduce the achievement gap for minority students. James Olsen paints a similar picture of success in Chapter 26 with computer-based assessment systems that can diagnose students' instructional needs and prescribe appropriate instructional activities accordingly. The empirical data he presents are very encouraging.

In summary, at CRESST we recognize serious problems in current testing and evaluation practice, but we remain optimistic about its potential to help improve educational opportunities. We are working directly on answers to some of the important issues raised by the chapters in this volume. Our work in writing assessment, for example, very early on demonstrated the importance and feasibility of moving beyond multiple-choice measures and using student essays to reliably and more validly assess writing skill. Our current work in content assessment carries similar issues forward into the social studies domain. Applying what we know about the structure of knowledge and about how students learn, we are developing alternative measures to systematically assess students' higher level understanding in particular subject area domains. Simultaneously, our work in instructional assessment is developing new, multipurpose approaches to evaluation and assessment so that a single set of measures can provide sound information for diagnosing individual student's needs; for detecting the effectiveness, strengths, and weaknesses of both instructional programs and school curricula; and for articulating strong, coherent course sequences that will help to assure student success at the secondary and postsecondary levels.

In still another example from current work, a project on school-based evaluation systems is investigating how best to configure the evaluation enterprise so that it will be useful to educators, focus attention on equity issues, and contribute significantly to school improvement. We will look forward to sharing our findings as they accrue.

REFERENCES

Baker, E. and Herman J. (1985). Educational evaluation: Emergent needs for research. *Evaluation Comment*, 7(2) (December).

Dorr-Bremme, D. W. & Herman, J. L. (1986). Assessing student achievement: A profile of classroom practices. *CSE Monograph Series in Evaluation, No. 11.* Los Angeles: Center for the Study of Evaluation.

Eisner, E. (1985). *The art of educational evaluation: A personal view.* Philadelphia: The Falmer Press.

Jenifer, F. G. (1984). How test results affect college admissions of minorities. In C. Daves, ed., *The uses and misuses of tests.* San Francisco: Jossey-Bass, pp. 91–106.

Nairn, A. and Associates. (1980). *The reign of ETS: The corporation that makes up minds.* Washington, DC: Ralph Nader.

National Commission on Excellence in Education. (1983). *A nation at risk: The imperative for educational reform. A report to the nation and the Secretary of Education.* Washington, DC: U.S. Department of Education.

Oakland, R., ed. (1977). *Psychology and educational assessment of minority children.* New York: Brunner/Mazel.

Phillips, B., ed. (1973). *Assessing minority group children.* New York: Behavioral Publications.

Williams, R. (1974). Black pride, academic relevance, and individual achievement. In R. W. Tyler and R. M. Wolf, eds., *Crucial issues in testing.* Berkeley, CA: McCutchan.

TWENTY

Framework for Effective Schools

Eric Cooper

The strength of our nation is a direct function of the ability of our schools to educate—majority as well as minority, women as well as men, children as well as adults. All students served, all students educated. This is not only a goal, but a necessity. An institution that provides "effective schooling" is one that is able to maintain sustained progress toward national goals and expectations for all students.

In this definition, it is important to note that a school with a "good" reputation may not be an effective school. The difference between the two relates to the concept of progress and whether or not all students are well served. To some, "good schools" develop high levels of achievement for a certain portion of the students served. Effective schools, on the other hand, hold to a higher standard. They sustain high levels of growth for all students.

The recent reports on reading and writing produced by the National Assessment of Educational Progress (NAEP) document well the fact that the average performance of students on the process outcomes of education is simply not high enough to meet the needs of the nation.[1] The nation is still at risk. Therefore, for effective schooling to become a reality, our schools must set and hold all students to higher expectations of performance on the process outcomes of education.

In order to provide effective schooling, an institution must set high goals and expectations, not only for the students served, but also for its administrators and its teachers and parents. And these goals and expectations must apply equally to students who are considered academically gifted and those who are considered educationally at risk. While equality in outcomes cannot be guaranteed, there is no place for differential opportunities or expectations for students.

Stating that an institution has high expectations for the students it serves is not enough for effective schooling. These expectations must be stated in concrete terms—in ways that can be observed and assessed. As an integral part of effecting schooling, student progress toward these expectations must be monitored continuously—by measures of valued educational outcomes as well as by other indicators of success. An example of the former would be the periodic assessment of student ability to write through the use of direct writing samples. An example of the latter would be evidence that the retention rate for at-risk students was as high as the retention rate for the academically talented.

In stating that measures of valued educational outcomes must be used to monitor student progress, it is important to define what is meant by "valued educational outcomes." Education is not simply the acquisition of subject matter knowledge—the facts and figures. Effective schooling involves the processes of learning—the processes needed to actually solve problems, read with comprehension, and develop an idea in writing, for example. Measures of these processes, rather than the discrete skills and facts, must be used to assess student progress toward these valued outcomes. No school can be considered effective without evidence of sustained progress for all students on these processes of learning.

In order to ensure that instruction is fulfilling student needs, appropriate tests that are in accord with real-world outcomes should be used. These tests should repeatedly show that students in all classrooms and at all ability levels are making satisfactory progress toward stated goals and expectations. They should demonstrate that students are successful on those optimally difficult learning tasks that ensure growth.

While it is important for teachers to use tests to monitor instruction, it is very important to distinguish these tests from those that show that students are making progress toward valued educational outcomes. These outcome measures should be used for the purpose of redesigning the curriculum and teacher-directed instruction so that ever-increasing progress is made toward the bottom line—toward attaining valued outcomes.

Two statewide testing programs stand out as exemplars in terms of their use of measures that focus on the process outcomes of education rather than the discrete skills and facts of education. In Connecticut and New York, outcome measures are used that permit the assessment of student progress toward expectations—absolute expectations set in terms of functional needs of the state and the nation rather than relative needs set in relation to the average performance of students on tests that are only norm-referenced.

Effective schools use a variety of assessments to provide information for informed decision making not only in terms of current problems, but also with respect to the need for attaining those levels of performance required to function effectively in the future. According to NAEP, for example, only one in twenty 17-year-old students can read at the "adept" level. It is obvious that we need to know what must be done in the future in order to plan for new and higher levels of performance.

Inadequate student performance is a cause for restructuring and redesign not only of educational programs, but also of the retooling of management and related support systems in the school and the community that are required for implementation of instructional programs that have been shown to work in similar educational systems. Effective schools are problem-solving institutions that serve all students in meeting their aspirations and the nation's need for informed, literate citizens in an increasingly competitive world.

In order to define and resolve problems, and sustain high levels of progress for all students, effective schools:

- Reallocate and/or allocate additional resources (e.g., time, teachers, and materials) to improve the performance of low-achieving students.
- Involve teachers and other staff in ongoing examination and revision of decisions and in collegial problem-solving regarding effective implementation of instruction within and across classrooms.
- Provide adequate resources to improve the delivery of instruction of the most important learning skills, particularly for low-achieving students, through school-wide staff development.

In drawing attention to the process of learning, such as the ability to solve problems, read with comprehension, and develop an idea in writing, we must take note of the fact that effective schooling requires that students be engaged in productive learning experiences, not simply time-on-task. Throughout the school year, the amount of time students are actively engaged in the learning process is critically important. Furthermore, teachers must be sensitive to the needs and abilities of the students served in order to engage them in productive learning experiences in the classroom. This means that the materials used to deliver instruction must not be so easy as to create boredom, nor too difficult to create frustration.

In effective schools, all students must have a demonstrable opportunity to develop cognitive processes to comprehend, think, and compute. This means that students should be actively engaged in a mixture of interactive and teacher-directed instruction for a significant portion of the school day. All students should also have an opportunity to learn in the content fields, such opportunities should be integrated with the development of processing capabilities. While the curriculum may be enriched for the gifted, it should not be trivialized for those who are at risk or who are more dependent upon the school for their development. Finally, effective schooling requires that teachers be sensitive to the art of classroom questioning, listening well to student responses, and providing constructive clues and feedback to facilitate the learning process.

While the above generalities hold for institutions that provide effective schooling, there are a number of additional requirements for institutions that serve high-risk students—students who are almost solely dependent upon schools for the development of the processes of education. The educational attainments of disadvantaged students, who are disproportionately Black, Hispanic, American Indian, and poor, serve as a barometer to determine whether a school is engaged in effective schooling. An effective school produces as much progress toward national goals and expectations for these students as it does for the educationally advantaged.

To provide effective schooling for the educationally disadvantaged, a school must assign some of the best teachers, allocate a disproportionate amount of resources, and provide small class sizes or otherwise address the problems of these students. Anything less, and the educationally disadvantaged will not be able to sustain progress toward the acquisition of the processes of learning. Finally, to sustain progress, particularly for at-risk students, attendance should be high and the school should aggressively resist the transferring of students in and out of classrooms for pull-out programs, unless they are fully and productively coordinated with regular classroom instruction.

Effective schooling requires that concrete and manageable plans be developed and in place for starting off a school year with complete programs and a fully professional staff ready to teach. The school year is too short to waste time on start-up processes and it is especially important to make sure that the at-risk students are served with the best staff from the very start of the school year. Effective schooling requires the systematic upgrading of instruction so that it is in accord with the state of the art in instructional fields as documented in various professional reports such as the NIE report entitled *Becoming a Nation of Readers*.[2]

Teachers and administrators who provide effective schooling are critical consumers of educational books, computer software, and other products, making sure that they have been validated for instructional use. Because these products overwhelmingly determine the nature of instruction, those involved in effective schooling frequently acquire updated products to support efforts at upgrading themselves.

Effective schools recognize the importance of teachers, parents, and community representatives and involve them in the planning, decision-making, and evaluation process of educating children. Effective schools do not depend on top-down mandates to improve instruction. Effective implementation of instructional reform requires a mixture of school-level decision making and top-level direction setting, with emphasis on on-going, building-level staff development and initiative focusing on how instructional improvements will be defined, implemented, and modified. Teachers must be deeply involved as scholar practitioners in determining, through collegial decision making, how improvements are shaped and delivered.

Evaluation indicators and criteria that can be employed in identifying institutions that provide effective schooling can be grouped under three major headings: (1) indicators of efficacy, (2) indicators of quality, and (3) indicators of equality. Examples of such criteria are as follows:

1. Indicators of efficacy:
   - Assessment of educational outcomes based on process measures such as work samples, direct writing samples, and holistic measures of comprehension. Specifically, tests that sample discrete skills rather than engage comprehension, writing, and computing processes should not be relied upon as indicators of educational progress. Attempts to legislate improvements in education through minimum competence testing programs fall short for students, especially students who are risk, because they focus attention on lower level discrete skills at the expense of comprehension, problem solving, and the expression of ideas orally and in writing.
   - Frequent monitoring of student progress toward outcomes by classroom teachers using a variety of formal and informal procedures.

2. Indicators of quality:
   - A supportive school climate that is also visible in the classroom.
   - Clear statements of school goals and expectations that are shared by students, school staff, parents, and other community representatives.
   - Other components of effective schools as identified in the literature, such as school mission, leadership, school climate, high expectations, instructional improvement, and assessment.

3. Indicators of equality:
   - Attendance rates for at-risk students that equal or exceed those for the entire school.
   - Retention and completion rates for at-risk students that equal or exceed that for the entire school.
   - Progress toward educational goals and expectation for at-risk students that is equal to that made by all students.

To employ such indicators in the identification of effective schools, it is important to remember that such data must be available on a disaggregated basis. Effective schools must collect, record, and retain quantitative and qualitative data in a fashion that supports longitudinal analysis of the performance of individual students and groups of students. Such analyses would include, for example, data disaggregated by race, ethnicity, gender, socioeconomic status, and grade level. Anything less and there is no way to ascertain whether sustained progress is being made for all students. Schools that provide effective schooling are humane and creative problem-solving institutions that engage students in academic learning processes, which enable them to become capable of full participation in a free society that needs intellectually capable citizens.

NOTES

The framework described in this chapter was developed by the College Board's Ad Hoc Committee on Effective Schools.

1. A. N. Applebee, J. A. Langer, & I. V. S. Mullis. *The Writing Report Card: Writing Achievement in American Schools* (Princeton, NJ: Educational Testing Service, 1986); and National Assessment of Educational Progress, *The Reading Report Card: Progress Toward Excellence in Our Schools: Trends in Reading over Four National Assessments, 1971–1984* (Princeton, NJ: Educational Testing Service, 1985).

2. National Academy of Education, Commission on Reading, *Becoming a Nation of Readers: The Report of the Committee on Reading.* (Pittsburgh: National Academy of Education, 1985).

TWENTY-ONE

Some Thoughts on How Testing and Evaluation Can Improve Educational Opportunities for Underachieving Minorities

Ernesto M. Bernal

This chapter will address both testing and evaluation or, rather, some new departures in both fields that I believe are definable in light of what is needed, or what has not yet been accomplished. I hope the ideas presented here will make you somewhat uncomfortable, in some cases for their speculativeness and in other instances for their departure from the current zeitgeist.

EVALUATION

I am gratified that the number of journals on evaluation have increased but concerned that the number of journal articles dealing with urban, minority, and compensatory education have not. A cynic, I suppose, could begin by asking, "Given that much of the financial impetus for the development of program evaluation as a field came from compensatory education and other government programs (Daniels & O'Neil, 1979), what has evaluation done to improve the lot of the underserved, the ill-served, nondominant groups in American society?" One of CRESST's guiding premises is the belief that testing and evaluation are important tools for promoting educational equity. Perhaps the chapters in this volume can be considered partial repayment. I believe it is necessary for us to distinguish between a moderately routinized, operational program evaluation and one that seeks to influence policy at levels that could affect a significant sector of educational practice, not just a parochial interest.

We also need to recognize that certain programs are likely to generate confusion and ill will when they deal with an already politically sensitive area (e.g., bilingual education), require extensive systemic change (e.g., Experimental Schools Program [Lenning, 1977]), or combine one or both of these elements with personal pride or finances (as in the case of career ladders). It is wise to note that for some proponents and opponents of controversial programs such as these, no amount of data or evidence will dissuade them. What we should attempt is to gain a balanced picture when analyzing large-scale, controversial programs. How do we best achieve such a balanced picture? One might consider, for example, letting out three small contracts instead of one large one. One proponent group and one contrary group would be in charge of analyzing the data that yet a third, ostensibly more neutral, group would collect to satisfy the analysts' designs. Comparing the results (reported in a uniform, juxtaposed format) might help us all to evaluate how well evaluation can handle controversy (see Duckett et al., 1982) and see just how Suchman's old (1967) pitfalls of evaluation ("eyewash," "whitewash," "submarine," etc.) apply today.

It is a testimony to our lack of imagination that compensatory education programs *look* so compensatory. (Like Henry Levin, in Chapter 1, I feel that comp-ed should be an enriching, alternative mode of delivery.) Such lack of imagination also impedes our evaluations of such programs. For example, we continue to look at national norms and "regular progress" as the touchstones for many minority programs. We need to think of how educationally disadvantaged *minority* children would do if they were placed in the *regular* program which after all does not want them (Bernal, 1984). (Why else were special programs created?) I am not sure how best to estimate these effects, but I am certain that this would be a more revealing comparison, both pedagogically and politically.

Since minority students are culturally (i.e., behaviorally) different, it is crucial that policy and program evaluations deal with naturalistic *settings* (Wardrop, 1971), particularly the way the schools (representing the majority culture, values, and expectations) interact through their rules and representatives with the minority cultures, children, parents, and neighborhoods. I recall an old ethnographic study by Spradley (1971), never picked up in the education literature, which found that minority school children, rather than being "culturally deprived," were often culturally overwhelmed. The study concluded that to succeed in school, minority students needed to possess a capacity not required of others, namely to become bicultural. This study illustrates how perceptions and protocol are critical intervening variables. *Real events*, not just official events, in terms of human transactions, must be documented (Charters & Jones, 1973).

In a similar vein, we need to stop fragmenting educational objectives without attempting a synthesis that transcends individual objectives (see Page & Stake, 1979). Many programs present an evaluator with goals and objectives that later experience proves to be excessive, undesirable, or positively misleading. I believe that controversial, complex programs are not only not evaluatable in their first year, but also that the task of the evaluator of these programs is to complete the evaluation design *after* the project is under way, and that the first year or two of the evaluation should be as fluid and formatively dynamic as the project itself (see Weiss, 1973).

Nor do we need to be naive to think that the goals and objectives provided us are the only ones we should measure. I suppose I am arguing against the disinterested evaluator role whenever policy issues are being investigated. The evaluator in a collaborative role, however, needs to have the courage to supply essential goals and to examine the data to see if they have been fulfilled. Among these are the long-term monitoring of achievement, placement, and retention of minority students to see if they have similar tracking options within the curriculum as White students do, over the long run. (See Oakes, 1987, for "indicators of equity.")

While systems exist for objectively discovering which goals are real and for prioritizing the maze of objectives that complex programs present us (e.g. Borich, 1984), what is needed, additionally, is a good model for detecting how objectives interact with one another, particularly how implementation of certain program features (how the attainment of certain objectives) might impede or facilitate the realization of other objectives. For example, the early reclassification and exit of limited English proficient students from bilingual programs may impede their long-term success in school and necessitate further special services, such as Chapter I programs. (Such "exits" from transitional bilingual education to another compensatory program instead of to regular education are a sham, in my opinion.) The possibility that objectives interact with each other means that a project's effects and impacts may be greater or less than the sum total of its individual objectives.

TESTING

My first and most basic recommendation for psychometricians is to move directly to de-bias tests of intelligence, aptitude, and achievement, even if you do not believe them to be biased! This effort would in any case be a more creative and engaging enterprise than defending current practices. The new goal is to measure *adequately* as well as validly without compromising other features of a test like reliability and usability.

I suppose that I see recent developments in the bias issue as portending even greater conflict, more serious confrontations. On the one hand, such programs as "teacher-competence" and student-achievement (basic skills) testing, are expanding and generating new hundreds of thousands of dollars to certain test-making and test-scoring enterprises yearly. On the other side of the political equation, groups that oppose testing in one or more of its forms are joining forces with consumer advocates and even with avowedly political action organizations. The underlying social issue, however, has to do with the real costs of these conflicts in terms of human potential lost, not to mention the professional energies that will be dissipated in formal judicial hearings and legislative manipulations.

Mercer (1979) has stated that psychologists generally are among the established American elites (in the sociological sense) and that they understandably perpetuate a psychometric belief system that provides a "scientific rationale for the continued ascendancy of politically dominant racial and cultural groups" (p. 112). She further points out that there are a few psychologists who hold a counterideology, one that rejects "a definition of 'intelligence' which is based entirely on an individual's knowledge of the Anglo core-culture and would include the language, skills, and knowledge needed to operate successfully in non-Anglo cultural settings" (p. 112). I wish to add that while many apologists for extant testing practices *claim* that measured mean differences between Whites and minorities are functions of differential educational opportunities, the testing industry has never really *studied* this particular question, a crucial hypothesis, really, which can be answered only by investigating several alternative possibilities at the same time.

The new tests that I envision might include a representative sampling of thinking, learning, expressive styles, and bicultural survival competencies (so that almost everyone does poorly on a few sections of the test, but not on the same ones). These tests should not be like the old "culture free" tests, with all their attendant problems, including lack of validity, but should address themselves to a wide variety of abilities (see Flaugher, 1971) that new research would show are important to success in life generally and in school as well. We must keep in mind that current predictor variables are not all that powerful (which occasionally gets tests into trouble even with White populations); hence a search for stronger and "alternative" cognitive skills and "nonintellective" (Lenning et al., 1974) factors is in order—predictors we do not yet tap. We could, for example, develop tests based on studies of extreme groups who do not perform as our contingency tables would predict, then compare these groups to each other and to groups of more consonant individuals. The application of computer-assisted testing may also be in order here, for the sake of both efficiency and humaneness, to reduce overall testing time and stress on such diverse sets of items.

While tests allow us to do some very sophisticated analyses of individuals and groups, we have to adopt a more user- and consumer-friendly approach:

1. We need tests of *achievement/placement* that yield not only reliable but also accurate scores without having first to subject minority kids to extensive test-taking skills training. In short, we need tests that are not so artificially constructed

that they mask the true abilities and achievements of minority students (see Bernal, 1986).

2. We need tests of *ability/diagnosis* that yield educationally and clinically meaningful *profiles*.

3. We need tests that *prognosticate* success or failure in the long run, not just the short run, so that we might better counsel both minority and majority students and prepare more appropriate interventions for those who may encounter only short-run difficulties.

Finally and very importantly, we need to stop testing for the prestige of it or to gain political approbation from the public. Teacher competency testing, where a test score effectively becomes either the sole criterion or part of a multiple cutoff system of screening for admission to teacher education or for certification, is an issue in point. The Pre-professional Skills Test (PPST) and the California Basic Educational Skills Test (CBEST) admittedly have little to do with actual professional outcomes such as classroom effectiveness. Glass and Ellwein (1986), who conclude that very few people ultimately fail these tests (given that some must retake the examinations), miss an important point: minorities fail these tests in disproportionately high rates and are not particularly successful on subsequent attempts, as the PPST data from Arizona indicate (Cropper & Nomura, 1987). When we use tests to satisfy political agendas—tests that have little or no relationship to professional competencies, but that severely and disproportionately impact minorities—one must suspect that hidden political agendas may include the limitation of opportunities for minorities to enter the teaching profession while reassuring the public that educational reform—and insistence on standards—is taking place.

CONCLUSION

Compensatory education has enjoyed some successes but perhaps not as many as it might have achieved had it embarked on a different course by offering a program more appropriately tailored to the needs of nondominant ethnic schoolchildren. In too many cases, compensatory education has merely presented a slower, less interesting, less challenging version of regular education to these youngsters (see Bernal, 1984). My own impression is that the results of these programs are ideologically disappointing although, realistically speaking, quite good, given how little innovation was invested in their design.

Evaluation can make a real difference in the configuration and delivery of programs for underachieving minorities if it begins to document what is really going on, how these events are perceived by different actors, and how these perceptions compare. My experience convinces me that to a very great extent parents, children, administrators, and teachers do not perceive the same educational events in the same way, and that they might accomplish a lot more if they knew what each of the others was thinking. I suppose I am arguing for more observation, more ethnographic monitoring, because I have encountered so many dissonant perceptions in my own studies. But because these require significant outlays of money, they may have to be reserved for major evaluative undertakings. What must be done in all cases, however, is to link these goings-on (programmatic features, events, variations) to student achievement, attendance, retention, and placement/tracking over *long* periods of time, since these criteria are closer to what educational equity is all about.

For the testing profession to make a contribution to minority education may require a major reorientation of both individuals and organizations, from defensive (albeit "scientific") posturing to creative problem-seeking and problem-solving. It would be far more socially beneficial and professionally challenging to discover the psychological sources of differential ethnic performance on both predictive and criterial measures than to continue to invest resources in the defense of traditional tests.

If such research proves fruitful, if it were possible to sift the "real" differences from the culturally/arbitrarily imposed biases/problems in the instruments, then new tests could be devised that would alter not the psychometrician's social role as gatekeeper (elite) but the demographic characteristics of the persons who would be most significantly affected by testing.

By ensuring that both our instruments and the criteria by which we judge their validity are unbiased, we could simultaneously assure ourselves, the public, and the school professionals whose programs we evaluate that our tests are not merely consequential but also germane. At a time when we spend such great efforts justifying current practice in test design and validation (Bernal, 1986) to no one's deep satisfaction (except for true believers), is this not the time to try?

REFERENCES

Bernal, E. M. (1984). The implications of academic excellence for the culturally different gifted. In L. Kavevsky, ed., *Academic excellence: Its role in gifted education* (pp. 65–83). San Diego: San Diego City Schools.

———. (1986). *Increasing the interpretative and practical utility of Hispanic children's scores on tests of maximum performance.* Paper presented at the Minority Mental Health Conference, Ohio State University, Columbus.

Borich, G. D. (1984). *Needs assessment and program planning techniques.* (Available from Gary D. Borich, College of Education, The University of Texas at Austin, 78712.)

Charters, W. W., Jr. & Jones, J. E. (1973). On the risk of appraising non-events in program evaluation. *Educational Researcher, 2,* 5–7.

Cropper, A. & Nomura, K. (1987). PPST report: Current status and plans for the future. Unpublished manuscript, Northern Arizona University, Center for Excellence in Education, Flagstaff.

Daniels, R. S. & O'Neil, C. (1979). The reverse RFR. *Educational Evaluation and Policy Analysis, 1*, 43–44.

Duckett, W., Strother, D., & Gephart, W. (1982). Evaluating the evaluator. *Practical Applications of Research*, March, p. 1.

Flaugher, R. L. (1971). *Minority versus majority group performance on an aptitude test battery* (Project Access Report No. 3). Princeton, NJ: Educational Testing Service, (Research Bulletin No. 71–48).

Glass, G. V. & Ellwein, M. C. (1986). Reform by raising test standards. *Evaluation Comment*, December. Los Angeles: UCLA Center for Research on Evaluation, Standards, and Student Testing.

Lenning, O. T. (1977). *The outcomes structure: An overview and procedures for applying it in postsecondary institutions*. Boulder, CO: National Center for Higher Education Management Systems.

Lenning, O. T., Munday, L. A., Johnson, O. B., Vander Well, A. R., & Brue, E. J. (1974). *The many faces of college success and their nonintellective correlates: The published literature through the decade of the sixties*. Iowa City, IA: American College Testing Publications.

Mercer, J. R. (1979). In defense of racially and culturally non-discriminatory assessment. *School Psychology Digest*, 8 (1), 89–115.

Oakes, J. (1987). *The distribution of excellence: Indicators of equity in precollege mathematics, science, and technology education*. (National Science Foundation Contract No. WD–2919/3–1-NSF.) Santa Monica, CA: Rand Corporation.

Page, E. B. & Stake, R. E. (1979). Should educational evaluation be more objective or more subjective? *Educational Evaluation and Policy Analysis, 1*, 45–47.

Spradley, J. P. (1971). Cultural deprivation or cultural innundation? *Western Canadian Journal of Anthropology, 2*, 65–82.

Suchman, E. (1967). *Evaluative research*. New York: Russell Sage Foundation.

Weiss, C. H. (1973). Between the cup and the lip. *Evaluation, 1*, 49–55.

TWENTY-TWO

Quality Indicators for Monitoring Equity

RAMSAY SELDEN

I am the director of the effort by the Council of Chief State School Officers to develop better indicators for education. The part of that job that is politically popular right now and the one that generates interest in the press is the issue of state-by-state comparison and comparative achievement testing. It is, however, a small part of what I believe to be the very important problem of developing better indicators for monitoring educational equity. We should have better indicators, but we don't, because it is not the primary task that is before educators whose primary task is making schools work for underachieving students. I think, however, that the development of educational indicators is a supportive task that can make educators' efforts work better and be more successful. I am in the business I'm in because I believe in indicators and their value.

We need better information on how schools are functioning for underachieving minorities. I would like to explain how that would work, in a sort of idealistic sense, and then tell you, from state policy maker's perspective, where we stand in terms of getting the information we need. This model of the distribution of excellence in the school system was developed by Jeannie Oakes of the Rand Corporation. It pulls together many of the things that have been presented in this book. According to this model, there is a process that results in inequitable outcomes in the school systems in this country.

This process begins at the elementary school level, where the extent of a child's interest and achievement leads to placement in one of two routes at the junior high level. If the elementary school child has an opportunity to develop interests and demonstrates achievement, that child is much more likely, according to the research, to be placed in a track that is preparatory for a high school level program and the opportunity to take initial high school courses at the junior high school level. That placement leads to the high school college prep program. Such a placement is characterized not only by the opportunity to take more academic courses, but also courses that are sequential in nature, courses that accumulate and build on one another, and courses that present advanced-level content. The advanced courses stimulate additional interest and persistence in studying academic subject matter beyond minimum requirements.

Down the other route, the elementary child who does not experience success in academic achievement early in school loses interest, and tends to be placed in intermediate or junior high programs that are remedial in content and practical in orientation. That placement leads them to high school programs that are vocational, general, or remedial, and that are characterized by fewer academic courses. Generally, such courses don't build upon one another, do address lower level content, and are not sequential. These courses promote a lack of interest, persistence, and further achievement on the part of the students enrolled in them. These students are much less likely to overcome that experience and be interested in going on to the high school or higher education levels.

Although these two paths are very logical and feel intuitive, the model was constructed by synthesizing research. The snowball effect described above is what really happens in schools. This is how kids get tracked down one route or the other. One of the most troubling aspects of this problem is the clear recognition that the process starts early, at the elementary school level.

Based on her model, Oakes developed a set of indicators to show the extent to which schools are engendering that routing and encouraging those patterns of success (or lack thereof) for minority students and for women. The distribution of excellence for minority students and women were both considered during the development of the indicators. Basically, the model includes two types of indicators. The first measures outcome or performance. The second measures the processes within schools that characterize how schools are serving different kinds of students.

A wide variety of outcome indicators are possible—for example, what students study and learn (achievement in basic skills or subject areas), the courses they complete, and their interest in and rate of high school completion. These outcomes can be monitored comparatively and over time. In order to determine the equity in school performance, all aspects of the outcome indicators should be analyzed by socioeconomic status, race, and gender. Such cross-tabulation by groups, however, needs to consider all three categorical groups simultaneously, rather than in isolation—not just by race without accounting for gender or SES. There are various differential inequity effects within racial groups when they are considered by gender and by SES. Means within groups should be looked at, and because the comparison of means tends to mask the fact that there is a great deal of variation within groups, the distributions across groups also should be considered.

The process indicators were developed to show if schools are delivering their services equitably. Looking at both the indicators of school and instructional process by group, then, gives educators a picture of how effectively and equitably programs are working, and signals areas in need of strengthening. For instance, a first step might be to monitor achievement in grades four, eight, and eleven by means, and by group, and by the distribution of groups across quartiles. This gives a sense of the extent to which students in racial and ethnic groups are evenly distributed across the performance range. As mentioned, this means the data needs to be broken down by SES, race, and gender, and cross-tabulated. The school might also keep track of the development of student interests, student confidence, and parental encouragement at each of the grade levels. As group differences in the variables emerge, the schools can then detect those differences and respond to them. Attitudes also should be monitored, especially those related to further study in the academic areas. That monitoring, in this example, would begin in the fourth grade and be repeated in the eighth and tenth grades.

At the elementary level, attention to process might mean keeping track of the instructional time spent in various subjects and amount of homework, again by SES and racial makeup of the school. We should look at participation by race and SES in high school courses, and the ratio of course enrollments to the proportion of groups in the school population. How disproportionate is student representation in courses like calculus or academic chemistry?

Next to be considered in Oakes' model are resource indicators within the school. These classify the school by its racial and SES makeup and look at things such as per-pupil expenditures, teacher salaries, pupil-teacher ratios, and class size. Are the schools within a district different in a way that is related to the socioeconomic and racial makeup of the school? What is the distribution of curriculum resources like laboratory facilities in instructional processes?

Schools must have a plan for raising minority achievement. Plans to boost achievement should contain supplemental programs, extracurricular activities and programs, staff development programs, curriculum development efforts, and special guidance programs. Data collected for process indicators can help target these five elements.

The Chief State School Officers are working on two projects that are helping us determine the extent to which we will be able to monitor this kind of comprehensive information at the state level. In one project we are looking at the core data base in education, which is collected by each state. We find, from the demographic indicators on a state level, that states do not have standard data on the locale of their schools, whether they are urban, suburban, or rural, or what types of neighborhoods these schools serve.

School enrollments are not cross-tabulated by race or sex. We have no standard SES indicator for schools that is collected and used by the states.

The national core data base for outcomes shows that state-level data that classify graduates by school and racial or ethnic group are not generally available. Some states have the figures, some don't. We don't have standard dropout data at the state level. We don't have standard dropout data at all; most states don't collect dropout data by student characteristic.

In the second project, undertaken in collaboration with the National Science Foundation, we are looking at the math/science indicators that are collected and used by each state. Almost 40 states have achievement data in subjects like math, science, and reading. We are currently studying whether they report that data by race, sex, and SES. Similarly, 4–7 states collect attitude and interest information. We are finding out now if they report that by student group. Only 7 states keep track of the postsecondary majors selected by students and they break that down by racial or ethnic group of the student in those 7 states. One state monitors time spent in different subjects in the elementary school by group of students served. Ten states monitor student enrollment by subject and ethnic group.

Some 38 states regularly keep track of the ethnicity of their teachers; 48 keep track of teacher assignments and certification. This information could be broken down by the kinds of students those teachers serve. We don't know yet, but I think that relatively few states are doing that now. Only 4 states observe teacher performance. If we wanted to know if teachers perform better with advantaged versus disadvantaged students, we would not have the information to do so.

Only 10 or 11 states keep track of the amount or type of professional development programs provided to teachers; only 2 states keep track of the extent to which teachers are involved in voluntary professional enhancement activities. In 23 states there is the potential of monitoring teacher knowledge of their subject matter; 36 states keep track of pupil-teacher ratios; and 15 or 16 record the classroom resources that are provided. We don't know yet if any of these data are broken down by the type of student served.

The main point is that the rudimentary information a state-level policy maker needs to determine if his or her school system is meeting equity concerns is not even available. We don't have the basics, let alone the breakdowns by student type that we need to monitor these issues. What I see as the first and most important problem is that people simply don't have a strong model and rationale for monitoring these equity concerns. I think this is where Oakes' model of the distribution of excellence has made a contribution. We intend to get our people to do some thinking about how they might apply such a model within their individual states.

Second, we are running into tremendous resistance to change. Existing data are sacred, and there is a horrendous reluctance on the part of state and local school people to change them. They think if they redefine the data or add information, somehow their continuity with the past will be broken. I don't know if this is the issue in every case, or if people just don't want to do additional data collection. There is a tremendous resistance to change. In 1986 we proposed that states start collecting standard demographic data on school enrollment in every school in the country, including the sex and race breakdowns within each school—not by grade, but by the school as a whole. We ran into tremendous resistance on the part of state data collection people. There is also something of a cost issue. It is less of an issue when it is a matter of expanding and tuning the existing data collection system, in which we now invest relatively little. A little bit of money would help us all offset some of the additional costs.

In order to take the recommendations that people have been making in this volume and monitor their implementation, we need to operationalize the recommendations as objective data that can be used to keep track of how the school systems are doing with their underachieving minorities. We aren't very well equipped to provide and use that data right now, at least among our constituents. There is a need to reformat data collection and, in many cases, add to the data collection that already takes place in schools. People have to accept that the value and importance of the information are worth the restructuring process, even if they increase the burden of collecting the data. We have a lot of work to do.

TWENTY-THREE

The Need to Assess Multiple Crucial Components in Evaluating Programs

DANIEL LEVINE

My goal in this chapter will be to provide several illustrations of the importance of attending to multiple crucial components of effective programs and determining how they may fit together to improve instruction for disadvantaged minority students. Such attention is critical in the identification, design, implementation, and evaluation of the effective programs.

One useful recent example of the general problems that arise in identifying and assessing crucial components has been provided in a "best-evidence" analysis of mastery learning research carried out by Bob Slavin of Johns Hopkins University.[1] Zeroing in on technically competent studies that compared mastery learning with traditional instructional sequences, Slavin concluded that mastery learning generally has not produced large, generalizable achievement gains in controlled experimental implementations.

This important finding points to the likelihood that mastery learning alone will not help low-achieving students in poverty schools or elsewhere unless it is implemented in conjunction with other key changes such as effective curriculum alignment and reorganization, if necessary, in grouping arrangements. In my experience, some schools that have attended to such imperatives as part of a unified approach to improvement have been successful in substantially raising student achievement through mastery learning. In short, mastery learning may be a crucial component in some successful efforts to improve achievement, but it alone is not sufficient to assure program effectiveness. Rather a multiplicity of crucial components is required.

Rather than negating the potential utility of mastery learning, Slavin's results can be viewed as helping to call attention to the concomitant changes that must be made if mastery learning is to be a useful component in a school improvement project. Unfortunately, his results likely will be used by some readers to support the conclusion that mastery learning cannot be helpful in improving the achievement of disadvantaged students.

One useful way to articulate the larger issue of multiple crucial components is to pose and try to answer a few questions as follows:

Q: If mastery learning or any single treatment by itself does not improve students' achievement, does that mean it is not potentially potent in helping to improve achievement?

A: No. Successful mastery learning at poverty schools requires, among other things, implementation in conjunction with unusually effective organizational arrangements for low achievers. (One possibility involves very small classes for students functioning very poorly.) In addition, by definition mastery learning requires more time to provide corrective instruction for low achievers. If mastery learning when properly implemented in conjunction with appropriate changes in organization and scheduling of instruction yields large achievement gains, then mastery learning can be an important approach for improving achievement. An exact analogy would be a medical treatment in which exercise and medication together, but neither separately, reduced subsequent incidence of heart attacks.

Q: What then can we learn about the effects of potentially important instructional changes when we vary conditions in order to test them in isolation?

A: Only whether they are effective in isolation, not whether they can be combined with other changes to produce improvement. Since instruction takes place in the complex setting of schools and classrooms, few if any innovations are likely to produce sustained and substantial improvement unless part of a larger effort to impact the larger setting. It is well established, for example, that substantial staff development, together with motivation to participate in it, is a prerequisite for successfully implementing a serious innovation. Given this interdependence, one should not reject an innovation after assessing its effects in settings with inadequate staff development or insufficient incentives and support.

Q: Is mastery learning the only instructional sequence available for improving the achievement of disadvantaged students? Is there a single best approach?

A: Obviously not. In fact, most of the unusually successful poverty schools I have seen or learned about have not used mastery learning as defined by James Block, Benjamin Bloom, S. Alan Cohen, Thomas Guskey, or other leaders in this field. In addition, I have not been able to find inner city senior high schools (or hardly any other high schools, for that matter) that have introduced mastery learning successfully on a schoolwide basis. On the other hand, successful inner city schools of necessity do use some approach to "mastery-type" learning—that is, their faculty go to whatever lengths are necessary to make sure that nearly all their students make progress in mastering agreed-upon learning objectives. Within this context, when mastery learning as defined by Bloom and others is implemented well, it does offer some particular advantages in terms of focusing instruction more effectively on the learning problems of initial low achievers.

A related problem occurs in situations in which the set of changes or variables one is assessing through research does not include those that actually were most important in bringing about improvement. One example of this occurred in the series of substudies that researchers at the old U.S. Office of Education conducted using data from the Equal Educational Opportunity (EEO) study directed by James Coleman.[2] Because the questionnaire administered at schools participating in the study did not include good items dealing with the leadership of the principal, there was no possibility that this variable could show up well in the substudy that contrasted unusually effective and ineffective schools.

Another possible example along these lines may be present in some of the publications prepared by personnel in the San Diego Unified School District. San Diego has carried out probably the most successful program in the United States for improving the performance of students attending concentrated poverty schools—the Achievement Goals Program (AGP). The descriptions I have seen of the AGP usually cite four main components: increased time-on-task, direct instruction, improved classroom management, and mastery learning.

However, there are reasons to believe that an equally or even more important intervention involved a radical curriculum change that removed basal readers from classrooms so that teachers no longer could proceed page-by-page at the pace of the slowest student. (This intervention is only hinted at in some descriptions of the four components.) If this intervention indeed was critical, as there is reason to believe it was, implementation of an AGP-like program elsewhere in the absence of radical curriculum alignment could result in nontransportability along with severe disappointment and discrediting of the four useful components identified as part of the program.

Among the implications of the preceding discussion are that program evaluation generally requires some attention to implementation analysis, whether formally labeled in this way or not, and that evaluators should have substantial knowledge of and familiarity with the schools at which they assess programs.

On the first point, it is apparent that evaluators must understand what schools actually are doing to implement program components. Further, schools must be helped to overcome obstacles to effective implementation, if components crucial to success are to be identified in the analysis.

Regarding the need for evaluators to acquire in-depth knowledge of how programs actually are being implemented and the actions teachers and administrators must take to assure their success, evaluators can spend time in classrooms themselves or obtain the opinions and perceptions of others familiar with participating schools, or combine these two approaches.

Of course, spending time in schools and obtaining information from knowledgeable observers do not guarantee that crucial components will be clearly identified, but failure to engage in these aspects of data collection will multiply the likelihood that program assessments will omit key considerations. Ultimately, it is these key considerations that determine success or failure among initial participants and subsequently at sites engaged in replicating promising innovations.

NOTES

1. R. Slavin. "Best-evidence Synthesis: An Alternative to Meta-analysis and Traditional Reviews." *Education Research*, 15(9) (1986), 5–11.

2. See, for instance G. W. Mayeske & A. E. Beaton, Jr., *Special Studies of Our Nations' Students* (Washington, DC: U.S. Government Printing Office, 1975).

SECTION B

Lessons from Success in Practice

TWENTY-FOUR

Persistence and Patience

TODD ENDO

> Commitment to the academic success of black students clearly requires
> a sensitivity to the need for resolving these crucial cultural conflicts
> between school and community. Persisting in the face of these conflicts
> is more than many students, who see themselves as powerless, can
> manage. The teacher must affirm those behaviors needed to demonstrate
> achievement in the larger academic community, while simultaneously
> understanding the cultural and learning style diversity that the minority
> student brings to the learning environment.[1]

Like the teacher and the student who must learn to persist in the face of
conflict and difficulty, the school system that seeks to improve the achievement of minority students must persist as well. Brilliance, creativity, and
political savvy are all desirable. Technically sound analysis and use of data
(even disaggregated data) are necessary but not sufficient steps to be taken.
Persistence, patience, and just plain plugging along are mundane but vital
ingredients that spell the difference between a good plan and a successfully
implemented program.

The Fairfax County (Virginia) Public Schools are in their second full year
of implementing a series of activities designed to improve the academic
achievement and aspirations of minority students. The Fairfax program features school-based planning, implementation, and evaluation to match the
identified needs of the students, skills of the staff, and potentially effective
strategies for improvement in individual schools. School-based planning is
conducted within a central mandate and framework. Other key ingredients
are a sufficient time line to develop and implement activities, additional
resources of money and time, intensive support and assistance from central

and area offices, careful monitoring and feedback, and above all dogged persistence and patience.

As the program has developed, there has been a continuing struggle to keep it on course. The temptations have been to speed up the process, to direct more and nurture less, to treat all schools like identical parts of the machine, to look for blueprints for the quick fix, to simplify the expected outcomes to standardized test scores, and to wash away the emphasis on minority student achievement in the tide of competing priorities and crises. By the end of the first full year of implementation in 1985–86, modest improvement in minority students' achievement occurred. However, being in only the second year of implementation, we must persist through the full stages of implementation and be patient before judging the success of Fairfax's minority students' achievement program.

This chapter first describes briefly the Fairfax program. Then it develops in more detail selected, important aspects of the program. Finally, it discusses some dilemmas, tensions, and unresolved issues in the program.

BACKGROUND FOR THE FAIRFAX COUNTY PROGRAM

Planning

In the summer of 1983, the Fairfax County Public Schools established a staff study group that analyzed 1982–83 school achievement data to determine the status of minority students' performance.[2] The study group purposely chose to examine regularly collected data that were broader than just standardized test scores. The eight indicators of achievement that were examined included:

- retentions in grade
- enrollment in higher level and lower level courses
- grades
- placement in special programs
- attendance
- dropout rates
- postsecondary school educational plans
- standardized test scores

Data on these indicators of achievement were analyzed by four ethnic groups: White, Black, Hispanic, and Asian. Inclusion in a specific ethnic group was determined by the response of parents on the student's enrollment card to a question that used the categories provided by the U.S. Office of Civil Rights.

The study group concluded that the achievement of Black and Hispanic students was unacceptably low and below that of White students on nearly every indicator examined. To address this identified problem, the study group concluded that the most promising strategies were directly related to the factors identified in the research on effective schools and effective teaching, namely: administrative leadership, high expectations for all students, defined instructional objectives, an orderly environment for learning, systems for regularly monitoring student learning, and parent and community support. The study group further concluded that improvement in minority students' performance was achievable as part of a long-range plan for school improvement that would benefit all students. Specifically, the study group proposed the following elements of a successful plan:

- Establishment of a major, long-range school board priority to improve minority students' academic achievement and aspiration.
- Leadership from the superintendent and other top school system leaders through providing direction, announcing expectations, generating momentum, and providing visible support and attention.
- Development of local school improvement plans that address the achievement and aspirations of minority students within guidelines established by the school board and superintendent.
- Commitment of additional resources (time, money, and staff) and the reallocation of some existing resources over an extended period of time.
- Development of a systemwide plan for program and staff development based on the effective schools' research and the sharing of successful strategies for improving minority students' academic achievement.
- Provision of additional evaluative tools and training to teachers and principals to monitor student achievement.

Implementation of the Program

Although the implementation of the minority students' achievement plan has evolved since its beginning in 1984–85, it basically has stayed true to the vision expressed in the initial staff report. The balance between direction, support, and monitoring by the school system and the development, implementation, and evaluation of school-based plans by school staffs has been critical.[3]

Central Direction

The school board, superintendent, and top-level staff persistently announce that the improvement of minority students' achievement is a major school system priority and that they expect the multiple indicators of achievement to show improvement over a number of years. This priority and direction are reflected consistently in the superintendent's annual operating plan for the school system, the divisionwide plan for the improvement of minority students' achievement, publications, speeches, remarks at school board meetings, memos, and a variety of other means of communication.

The divisionwide plan issued at the beginning of the 1985–86 school year stated a series of objectives and evaluation strategies that relied on the eight indicators of student achievement used in the study. At the same time, the superintendent emphasized that while he planned to monitor results in terms of student outcomes, he believed that the best place for program planning and implementation was at the school level. He also indicated that the role of the central and area offices was to "support both divisionwide emphases and school-community identified objectives." This focus on school-based planning was also contained in the superintendent's annual operating plan. He directed the schools to develop, implement, and evaluate plans according to an established time schedule and committed systemwide resources to support the schools' efforts.

School-Based Planning

The central element of the program is school-based planning. The process involves an annual cycle of activities:

- Development of final objectives, strategies, and evaluation plans in the early fall
- Submission of plans by the end of October
- Review of plans and return of individualized written responses to principals by the superintendent in November
- Implementation of the plans throughout the year beginning in September
- Collection and analysis of data at the school throughout the year
- Review of activities, progress, and concerns by the area superintendents and the deputy superintendents at midyear
- Submission of an annual evaluation report in June that describes results and discusses implications for the next year's plan
- Review of evaluation reports and return of individualized written responses to principals by the superintendent in July that include advice and requirements for the next year's plan
- Repetition of the cycle

Often merely a paper exercise, this process gains vitality through a number of strategies. First, school system leaders visibly and repeatedly announce their intentions and expectations. Second, they follow up by personally showing specific interest by responding to individual school plans and reports, participating in midyear review meetings, visiting schools, and discussing evaluation reports. Through these interactions, they encourage collaborative planning by members of the school community, recognize differences in plans due to differences in school circumstances, encourage changes in plans if the situation or data call for them, and support continuity in plans if all is going well. Third, central and area offices provide extensive and intensive support and assistance.

With the steady stream of new priorities that flow across the experienced principal's desk, it is no wonder that his or her typical response to another new priority is "this too shall pass." Visible persistence is required to convince principals that the minority students' achievement priority will remain. The school system leaders reinforce the message that they mean business by committing the resources and giving the assistance necessary to enable schools to succeed.

Persistent reinforcement is also needed to convince school staff that their ideas are sought and that good school-level plans will be approved. Many school staff are in the habit of trying to guess what the superintendent wants. Top-down management is part of the system culture. Principals, with good reason, often greet the call for bottom-up initiative with skepticism.[4]

Schools developed their first plans in the fall of 1984. Because of the late start, the first full planning and implementation cycle was completed in the 1985–86 school year. Individual school plans addressed one or more of the eight indicators specified by the school system. In addition, they developed objectives and activities determined by the school. These included quantity and quality of student writing, reduction of disciplinary problems, more parental involvement, greater participation in school activities, and progress through reading text books.

Systemwide Support and Assistance

The school system supported its plan with action that gave credibility to its claim that minority students' achievement was indeed an ongoing priority:

- Beginning in 1985–86, money was set aside to fund school-based proposals. This strategy not only provided additional resources to schools but also reinforced the notion of school-based plans. The total available funds for grants has increased steadily to meet demand.

- Also in 1985–86, a coordinator was hired and resource teachers were provided to manage the program and provide assistance to schools.

- To help schools plan and implement, written models were provided, workshops were conducted, and individual assistance was given.

- To help schools monitor and evaluate the effects of their strategies, resource manuals were provided, workshops were conducted, group and individual assistance was provided, and on-going follow-up was provided at the individual school level.

- Systemwide staff development programs were offered to volunteer school staff. Examples included the Teacher Expectations and Student Achievement (TESA) program and the Classroom Management Training Project begun in the 1984–85 school year. These programs reinforced the idea that strategies to improve minority students' achievement can be integrated with strategies for school improvement.

• Centrally based activities were conducted to pursue the system's direction and to support school-based activities. Examples included a review of procedures to select students for special programs, training for guidance counselors, overall coordination of the program, review of proposals for school-based grants, and initiation of some instructional programs.

• Related initiatives were linked to the minority students' achievement priority. For instance, for the 1985–86 school year, the school board approved a proposal written by a group of principals to allocate additional resources to schools with a high proportion of students with special needs. In addition, in the spring of 1986, the school board approved the superintendent's recommendation for a new priority "to develop a system for school-based management."

The provision of supplemental resources was crucial to convince schools that the school system was serious. Perhaps more important were the individual attention given to schools and the accompanying message that school-based efforts were indeed supported. For rhetoric to become reality, persistent effort was required as evidence.

School System Monitoring

Based on the original staff committee report, an annual report on minority students' achievement is issued each year in the fall. The report provides system-level trend data by ethnic group on each of the eight original indicators. This report is presented at a school board meeting and publicized through the media. In addition, analyses are conducted to answer specific questions about subsets of schools or students. These analyses are provided to the requestor on an ad hoc basis. Moreover, area superintendents monitor progress through their related planning process. As mentioned earlier, they review the individual school plans and evaluation reports. They also are provided with school-level data on their schools for use in supervision.

Schools are provided data on their students using the same indicators and ethnic group classifications used for the systemwide report. They use these data for planning, evaluation, and reporting purposes. Finally, a community advisory board reviews the process and progress and gives advice to the superintendent.

Results to Date

School plans were developed during the 1984–85 school year and the first full year of implementation was the 1985–86 school year. The annual report issued in October 1986 provided trend data for four years culminating in the first full year of implementation.[5] The summary of the report stated:

During 1985–86 the standardized test results showed improvements, especially for black students. Of all ethnic groups, black students made the greatest gains on the SRA [Science Research Associates] tests over the last four years. In grades 8 and 11, black students have made gains each year, increasing cumulatively by as much as ten percentile points in grade 11. On the Virginia Minimum Competency Test, the percentage of black students who passed the tests increased substantially in 1986.

In addition, the percentage of Black students scoring above the 50th percentile increased by three percentage points over the three-year period. Other minority groups improved on this measure slightly, while the performance of White students declined slightly. The percentage of Black students scoring below the 20th percentile declined by four percentage points over this same three-year period, while the performance of all other groups stayed the same on this measure.

On the other seven indicators of achievement, the message was mixed. Placement of Black students into programs for the emotionally disturbed and mildly mentally retarded showed steady declines over the four-year period. The intention of Black students to attend four-year colleges steadily increased. On the other indicators, no strong trends were noticeable. The report concluded: "Clearly, minority student achievement is not at the levels it should be. While the first full year data in this report show some progress, justifying the Board's long-term commitment, only in the long term will minority achievement reach satisfactory levels."[6]

Next Steps

Fairfax is now in the second full year of implementation of its minority students' achievement activities. For this year and the foreseeable future, reinforcement of the existing activities is planned. We expect that persistence will pay off.

In addition, some new activities are planned that reflect a more advanced stage of development. For instance, promising school-based practices will be identified and described. In printed form and through personal contact, school staff will share these practices with their peers. Perhaps grants will be given to schools so that they may adopt and adapt promising practices developed by others.

Also, because the program is approaching the end of the second full year of implementation, longitudinal data will be available on students. For example, students from the four major ethnic groups with similar achievement in grade six will be tracked on subsequent indicators of achievement, such as test scores, enrollment in higher level and lower level courses, grades, and placement in special programs.

In the next few years, the minority students' achievement emphasis will be integrated with and reinforced by other major school system initiatives.

Clearly, the emphasis on school-based planning will be reinforced by the school board and superintendent's priority to develop a school-based management program. As part of this program, a new process for selecting, training, asssigning, and evaluating principals and other school-based administration is being developed. This new process should help clarify the role of all administrators and enhance the possibilities for success of both school-based management and the minority students' achievement emphasis.

Also related to the minority students' achievement emphasis is the school system training based on *The Skillful Teacher*, a generic instructional and supervision model developed by Jon Saphier.[7] This model provides the framework for the instructional focus expected of school-based administrators and teachers, and it is integral to the new performance evaluation program being developed in Fairfax County. The cumulative effect of these initiatives will be to enhance the role of school-based staff to design, implement, and evaluate improved instructional strategies with a particular emphasis on minority students.

CONTEXT AND ASSUMPTIONS OF THE FAIRFAX PROGRAM

The Context Is Fairfax County

The process for improving the achievement of minority students described in this chapter may be suitable only for Fairfax County. Just as there is no one best educational system, there is no one best strategy for improving the achievement of minority students. Fairfax County is a large, metropolitan Washington, DC school district in which minority students represent about 22 percent of the enrollment. Fairfax has sufficient staff and financial resources to support minority students' achievement programs as well as most other identified priorities. Most students achieve well and the public is generally happy with the school system. Standard operational functions relating to personnel, budgeting, accounting, purchasing, planning, and transportation generally happen routinely. A standard framework for curriculum and instruction is in place. Basically, this is so because the school-based and centrally based staffs are competent and have put into place systems to handle the routines. Though not without crises, Fairfax can afford to build on a solid foundation and plan carefully selected strategies for improvement.

Assumptions Underlying the Fairfax Program

The Fairfax program is built on many explicit and implicit assumptions, which rely on much of the research on effective schools and school improvement. However, competing models are also based on research.[8] Without discussing which model is more true, I will state some of the assumptions of our program:

- The school is the basic unit of school improvement.
- The school board and superintendent should establish priorities and give general direction, but a school staff is in the best position to develop the specific plans to enable its school to move in the desired direction.
- The emphasis on minority students' achievement is not an add-on and should be integrated with systemic efforts to improve instruction.
- There is no magical solution or panacea. The task is to put together a set of available ideas and commit the system to implement the ideas with sufficient resources over an extended period of time.
- The improvement process takes time.
- The improvement process requires varied strategies to provide support and supervision.

The remainder of this section will expand on each of these assumptions.

The School Is the Basic Unit for Improvement

Fairfax recognizes that the desired improvement at the school-system level is composed of improvements made school-by-school and teacher-by-teacher. In addition to systemwide activities, great efforts must be expended in each school. The focus on the school implies a recognition that the whole is greater than the sum of its parts. That is, while the individual teacher is important, the school is more than a collection of individual teachers. In fact, there is a need to break down some of the isolation that teachers and administrators feel, to develop more collegial and collaborative relationships, and to develop a sense of a common school mission. From this perspective, a school system could impose a uniform program and then implement it school by school. Fairfax took a different tack.

School Staffs Are in the Best Position to Plan and Implement Activities Within Their School

This statement contains within it a number of further assumptions. First, because each school is different, the school system should be careful of what it demands that all schools do. The superintendent has stated that he wants to hold principals accountable for results and give them flexibility in terms of the means.

Second, most principals and teachers have sufficient skills, interests, and ideas to be entrusted with the development of school-based plans. In most schools, the principal and teachers can learn even if the central office is not teaching. Just as higher expectations for students are desired, the assumption is that high expectations for school staffs will lead to higher achievement.

Third, if the staff is more involved in making program decisions, their commitment to the effective implementation of these decisions will be greater and the results for students will also be greater. Central and area office staff tailor their support and assistance to the needs of the individual school and principal. While some large-group instruction is given, most activities are designed for small groups of like-minded staff or for individuals. This strategy is similar to a teacher designing total class, small group, and individualized instruction.

Minority Students' Achievement Is Not an Add-On

Since there is a tendency to view a new initiative as an addition to the existing program, Fairfax is emphasizing that minority students' achievement activities should be integrated into the ongoing instructional program, not added on to it. Therefore, Fairfax is encouraging improvement in the regular functions of a school; for instance, counseling students into existing higher level courses, better monitoring of individual student progress, involving more parents of minority students in the ongoing life of the school, improving teacher expectations, examining screening procedures for special programs, and focusing on writing or thinking skills across the curriculum. Fairfax is not encouraging greater grouping of minority or underachieving students or pulling out identified students from regular classes for special instruction.

There Is No Magical Solution, or, Persistence Pays Off

The superintendent has emphasized that there is no magical solution to the problem of improving minority students' achievement and that only a persistent effort over a number of years will succeed. A review of what the school system and each of the schools are doing reveals no dramatically new instructional ideas. The ideas are good but were culled from personal experience and reflection, discussions with colleagues, and insights from external publications and workshops. What does contribute to success is the persistent attention paid to planning, implementation, and evaluation. Persistent attention means that the improvement process takes time.

The Improvement Process Takes Time

The downfall of many new initiatives is the belief that policy decisions are self-implementing or are easy to implement. By their statements and actions, the school board and superintendent are attempting to resist the pressure to speed up the process. The superintendent has emphasized the need for a long-term persistent effort that will yield slow but steady improvement.

On many topics he has been quoted to say, "Just because we've planted the seed and it's germinating doesn't mean you can keep picking up the plant and looking at it every day." The school board considered the annual report, presented in October 1986 after the first full year of implementation, to be a progress report, not a summative report on the program's successes or failures. In the midyear reviews, the deputy superintendents stressed that the priority will remain for the foreseeable future because the improvement process takes time.

A second dimension of time is the "life space" needed by all staff, but especially principals and teachers, to plan, implement, and evaluate school board plans thoughtfully. Principals' and teachers' days are full of countless important and mundane events. It is too much to expect that school staffs will plan effectively on top of everything else they do. Time as a resource must be provided. This kind of time to plan, implement, and evaluate can be provided in three ways. One is to take away other tasks (e.g., some competing priorities, some unnecessary meetings, some externally or internally imposed expectations, some paperwork). A second way is to provide substitute days and days before or after the contract year. A third way is more a state of mind than real time. We assume that when a staff believes it is the creator and owner of the plan, it willingly commits additional time to do the right job and to do the job right. When faced with the task of implementing a school system mandate for which it feels no ownership, we assume that a school staff tends to devote only enough time to comply.

The Improvement Process Requires Varied Strategies to Provide Support, Assistance, and Supervision

Besides time, the school-based improvement process requires support from the central and area offices. As described in the section on "systemwide support and assistance," this support has taken the form of money, time for school staffs to plan, staff to coordinate efforts, and resources to assist school staffs plan and implement better.

Just as assistance is tailored to the individual school, so is supervision. Through the monitoring activities, some schools are recognized as being on the right track. For them, little change is demanded and praise is given. Deficiencies are noted in other schools' efforts. The area superintendent supervises these schools more regularly, giving more explicit instruction and direction.

THE ROLE OF THE OFFICE OF RESEARCH AND EVALUATION

While many departments of the school system contribute to the effort to improve minority students' achievement, this section focuses on the role of the county Office of Research and Evaluation (ORE) because the activities of this office illustrate most of the basic components of the program and because I know the activities of ORE best. Much of this section could also be written about the activities of the coordinator of minority students' achievement, the area minority student achievement resource teachers, and other area and central departments.

The Office of Research and Evaluation has played a central role in monitoring the achievement of minority students and in providing support and assistance to schools. Some ORE staff monitor the indicators of achievement for the school system, for identified groups of schools, and for individual schools. They provide data and analyses of data to decision makers, produce reports on the academic progress of minority students, and discuss the implications of the findings for program activities.

Other staff in ORE provide support and assistance to individual school staffs in the development and implementation of school-based plans. The process for support and assistance is tailored to the needs of the individual school staff and, thus, is time consuming. In its highest form, an ORE staff person meets with the principal and/or member of the school staff to plan a needs assessment, discuss possible elements of the school plan, propose alternative evaluation strategies, and review drafts of the school plan. In an intermediate form, the ORE staff provides intensive assistance to schools in the development of their evaluation plans, the implementation of the plans (including methods of collecting and analyzing data), and the writing of the evaluation reports.

In its most extended form, ORE has conducted two-year projects with volunteer schools. These are designed to assist school staffs increase their capacities to identify, clarify, analyze, and use factors within the school in order to develop, implement, and evaluate a long-range, comprehensive plan for improving student achievement with a special emphasis on minority students.[9] The framework for this effort drew freely from the experiences of the staff, from the writings of Fullan, Hall, Little, and Joyce and Showers on school improvement, leadership, and staff development,[10] and from a variety of effective school projects across the country.

The major explicit tasks of the first year of the project were to help school staffs conduct a needs assessment at the school and develop a plan to address these identified needs. Behind these explicit tasks were two implicit but necessary tasks. These were to develop both readiness in the staff to "own" the project and the staff skills in planning.[11]

The formal activities of the first year included monthly meetings of the school-based planning team and two full-day workshops on the planning process and planning objectives, activities, and evaluation strategies relating to identified needs. In addition, many informal meetings were held among the school staff and between members of the school staff and ORE staff. The role of the ORE staff was to initiate and develop, in conjunction with the principal, most of the planning activities for the monthly meetings and workshops; to circulate appropriate articles and otherwise link the school-based planning teams to useful resources; to develop data-gathering instruments and analyze some of the needs-assessment data; and generally to serve as a sounding board and consultant to the principal and teacher chairpersons.

By the end of the first year, each school had developed a school improvement plan. In the process, the planning committees developed strong collegial relationships, a sense of school mission to guide classroom responsibilities, ownership of the planning process and the plans, familiarity with much of the research literature, and knowledge and skills related to data collection and analysis.

The second year featured implementing the plan and evaluating activities. The major responsibility for the project shifted to the school staff. The ORE staff still conducted workshops and influenced events, but their role became more one of support than of leadership, of responder than of initiator. Major emphasis in the second year was on broadening the staff's repertoire of evaluation strategies and developing real use of selected strategies for school-based improvement. The repertoire included systematic use of peer and principal observations, teacher and student interviews, report card data, office records, basal test information, anecdotal records, instructional grouping information, teacher and principal anecdotal records, records of attendance and participation, and various types of standardized and teacher-made tests. By the end of the second year, each school had completed the first year's implementation and the first report of progress.

School-Based Evaluation Is Not as Easy as It Sounds

We were surprised by how hard it was for some schools to develop school-based evaluation plans that would help them improve their programs. Use of data by school staffs to help improve instruction for students did not occur just because the data were available and technical assistance was given. Our reflections on the reasons for this difficulty may offer insight into the change process and why it is necessary to persist over time.

Talking about testing, a researcher once noted that everyone thought testing was important—for someone else. Teachers thought testing was important for principals, principals thought testing was important for the superintendent, and the superintendent thought testing was important for teachers. But few people thought testing was important for themselves.

Similarly for evaluation, the prevailing image was hard to break. School principals and teachers generally had the view that evaluation was something done *to* them by *someone outside the school*, usually with negative consequences. In planning evaluations, many of them initially focused on summative not formative evaluation, hard data not soft data, and pretesting and posttesting. Perhaps because of the view that evaluations were negative accountability strategies, many principals tended to focus on activities they could control (e.g., number of staff development sessions held), rather than on outcomes for students or others. They tended to view evaluation as a game in which the object was to state objectives that could be accomplished.

Aaron Wildavsky, a political scientist, wrote an article entitled "The Self-Evaluating Organization," that addresses some of these same difficulties.[12] Wildavsky reflects on his intellectual journey: "I started out thinking it was bad for organizations not to evaluate, and I ended up wondering why they ever do it." He explores why evaluation and organization tend to be in tension: "Evaluation and organization may be contradictory terms. Organizational structure implies stability while the process of evaluation suggests change. Organization generates commitment while evaluation inculcates skepticism. Evaluation speaks to the relationship between action and objectives while organization relates its activities to programs and clientele."[13] As part of a school organization, then, principals and teachers were, at the least, in tension over the call to evaluate themselves.

It was only through persistent and intensive efforts that some progress was made in dealing with these tensions. Part of the success can be attributed to the distribution of a resource notebook for school-based evaluation, workshops on the subject, technical assistance in small groups and individually, and more intensive effort such as that described in the previous section. Part of the success also resulted from persistent feedback that objectives should be stated in terms of outcomes, that use of nontest data is encouraged, that data derived from teacher journals are acceptable, and that nonattainment of objectives is more a signal to improve than to condemn. Much of the success also came from principals and teachers realizing that not only do good evaluation plans and reports gain external praise, but also that the data are useful to them as they seek to improve instruction. Finally, part of the success came about only because the ORE staff and the school staff persevered and eventually came to trust and rely on one another. Still, it would be foolish to say that self-evaluation is now the norm of the school system.

The School Improvement Process

What we experienced in the project reinforced our view that "change is a process, not an event,"[14] and that the process is a long and difficult one that requires more time and persistence than anticipated. A major reason for the length and difficulty of the process is the necessity for some basic changes to occur in the culture of the school, the culture of the school system, and the perception of roles by principals and teachers. It is not easy for teachers and principals to move out of their isolation toward a sense of school community with a definite mission. It is not easy for teachers and principals to believe that they can make important decisions and to act on that belief by taking ownership of ideas and pursuing them. It is not easy for colleagues to develop enough trust to open up areas of uncertainty, to question oneself and others, to make mistakes in front of others, to rely upon one another. It is not easy for a school staff to really believe that the central office is there to help them. It is not easy because control, compliance, hierarchy, isolation, and doing the thing right are stronger elements of the culture than school-based decision making, collaborative planning, collegiality, mutual problem solving, and doing the right thing.

Wildavsky and Judith Warren Little discuss some of these difficulties and agree on some of the positive characteristics of improving and evaluating schools.[15] Little describes "a norm of collegiality," while Wildavsky states that "an extraordinary degree of mutual trust" is a requirement of a self-evaluating organization. Our findings support that a context of trust and collegiality is a prerequisite for the honest use of data for self-evaluation.

Little also describes "expectations for analysis, evaluation, and experimentation: a norm of continuous improvement." She talks about the need for "aggressive curiosity and healthy skepticism" and concludes that "where analysis, evaluation, and experimentation are treated as tools of the profession, designed to make work better (and easier), and where such work is properly the work of the teacher, teachers can be expected to look to staff development to help provoke questions, organize analysis, generate evidence of progress, and design differences in approaches."[16] Wildavsky agrees on the need for a "climate of opinion that favors experimentation" and skepticism and states as an example that "organization members would have to be rewarded for passing on bad news."[17] Merely to state these points is enough to realize how far away most schools and school systems are. However, as Little and we have shown, in some schools such a supportive culture exists. But progress is slow. Persistence and patience is called for.

TENSIONS, ISSUES, AND DILEMMAS

Bottom-Up and Top-Down

This is purposely posed as a both/and statement. Minority students' achievement is both a top-down and a bottom-up enterprise. The trick is to know what to mandate from the top-down and what to encourage to emerge from the bottom-up. Basically we mandate from the top the expectation that minority students' achievement will improve as measured by the eight indicators, the school-based planning process and format, and a monitoring system. At the same time we encourage local school initiative and creativity. Where it is difficult to know whether to operate bottom-up or top-down include the following situations:

- Reviewers of plans and reports conclude that the efforts of the school are inadequate and can be improved. When should the principal be encouraged? When should he or she be directed? When should he or she be removed?

- When is something deemed so good that it should be used more broadly? For instance, *The Skillful Teacher* training has been well received and eventually all schools will be involved in the training. One consideration in the selection of this model was that it is generic and not prescriptive. Thus, within its framework, it allows great flexibility to accommodate individual teacher and school differences.

- When is there a window of opportunity that must be used even if the system and the schools are not ready? For instance, at a given time, the political climate may be right, important actors in agreement, or additional funds available.

There is a natural tendency and pressure to centralize this process. However, it is important *not* to overcentralize. Although it may seem more efficient to direct schools to implement the same strategy, the effectiveness of such an approach is questionable. For those who monitor the program, it is easier to feel that you know what is going on if all schools are implementing the same program; and it certainly is easier to describe. The parents, community, and other external audiences can more easily understand a centralized program and thus may develop greater confidence in the effort. It is hard to persist against these pressures and tendencies, but it is important to do so.

The Pace of Change

The resolve of the school board and superintendent to expect a slow but steady improvement in minority students' achievement runs up against the pressure to show results quickly. The Black and Hispanic communities are understandably impatient. The desire to show positive results in the local and national press is also understandable, as is the desire to compete with the neighboring school systems. Pressure to do it faster, cut corners, and be more efficient is hard to resist. It is easy to understand that Wood's readiness and maintenance phases of the change process frequently are short-changed.

The Definition of Minority

The focus of the program can be on different groups of students and the choice can reflect different purposes for the program. In Fairfax there has been continuing discussion of the alternatives. The initial school board priority emphasized improvement in the achievement and aspirations of minority students. In practice, the emphasis was placed on Black and Hispanic students because the data indicated that Asian students were generally doing well. The priority purposely did not emphasize low-achieving students in general or low-achieving minority students in particular. The priority was intended to include the moderately achieving student who could do better as well as the low-achieving student. The continuing debate resulted in a change in the annual operating objective for 1986–87. The revised objective calls for "improving the academic achievement and aspirations of underachieving students, with emphasis on meeting the needs of minority students."

Focus on Test Scores

Test scores as a measure of student achievement are accepted by a variety of audiences. Researchers use test scores to judge the effects of a new program. The newspapers feature the results of the College Boards, norm-referenced tests, and minimum competency tests and rank school systems and schools on the basis of these. Parents, realtors, and the general public want to know what the test scores are. Yet thoughtful principals, teachers, central office staff, and researchers realize that test scores give only a partial picture of student achievement. If we want principals and teachers to take ownership of school-based evaluation, we must support the use of more than test scores as a measure of student achievement.

Fairfax consciously chose a variety of indicators of student achievement to assess the success of its effects to improve minority students' achievement. Spokespersons consistently speak about all the systemwide indicators and the variety of school-based indicators in order to curb the powerful impulse to simplify the criteria to one only of test scores. It helps to use illustrations, such as the classic underachiever who has high test scores, uneven grades, and low attendance. It is also important to talk about what decisions are made as early as the sixth grade in order for a student to take and succeed in calculus in the twelfth grade.

A more powerful reason to emphasize indicators other than test scores may be emerging from our data. Test scores are rising, but most other indicators are not showing much, if any, improvement. This may reinforce the view of the sometimes cynical principal who said that he could raise test scores, if that was what was wanted, even though student achievement would not improve. Use of multiple indicators will give a more complete picture of the changes.

Closing the Gap?

Most of the recent discussion concerning minority students' achievement talks about closing the gap between the achievement of minority students and the achievement of nonminority students. Fairfax has tried to resist this characterization of the goal. Instead, it has stated as its goal to "improve the academic aspirations and achievement of minority students." It has done this in order to compare minority students' achievement with itself or with the nation and not with other student groups in Fairfax.

An example will illustrate this difference. If the pass rate of minority students on the state minimum competency test increases by 5 percent, is the improvement any less if the pass rate of nonminority students also increases by 5 percent? For this reason, charting the change in the percent of minority students who score above the national norm on the test is more important than comparing the mean scores of minority and nonminority students. It would be fine if the achievement of minority students improved and the gap is narrowed in comparison with nonminority students. But the program can succeed if minority students' achievement improves even if the gap is not narrowed.

The Science and the Art of Education

The prospectus for the symposium from which this book emerged promised contributions to the creation of a science of education. I'm not sure my contribution will advance that cause. In my view education is more an art or craft than a science. Using creative analyses of available data is an important tool in the effort to improve the achievement of minority students and all students. But, in my view, data analysis is but one tool in the hand of a craftsperson and not the most important one. My image of the good superintendent, principal, teacher, and even the director of research and evaluation is the master craftsperson, not the eminent scientist.

I hope that no one attempts to replicate the "Fairfax model" in their situation. What I do hope is that readers will run the ideas and experiences presented here through the filter of their experiences, values, beliefs, hunches, and situation and shape what remains into something that makes sense to them. Then, persist and be patient.

NOTES

1. As I was finishing this chapter, a new booklet appeared on my desk: Bessie C. Howard, *Learning to Persist and Persisting to Learn* (Washington, DC: Mid-Atlantic Center for Race Equity, 1987). It caught my attention first because its title contained a major theme of this chapter—that is, persistence is a crucial factor—and also because it was about improving the academic achievement of minority students. As I read the booklet, I realized that much of what it said about the conflicts between minority students and the routines and expectations of the school system could also be said about the conflicts between principals and teachers, who are instructing minority students, and the routines and expectations of the school system.

2. The background and implementation sections of this chapter are adapted from three Fairfax County Public Schools reports: "Minority Students' Academic Performance: A Preliminary Report" issued in January 1984; "Report of the Advisory Committee on the Academic Performance of Minority Students in the Fairfax County

Public Schools" issued in May 1984; and "Report of Minority Students' Achievement for the 1985–86 School Year" issued in October 1986.

3. A useful think piece exploring a similar view in more depth is contained in Philip Schlechty's chapter, "District Level Policies and Practices Supporting Effective School Management and Classroom Instruction," in Regina Kyle, ed., *Reaching for Excellence: An Effective Schools Sourcebook* (Washington, DC: U.S. Government Printing Office, 1985).

4. A description of a bottom-up activity in Fairfax County and thoughts on how to encourage more such activities is contained in a paper, "Bottom-Up from the Top-Down," by Todd Endo, and published in *Reflections*, a journal of the National Network of Principal Centers. Copies can be obtained from the author.

5. "Annual Report on the Achievement and Aspirations of Minority Students in the Fairfax County Public Schools," Office of Research and Evaluation, October 1986, Executive Summary.

6. Ibid.

7. Jon Saphier and Robert Gower, *The Skillful Teacher* (Carlisle, MA: Research for Better Teaching, 1982).

8. A very thoughtful description and analysis of various models for school improvement and the development of effective schools is contained in Larry Cuban, "Transforming a Frog into the Prince: Effective Schools Research, Policy, and Practice at the District Level," a report for the National Institute of Education, June 1983.

9. This section is a summary of a more extensive informal report, "Effective Schools Project Report," written by the major developers of the project, Ann Cricchi and Mike Harrison, of the Office of Research and Evaluation.

10. M. Fullan, *The Meaning of Educational Change* (New York: Teachers College, Columbia University, 1982); G. Hall, "Concerns-based Approach to Educational Change." *Educational Horizons*, 4(57) (1979), 202–8; J. Little, "School Success and Staff Development: The Role of Staff Development in Urban Desegregated Schools," paper presented at the Annual Meeting of the American Educational Research Association, Los Angeles, April 1981; B. Joyce & B. Showers, "Improving Inservice Training: The Messages of Research." *Educational Leadership*, 37(5) (1980), 379–85.

11. The term "readiness" is used in the context of the RPTIM (readiness, planning, training, implementation, and maintenance) model described by Fred Wood et al. in "Practitioners and Professors Agree on Effective Staff Development Practices," *Educational Leadership*, October 1982, pp. 28–31. We have used many of the concepts contained in this and other articles by Wood and especially agree with his comment that in most staff development activities the readiness and maintenance stages are the most short-changed.

12. Aaron Wildavsky, "The Self-Evaluating Organization," *Public Administration Review*, September/October 1972, pp. 509–20.

13. Ibid., p. 510.

14. This quote is from Gene Hall, "The Concerns-based Approach to Facilitating Change," 202–8. We have benefitted greatly by this and other work by the Research and Development Center for Teacher Education.

15. Judith Warren Little, "School Success and Staff Development in Urban De-

segregated Schools: A Summary of Recently Completed Research," a paper presented at the American Educational Research Association annual meeting in 1981.

16. Ibid., p. 11.
17. Wildavsky, p. 519.

TWENTY-FIVE

Monitoring and Improving School Learning

Walter Hathaway

INTRODUCTION

One of the greatest challenges facing education in the United States in the second half of the twentieth century has been the differences in achievement among students of different ethnic groups. Today, some 35 years after *Brown vs. Topeka*, and almost 25 years after the Elementary and Secondary Education Act of 1965 propelled our nation along the road to equitable and excellent education for all children, there are signs that the achievement of minority students is beginning to catch up with that of nonminority students on a nationwide basis. The remaining gaps in achievement test scores and other indicators of student performance, however, are still large and perplexing. Excellent and innovative educational assessment and progress reporting has and can help us respond to that challenge both by targeting instruction on specific student needs and by focusing the attention of policy makers and other problem solvers on the larger underlying issues. Ron Edmonds pointed to this promise of assessment in his seminal work on school effectiveness when he included "frequent assessment" as one of the key factors in improving schooling for all students, but particularly for previously underachieving minority children (Edmonds, 1979).

The Portland, Oregon, school district has pioneered a number of improvements in achievement testing and test results reporting that have helped teachers improve the performance of all students while reducing the achievement differences among students of differing background. The Portland district also has begun to use test and evaluation data disaggregated by ethnic group to identify and respond to the needs of previously underachieving minority students by improving programs, policies, and resource allocations.

This chapter first summarizes some of the national data on student achievement test results by ethnic groups. It then briefly describes some of the innovative features of the Portland testing program that have helped improve the effectiveness and equity of instruction. Finally it reports why and how the Portland school system has begun reporting and using disaggregated student and system data at each of the key levels in the system, what some of the initial findings have been, and what some of the effects of such reporting have been.

THE NATIONAL ACHIEVEMENT GAP

According to a 1986 report by the U.S. Congressional Budget Office (pp. 74–75), there is evidence from a variety of tests administered to students of various ages in different localities that:

recent years have seen a shrinking of the long-standing difference between the scores of Black and nonminority students on a variety of achievements tests. The evidence pertaining to other ethnic groups is more limited but there are suggestions of relative gains by Hispanic students as well. While the change has been small relative to the remaining gap between the minority and nonminority students, it has been consistent from year to year and could prove substantial over the long run (see Figure 25.1).

Although this Congressional Budget Office report raises cautions about the limitations of the data upon which this trend is based, its authors conclude that the patterns observed seem genuine.[1] For example, they observe that in general, it appears that the average scores of students:

- declined less than those of nonminority students during the later years of the general decline;
- stopped declining, or began increasing again, earlier; and
- rose at a faster rate after the general upturn in achievement began.

Recent evidence of progress toward diminishing the national achievement gap has, however, only begun to mute the sad, national litany of indicators of the severe educational achievement disadvantage of many minority children. It goes beyond achievement data and includes:

- The dropout rate for minority students is as high as 80 percent, versus a national average of less than 20 percent for nonminority students.
- Minority students are often two to three or more grade levels behind on achievement measures. For example, the Southern Regional Education Board (SREB) reports that on National Assessment Tests, "the reading achievement levels of Black eleventh grade students is basically the same as for White seventh graders" (SREB, 1986, p. iv).

Figure 25.1
Trends in Average Reading Proficiency for White, Black, and Hispanic Students, by Birth Year, 1954–74

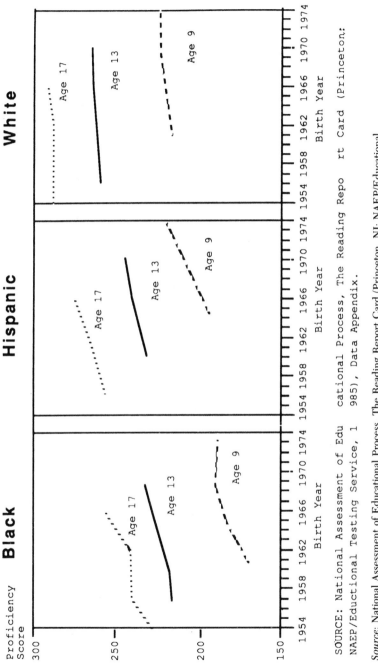

SOURCE: National Assessment of Edu   cational Process, The Reading Repo   rt Card (Princeton: NAEP/Eductional Testing Service, 1   985), Data Appendix.

Source: National Assessment of Educational Process, The Reading Report Card (Princeton, NJ: NAEP/Educational Testing Service, 1985), Data Appendix.

- In 1985 Black students had SAT Mathematics and Verbal scores that were 115 and 103 points lower than White students. Hispanic students scores were 65 and 67 points lower.
- Black students are approximately three times as likely to be in a class for the educable mentally retarded but only half as likely to be in a class for the gifted and talented as White students.
- Only about one-third of the estimated 2.7 million limited English proficient students aged 5 to 14 receive special help congruent with their linguistic needs.
- Black and Hispanic students are two to three times as likely to be suspended or expelled and only half as likely to be enrolled in courses that lead to a college education.

And the list goes on.

Almost daily the superintendents, boards of education, staffs, and communities of school systems such as those represented in the chapters of this volume find themselves searching for answers to the serious and complex questions of equity, efficiency, and excellence in education posed by such differences. Their colleagues in other districts throughout the nation share this quest. The encouraging nationwide trends in reducing the achievement gap are due in large measure to such efforts.

The questions that continuously emerge as we strive to develop policies and programs to improve the academic and social performance of all our students and to regain the confidence and support of our publics include:

- How to improve student motivation and behavior and thus reduce such crippling and costly problems as dropouts, absenteeism, violence, and vandalism?
- How to better assess and improve the performance of our students and the effectiveness and success of our programs?
- How to better identify and respond to the needs of special student populations— for example, disadvantaged, handicapped, bilingual and multicultural, gifted and talented?
- How to better select for and support improved staff competence in helping students gain academic, instructional, social, and personal skills?
- How to better gain and equitably utilize funding for our systems that is adequate and secure?
- How to improve communication with and involvement of our parents and community?

Answers to these pressing problems of education may be discovered if we continue to work toward creating:

- Accurate, accessible, and timely data on the nature and extent of the needs of our students;
- Valid, reliable, and efficient measures of the progress our students are making so

that we can identify the programs and practices that help them overcome the impediments to success in school; and

- Field-based as well as fundamental research on new teacher and technology-based approaches to enhancing the productivity of instruction and schooling in responding to our students' needs.

The Portland school district has taken the data-based research and evaluation approach to defining and seeking answers to the perplexing educational, social, moral, and political problems of differences in average levels of student achievement among student groups of differing ethnic backgrounds.

THE PORTLAND EXPERIENCE

It was to help us answer questions such as the above that led the Portland school district to develop an innovative testing system and to begin analyzing and reporting student achievement data as well as other student performance and status data by ethnic group.

Testing and Test Results Reporting Innovations

A decade and a half ago, a small group of researchers and test developers in the Portland school district realized the potential of Item Response Theory for developing tools for better educational measurement. The purposes we wanted our citywide testing programs to support included equitable, effective, valid, and reliable

- Grouping and placing of students
- Targeting instruction on individual student learning needs
- Evaluating student progress over time
- Identifying neglected areas of the aligned curriculum and evaluating and improving programs and services at the student, classroom, grade within school, and grade within district levels
- Providing accountability to the school board and the community

In order to meet these needs, we needed an educational measurement system that would answer the following questions:

- Is the current *rate of gain* of this student, class, grade, or program satisfactory compared to his/her/its age, grade, program mates and the previous pattern of gains observed?
- What are the current *strengths and weaknesses* (in terms of goal areas needing further diagnosis and possible work) of this student, class, grade, school, or program, and how have they changed over time?

- Is the *level* at which this student, class, grade, or program is currently performing satisfactory compared to his/her/its age, grade, or program mates and the previous pattern of levels observed?

We could not find any available measurement program that would help us answer these questions and meet these needs adequately, so we set out to build one ourselves.

There followed a period of extensive collaborative research and development, much of it within the framework of the Northwest Evaluation Association, which was created to foster regional cooperation in and mutual benefit from this effort. The result today is a system of three comprehensive basic skills Rasch calibrated item banks in Reading, Mathematics, and Language Usage. The constantly growing item banks in Reading and Language Usage each have over 2,000 field-tested, calibrated items linked to a common, continuous curriculum scale for each subject. The Mathematics item bank now has over 3,000 such items. State and local school systems including Portland have been using these item banks since 1977 to construct effective, efficient survey achievement tests, competency tests, and other instruments that combine the best qualities of criterion-referenced and norm-referenced measurement. These excellent measurement systems have been the cornerstones of state, district, and school renewal efforts that anticipated *A Nation At Risk* (National Commission on Excellence in Education, 1983) by at least five years. The ongoing collaboration is now resulting in similar item banks in Science and Direct Writing, and yet another in Social Studies is on the drawing board.

Some of the characteristics of the testing and test reporting system developed by the Portland school district that improve school and classroom effectiveness include:

- Matches the local curriculum.
- Emphasizes student gain over time (rather than just level of performance at the current time).
- Gives every student a challenging testing experience at which he or she will succeed (functioning level testing).
- Reports goal areas in which students may need help as well as overall performance in each subject.
- Monitors student progress toward mastery of graduation competency requirements starting with the beginning of third grade.
- Invites parent involvement with teachers in planning to help students learn better.

We are working on two additional computer-based testing and test reporting innovations:

1. Offering districtwide a school-based microprocessor test reporting system. Over the past two years, a group of seven principals, along with the

data processing department and the research and evaluation department, has worked to develop this computer system for local building controlled reporting and analysis of test data. The pilot system began with four goals in mind. We were interested in finding a program that would run on building microcomputers that would accomplish the following:

• Provide a complete individual student test history to building staff immediately on request.
• Produce test reports by instructional group.
• Provide analyses of longitudinal student group data when and as the building needed them.
• Improve the turnaround time of test reports.

We now have a program that gives local buildings the ability to meet these four goals and we have offered it to all schools in the district.

2. Creating a school-based computerized adaptive testing (CAT) system allows building personnel to continuously monitor the progress of students as they advance through the basic skills curriculum. This system involves putting a sufficient bank of field-tested and calibrated items inside a computer along with the requisite software to build a unique, individualized test for each student at the time when building staff feel it is needed. The advantages of CAT include:

• Increased measurement accuracy
• Increased testing flexibility
• Improved use of testing as an integral part of the instructional process
• Enhanced test security
• Decreased testing time
• Increased ability to measure high-level educational goals such as problem solving
• Immediate feedback of results

Our research and evaluation department has mounted the pilot CAT program in cooperation with the information services department, directors of instruction, and principals. The purpose of this pilot is to gain the information necessary to design a cost-effective CAT system that will serve the future testing needs of all our students and our schools.

Tested theories of effective education now reveal what we must do to improve schools and to help every child learn as much as he or she can as effectively and efficiently as possible. They indicate that our educational leadership must support the development of learning environments in which the following sorts of things happen for each of our students:

- The student's current, most pressing learning needs within a well-planned curriculum must be identified.
- The student must be helped to set clear, relevant, attainable learning objectives to meet those needs.
- The student must be expected to succeed in attaining the learning objectives and must want to learn them.
- The student must receive individualized instruction directly related to the learning objectives designed to meet his or her current learning needs.
- The learner must use the time allocated for instruction to work intently and seriously on the task of learning.
- The student must know when he or she has succeeded and when not, and must experience a reinforcing sense of accomplishment and achievement as a result of knowledge of success.
- The learner must receive and return a sense of caring, personal concern, interest, respect, and commitment that provides the psychological support necessary to want to learn and to work to learn.
- The student must receive and accept parental and community support and encouragement for success in learning.

The main barrier to our putting such models of effective instruction and education into practice up until now has been the lack of accurate data and information about:

- Each student's individual learning-needs
- What learning activities and experiences are matched to diagnosed student needs and to established learning objectives and how to help the student engage in such tailored instruction in a timely fashion
- When the student has mastered the objectives and is ready to move on
- The degree of overall success of staff and programs in promoting student learning
- What is and is not working to help students learn

We are now, however, at long last beginning to evolve the comprehensive assessment and information systems needed in order to create the more effective, equitable, and efficient education systems required for real and meaningful educational reform and even reinvention of schooling.

Guiding Values, Principles, and Goals of the Portland Effort

The Portland initiative in using assessment data to improve school effectiveness, especially for underachieving minority students, is founded upon the following values, principles, and goals:

1. *All students can learn.* We categorically reject the suggestions in some quarters that the observed differences in the achievement levels of students

of various backgrounds are intrinsic. Instead we believe that the barriers to high levels of achievement by all students are surmountable and that research-based solutions can be used to create schools in which all students achieve at levels that will help them be productive members of society while meeting their personal goals.

2. *Helping all students learn up to their maximum potential will require complex solutions to complex problems. There are no simple solutions or panaceas.* We recognize that the existing research on obstacles to student achievement indicates that the underlying problems are often long-term—beginning as early as the prenatal environment; and both complex and pervasive—with elements being found in the home, community, peer, and school environments and cultures.

We have resisted the temptation to extrapolate from current trends and to project when the "achievement gap" will be closed. We are using the best data available at each level in the system to understand why some students are not currently making the progress or performing at the levels we hope, and we are developing and carrying out collaboratively developed plans to raise the achievement of each individual student and each student group now lagging behind.

3. *Teachers, principals, students, and parents are vital partners in this effort.*

Disaggregating Reporting

A key event in the maturing of this commitment was the decision of Superintendent Matthew Prophet and the Board of Education in 1985 to begin issuing an annual report entitled *A Statistical Portrait of the Multicultural/Multiethnic Student Population in Portland Public Schools.* This report represents only the "tip of the iceberg" of the district disaggregated data reporting system, which extends to every level of the school district. It pulls together relevant districtwide analyses of data on culturally diverse children in the Portland public schools to assist district decision makers in developing a general understanding of the status of these children in the district. The districtwide report presents findings on which the district bases planning of its efforts to address concerns regarding culturally diverse children. Similar data are reported and used at the program, building, and classroom levels. This promotes problem identification and solving at each key level in the system.

At the district level the availability of disaggregated data helps the superintendent, the Board of Education, and the administration to work with the community to muster resources and to formulate and monitor efforts to raise the achievement and education levels of all students, especially those lagging behind. Data-based research and evaluation on the causes of and solutions to problems causing lack of educational progress become possible at every level. Program directors and building managers are helped to monitor and improve their units' efforts to bring about improvements. Teachers and others directly involved in instruction can evaluate and improve the effectiveness of their efforts to help all student groups and individual students progress through the curriculum. It is reasons such as these that have led Portland to take research, evaluation, and assessment-based approaches to understand and respond to the needs of underachieving minority students.

This districtwide report of data disaggregated by ethnic group was undertaken in collaboration with the district's Desegration Monitoring Advisory Committee (DMAC), a consortium of representatives of community groups concerned about equitable and excellent education and for education that is truly multicultural. The district's Management Information Systems group coordinated the data collection, analyses, and reporting effort. The assistance of the Northwest Regional Laboratory was obtained in designing and developing the initial report.

The Portland Findings

The Portland school district registers its students as White, Black, Asian, Hispanic, or American Indian. For the 1986–87 school year, the student enrollment was 73.0 percent White, 15.3 percent Black, 7.5 percent Asian, 2.1 percent Hispanic, and 2.1 percent American Indian. The district has enjoyed a high level of desegregation and has never been under a court order to desegregate. It does have a voluntary desegregation/integration plan focused on improving student achievement and the DMAC composed of representatives of community groups having a stake in educational equity and excellence.

In developing our districtwide Statistical Portrait of the Multicultural/ Multiethnic Student Population in the Portland public schools to symbolize and carry out our commitment to collaborative problem identification and solving with our community, we used a variety of sources to identify areas of districtwide concern regarding culturally diverse children. These included concerns expressed by the lay public and local school personnel. In addition we conducted an extensive review of the current literature and media stories to gain a broader perspective on concerns of local relevance. Through this process, we identified the following five general areas for analysis:

1. *Student Achievement.* At what levels do culturally diverse children in the district demonstrate achievement?

2. *Program Access.* To what extent do culturally diverse children participate in district programs?

3. *Multicultural Curriculum.* In what ways does the district's curriculum address appreciation and knowledge of one's own culture or the cultures of others?

4. *Teaching Personnel*. To what extend does the district's teaching staff reflect the cultural diversity of its students?

5. *Policy Representation*. Do groups that formulate district policies reflect the cultural diversity of the students?

The report itself does not attempt to deal with the causes of the conditions it profiles. Instead, it presents an honest and accurate statistical portrait of culturally diverse children in the district on selected variables for which data are available by ethnic group. The problem identification and solution process is inspired and guided by the data in the profile. A summary of findings follows to convey the nature and the power of the data presented. These data are revealed in far greater detail in the district's profile report and are articulated further at program, building, and classroom levels where they are used as an integral part of school and classroom improvement, evaluation, and planning.

Student Achievement

We looked at five student achievement indicators: test scores, school grades, absences, dropouts, and suspensions. In general, results from the elementary Portland Achievement Levels Tests showed that White students had a higher level of achievement test scores than other ethnic groups in both reading and mathematics. Minority groups, particularly Blacks, showed lower levels of scores. Longitudinal data obtained from the 1980–81 through 1985–86 school years, however, provided some evidence that while the average levels of minority students scores were lower than the average levels of White student scores, the differences were generally becoming smaller over the years. In many cases, minority students have been making greater gains within a school year than White students. The result has been a convergence upon and in many cases surpassing of the national average as well as a trend toward closing of the "achievement gap" in many instances (see Figure 25.2).

Approximately 7.6 percent of high school seniors were ineligible to receive a standard high school diploma in 1987 due to their inability to pass the district's basic skills Graduation Standards Tests (GST). This was up from 5.8 percent in 1984–85 and 6.0 percent in 1983–84. A generally disproportionate percentage of the students not passing the district's GST have been minority students. This disproportion has been declining, however. It has occurred primarily among those students who were recent Southeast Asian refugees. In 1983–84, 52.3 percent of the students not passing the GST were Asian; in 1984–85 this dropped to 50.2 percent; and in 1985–86 the percentage dropped substantially to 35.5 percent. The percentage of Black students not passing the GST has also decreased over the past three years. In 1983–84, 22.8 percent were Black; in 1984–85, the percentage had

Figure 25.2
Graphic Presentation of the Percent of Portland Public Schools' Elementary
Students Above National Test Publishers' Norms

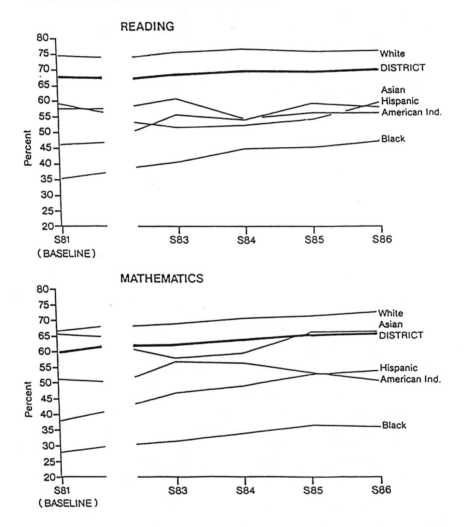

dropped to 18.6 percent; and in 1985–86, 17.3 percent were Black. The number of Hispanic and American Indian students not passing the GST was consistently low over the same three years.

Asian and White students received the highest percentage (34.0 and 25.2, respectively) of As and the lowest percentage (5.2 and 10.2, respectively) of Fs in their schoolwork. In proportion, Blacks received the smallest percentage of As (13.3 percent) and American Indians had the largest percentage of Fs (20.5 percent).

Asian students have the highest grade point average (GPA) and averaged a total GPA of 2.80 (B−). White students had the second highest GPA and averaged 2.43 (C+). Hispanic, American Indian, and Black students averaged a total GPA of about 2.0 (C).

Asian students showed the smallest number of class absences, averaging 3.5 absences in the first class of the day during the second quarter of 1986–87. American Indians, Blacks, and Hispanics had above-average class absences during the same period of time. White students averaged 5.2 absences, the same as the district average.

There has been a general decrease in the rates in which students have dropped out of school in any one school year. Asian students showed the lowest dropout rate, averaging 5.1 percent for 1985–86. American Indians had higher dropout rates, averaging 13.0 percent for the same year. Dropout rates for White and Hispanic students were close to the district average of 7.3 percent. Black students' dropout rates were well below the district's, averaging 6.0 percent for the 1985–86 school year.

The percentage of high school graduates differed substantially among the ethnic groups. Hispanic, White, and Black seniors demonstrated higher than average rates of graduation (96, 90, and 89 percent, respectively). American Indian and Asian seniors had a slightly lower than average rate of high school graduation.

Suspension rates have generally declined over the past several years for most ethnic groups. Black students, however, still showed a relatively high rate, averaging 5.9 percent for 1985–86 as compared with the district average of 3.7 percent. Asian students had the lowest rate, averaging only 1.2 percent for the same year. Hispanic and White students showed suspension rates lower than the district average. American Indian students' suspension rates were up during the 1985–86 school year, but numbers of American Indian students suspended are so small that percentages are generally not consistent from year to year.

Program Access

In this analysis, we examined six program areas: talented and gifted (TAG) programs, high school magnet programs, special education programs, ESL/bilingual programs, Chapter I programs, and Project SEED.

Asian and White students showed the highest participation in TAG. Their rates—8.5 and 8.1 percent, respectively, in 1986–87—were more than twice as high as those of other ethnic groups. American Indian, Black, and Hispanic students had a participation rate of about 3 percent.

Black students have the highest participation in the magnet programs, averaging 11.2 percent in 1986–87. Hispanic students also showed an above average rate of 9.3 percent for that year. Participation rates of American Indian, White, and Asian students were slightly below the district average of 8.6 percent.

There was a slight increase in special education enrollment through 1984–85 and since then there has been a slight decline. In 1986–87, the percentages of American Indian (12.3 percent) and Black (12.8 percent) students receiving special education services were higher than those of the other ethnic groups. Asian students, on the other hand, had the lowest rate of participation, averaging 2.2 percent. Enrollment of White and Hispanic students was slightly below the district average of 8.5 percent.

For the 1986–87 school year, Black participation in Chapter I (22.6 percent for reading and 17.0 percent for math) was more than twice as high as the district averages of 10.1 and 6.7 percent. Participation rates for Asian, American Indian, and Hispanic students were higher than the district average. White students had the smallest enrollment in Chapter I, averaging 7.0 percent for reading and 4.2 percent for math.

In proportion, more Black students were enrolled in Project SEED than any other ethnic group.[2] Their participation rate of 7.3 percent for 1986–87 was more than four times as high as the district average of 1.6 percent. Asian, White, and American Indian students had the lowest rate, averaging approximately 0.5 percent. Hispanic students were close to the district average at 1.7 percent.

Multicultural Curriculum

The district appears to have made a concentrated effort to strengthen its multicultural curriculum. The Curriculum Department has identified six major geocultural groups that have contributed to the American cultures, and has used this categorization to organize its multicultural curriculum. Each of the eight core curriculum areas has goals and objectives for teaching content that is multicultural with specific reference to the six major geocultural groups. The department has developed a cross-referenced grid linking existing planning documents, instructional materials, and key cultural concepts with the major ethnic groups.

In addition, the Educational Media Department, through the district's Professional Library, its Central Audiovisual Library, and individual school media centers, provides resources for both teachers and students in multicultural education. And the ESL/Bilingual program provides new student orientation, appreciation, and support for home language and culture, and awareness of America's multicultural society; it has developed curriculum materials for students from diverse linguistic and cultural backgrounds.

Teaching Personnel

At each individual school, the ethnic distribution of teachers somewhat corresponds with that of its students. Schools with an above-average percentage of one group of students often have an above-average percentage of teachers of the same group. Looking at the district as a whole, however, one finds a consistent pattern of discrepancies. Except for White students, teacher percentages are generally less than one-half of the respective student percentages. There is a discernible pattern that teachers of groups other than Whites are underrepresented in the teaching staff. The discrepancies between teacher and student ethnic distribution are most pronounced at the high school level. In addition, for the past two years nearly 90 percent of all newly hired teachers have been White in spite of intensified efforts to recruit minority candidates.

Policy Representation

We have reviewed the ethnic composition of district central administration, school principals, Citizens Advisory Committees (CACs), and the Desegregation Monitoring Advisory Committee. The data indicate that three groups (American Indian, Asian, and Hispanic) were consistently underrepresented in such policy groups. Blacks were overrepresented in central administration and DMAC but underrepresented in CACs.

In each area of review, the district has developed plans to improve the education of its culturally diverse children. For example, the district will expand testing to include more subject areas (e.g., science and social studies) and grade levels. It will continue to review test items and testing procedures for potential bias and develop more sophisticated ways of analyzing data on student growth. In addition, the district is working on data systems that will allow for longitudinal tracking and analysis of student data on school grades, absences, dropouts, and suspensions.

To improve program functions and outcomes, the district is reviewing and analyzing ways in which it has operated its special programs, including TAG, magnet, special education, ESL/bilingual, Chapter I, and Projects SEED and MESA.[3]

The Curriculum Department has developed a series of plans to revise and expand its multicultural resources and materials as well as in-service training for teachers. The Personnel Department is working to find ways of attracting and retaining minority teachers. The superintendent is working with several community groups in an effort to encourage and support involvement of our culturally diverse citizens in school district affairs.

Syntheses

Table 25.1 presents the difference between the averages for each ethnic group and the district averages on the variables studied. For student achievement data, ethnic group averages are compared with averages for all students. For program access data, participation rates of each ethnic group are compared with the district participation rates. Comparing ethnic group and district averages provides a picture of above-district achievement, below-district achievement, overrepresentation, and underrepresentation. In Table 25.1, a plus sign indicates that the ethnic group is higher than the district average; a minus sign indicates the group is below the district average.

As the districtwide synthesis in Table 25.1 indicates, there are still significant discrepancies in indicators of student performance among student ethnic groups in the Portland school district. Although, as noted earlier, some progress has been made in reducing lag in achievement test score level by greater gains by minority student groups, the most encouraging progress is indicated by other indicators, such as reduced dropout and suspension rates. The key philosophical and procedural difference is that we are using such data at all appropriate levels throughout the system to plan, implement, and monitor the success of efforts to reduce discrepancies. One key early benefit of this open data sharing has been an improvement in the climate of community relations.

Some of the major causes of this improved success of our students and our school system are the implementation of carefully screened and piloted specific programs and implementation of the general effective schools philosophy, including:

- Improved classroom management aimed at helping students become more motivated and more responsible for their behavior and their learning. This results in fewer interruptions for teachers and students and more time on the task of learning.

- Clear and high goals for achievement in the basics and beyond. Our teachers know what they want students to learn and students understand what is expected of them.

- Well-selected and appropriately challenging curriculum materials, instructional systems, and learning tasks.

- Instruction designed to challenge every student to succeed and targeted on his or her current diagnosed learning needs. Such individualized and personalized instruction brings out the best in each learner.

- Effective and efficient special programs aimed at helping teachers meet the special needs of students.

Table 25.1
Summary Information on Culturally Diverse Student Groups, 1986–87

Variable	American Indian	White	Black	Asian	Hispanic
8th Grade Reading					
Level	−	+	−	−	−
Gain	+	−	+	+	+
8th Grade Math					
Level	−	+	−	+	−
Gain	+	−	−	+	+
Passing Graduation Standards Tests	+	+	−	−	−
School Grades					
A's	−	+	−	+	−
F's	+	−	+	−	+
Class Absences	+	−	+	−	+
Graduation Ratio	−	+	−	+	+
Dropout Rates	+	+	+	−	+
Suspension Rates	+	−	+	−	−
Program Access					
TAG	−	+	−	+	−
Magnet	−	−	+	−	+
Special Ed. (84–85)	+	−	+	−	−
Chapter I	+	−	+	+	+
SEED	+	−	+	−	−
Teaching Personnel					
Elementary	−	+	−	−	−
Middle	−	+	−	−	−
High	−	+	−	−	−
Policy Representation					
Administration	−	+	+	−	−
Principal	−	+	−	−	−
CAC	−	+	−	−	−
DMAC	−	−	+	−	−

Note: Only the most recent data are included in summary.

+ = Above district average
− = Below district average

- Partnerships with parents and with community groups in supporting student learning.

- Prompt, accurate, and frequent feedback to students, parents, teachers, support staff, program personnel, district managers, and policy makers on the success of their efforts at learning and at fostering learning.

- Systematic recognition, rewards, and incentives for excellence in the level of achievement and progress in learning.

CONCLUSION

A variety of theories and hypotheses have been advanced to explain the observed differences in performance by various groups of students. Environmental theories held sway in the 1950s and 1960s, with an emphasis on family and school environments. These theories gave rise to the school desegregation and compensatory education movements. In the late 1960s theories of cultural difference were developed. These paved the way for the multiethnic/multicultural movement of the 1970s and 1980s. A parallel development during the same period has been the emergence of the mastery learning and effective schools' movements with their emphases on the ability of all students to succeed given clear and high expectations, the basics, a safe and orderly learning environment, instructional leadership, and regular monitoring and reporting of student and program success (Edmonds, 1979).

The fact remains that there are considerable differences in the observed average levels of academic achievement of students of different ethnic groups as early as first grade or even kindergarten. While research has established that many of the observed differences are correlated with socioeconomic variables and while recent trends point to above-average gains for previously low-achieving student groups, there is still much to be done to understand and deal with differences in student and system achievement and performance levels and with the subtle and complex educational and social issues that underlie them.

The steps being taken by Portland give hope of data-based and measurement-supported understanding and progress. We are developing and sharing with our staff, students, and communities honest, accurate information on the performance of student groups and we are using that information to plan change and to monitor student and program success. As much as we would all like things to be perfect, as educational managers and as educators, we are responsible for knowing what is the case, in working to make things as good as we can, and for knowing when, why, and how we have succeeded and failed and then trying to do better next time.

The staff of the Portland public schools are proud that we have risen and are continuing to rise to the difficult challenge posed by student performance differences between student ethnic groups. In general our efforts have been well received by our community, which welcomes accurate, timely, and freely available information on how their children are doing and who value the new opportunities we are creating to work together to improve education for all students.

NOTES

1. In a May 1987 report Lyle Jones questions whether young Black children in impoverished rural and urban areas are participating in the overall closing of the Reading NAEP Achievement Gap.

2. Project SEED (Special Education for the Educationally Disadvantaged) is a supplementary math program that uses the Socratic group-discovery method to help educationally disadvantaged elementary students learn conceptually oriented mathematics.

3. MESA (Mathematics, Engineering, Science, Achievement) is a program designed to increase the pool of minority students who are eligible to pursue careers in math-based fields. Students in the program are encouraged to take secondary-level courses that are required for admission to the University of California system and that will give them the background that is expected of students who major in math and science.

BIBLIOGRAPHY

Banks, J. A. (1983). Multiethnic education and the quest for equality. *Phi Delta Kappan, 64*(8), 582–85.

Bell, D. (1983). Learning from our losses: Is school desegregation still feasible in the 1980's? *Phi Delta Kappan, 64*(8), 572–75.

Brandt, R. (1982). On school improvement: A conversation with Ronald Edmonds, *Educational Leadership, 40*(3), pp. 4–11.

Congressional Budget Office. (1986). *Trends in Educational Achievement.* Washington, DC: Author.

Edmonds, R. (1979). Effective schools for the urban poor. *Educational Leadership, 37*(1).

Feistritzer, C. E. (1985). *Cheating our children.* Washington, DC: The National Center for Educational Information.

Foster, R. W. (1983). Desegregation in Denver: Down for the count? *Phi Delta Kappan, 64*(5), 331–33.

Gay, G. (1983). Multiethnic education: Historical developments and future prospects. *Phi Delta Kappan, 64*(8), 560–63.

Howe, H. & Edelman, M. W. (1985). *Barriers to excellence: Our children at risk.* Boston: The National Coalition of Advocates for Students.

Jones, L. (1987). Achievement trends for black school children, 1970–1984. Paper presented at a collegium on Black Families and Public Policy, Historical and Contemporary Perspectives, May, Yale University.

Lanasa, P. J., III & Potter, J. H. (1984). Building a bridge to span the minority-majority achievement gap. Paper presented at the National Conference on Desegregation in Postsecondary Education, October.

Messick, S. (1984). Assessment in context: Appraising student performance in relation to instructional quality. *Educational Researcher, 13*(3), 3–8.

Mullin, S. P. & Summers, A. A. (1983). Is more better: The effectiveness of spending on compensatory education. *Phi Delta Kappan, 64*(5), 229–343.

The National Commission on Excellence in Education (1983). *A nation at risk: The imperative for educational reform. A report to the nation and the secretary of education.* Washington, DC: U.S. Department of Education.

Ornstein, A. C. (1982). The education of the disadvantaged: A 20-year review. *Educational Research, 24*(3), 197–210.

Pugh, G. E., and Krasmakevich, J. (1971). *School desegregation with minimum busing.* Arlington, VA: Lambda Corporation.

Southern Regional Education Board (SREB). (1986). *Measuring Student Achievement.* Atlanta: Author.

Stickney, B. D. & Plunkett, V.R.L. (1982). Has Title I done its job? *Educational Leadership, 39*(5), pp. 378–83.

TWENTY-SIX

Learning Improvement Results from Integrated Learning Systems for Underachieving Minority Students

JAMES B. OLSEN

INTRODUCTION

Classroom teachers with minority students face a prodigious and extremely work-intensive job to provide instructional planning, individualized instruction, and assessment for all students within their classes. In a typical class, the teacher must provide instruction and assessment appropriate for a group of at least 20 students and often many times more. Each of the students has different levels of entering achievement, ability, and personal experience with the school curriculum content. Each of the students also exhibits a wide range of achievement and learning outcomes during the course.

The recent revolutions in technology and information processing offer significant promise for helping to assist and support the teachers in successfully accomplishing their daily teaching, assessment, and instructional management activities. Technology can indeed enhance and supplement the traditional teaching activities in support of learning improvement. Nancy Cole envisions such a technology-enhanced school classroom as follows:[1]

We begin this fantasy by entering an elementary school classroom. What strikes us first is that on every child's desk is a small computer and screen and at several locations in the room are large screens visible to the whole class. The teacher is talking to a group of 10 youngsters about social studies and uses the computer at hand to call up a short film on one of the large screens to illustrate a point. As the lesson ends, each child activates his or her own computer and is given questions over the material covered that day. When a mistake is made, a hint is given and the child tries again and each student may receive a different set of questions depending on earlier answers. The student types in short answers to some questions. While this group of students moves on to lessons in science or art, the teacher calls up a display of the results of the children's performance on questions asked, which includes an error analysis identifying particular children with incorrect conceptions or misunderstandings of the content. . . . That evening at home, each child would contact the school computer to get a report on that day's activities for the parents. These reports indicate each student's progress and areas needing special work and describe the child's own individual homework assignment based on the day's performance. . . . Meanwhile the principal, with several classes at this grade, wishes to check on the children's progress in science in each classroom and calls up a summary report by classroom. . . . The report to the school board will include norm-referenced information on the students' standing in relation to students nationally but will not require special testing. Instead it uses particular questions from the students' regular daily and end-of-unit review questions administered by the computer.

Though much of this vision remains at the moment a dream for the future, much of the required technology already exists; and it is only a matter of time before such technology-enhanced education described by Cole becomes part of tomorrow's classrooms.

As a significant step toward the classrooms of the future, several integrated computerized instruction and assessment systems have been developed over the past ten years and have been successfully implemented in schools for teaching minority students. Typically, these computerized instruction and assessment systems are referred to as integrated learning systems. An integrated learning system includes at least the following major components.

- a computerized school learning system
- comprehensive courseware curricula
- sophisticated learning management capabilities
- advanced assessment and testing programs

The following sections describe and illustrate each of these major features and capabilities of integrated learning systems that have been used very successfully for improving achievement of underachieving minority students.

School Learning Center Features

Integrated learning systems are currently being implemented in schools using a learning center or "computer lab" configuration. The learning center provides lessons that are tailored to the individual learner. Interactive exercises encourage students to develop higher order thinking skills. Drill and practice lessons are also included. Teachers receive up-to-the-minute student management reports, which permit them to monitor student performance and progress and identify areas where students require individualized attention.

The learning center allows each student to work on different courseware lessons all at the same time in the same lab. The learning center management and student workstations have been designed to be easy to learn and to operate. In the learning center each student can take computerized achievement tests and receive appropriate prescriptions to a comprehensive integrated curriculum. Student responses to the courseware and testing materials are monitored and teachers receive reports on individual performance as students proceed through the materials at their own pace.

The learning center courseware uses an extensive graphics library to stimulate student interest and motivate students toward higher performance. Students see learning exercises that are acted out in vivid animation. The learning center configurations include high-quality, speech-like audio, which is educationally beneficial for beginning reading instruction, activity directions, language instruction, feedback, and reinforcement.

Courseware Features

With an integrated learning system the reading courseware allows students to select electronic newspaper articles or stories to read. The newspaper editions available to the student include a mix of stories on the student's reading grade level, one year above reading level, and one year below reading level. From the edition list presented, the student selects a specific newspaper edition to work on and one of five possible news story articles available in the edition. The student must respond correctly to 80 percent of the questions on three stories within one reading level before advancing to the next level. Various prompts and helps are available to students during the reading exercises. The reading courseware teaches critical thinking skills and shows students how to apply these skills in a logical process to understand printed material. The reading courseware teaches students to draw inferences and conclusions, and to make predictions from text; to provide justification for conclusions, inferences, and predictions; to judge the validity of an argument based on stated criteria and evidence; to determine the relations of parts of a passage to its total meaning; to interpret data presented in graph, chart, or tabular form; and to identify appropriate summaries of text passages.

The mathematics courseware includes concept development activities that provide graphic models to promote mental images of concepts and insight into the relationships between concepts and symbolic math skills. Practice activities with problem-specific feedback reinforce the math skills and help provide additional support for students who need it without intruding on students who do not. Drill activities encourage immediate recall of facts. Problem-solving activities promote productive problem-solving habits and challenge students to thoughtfully apply previously learned math concepts in real-life contexts. Rich, animated graphics demonstrate math concepts and principles along with prompts and questions that guide the student through an interactive discovery approach to learning mathematics.

Learning Management Features

As each student progresses through the courseware, teachers can request several standard management reports, which include information on individual student and class progress. These management reports indicate the lesson difficulty for each student and class, time on task for the student and class, the number of trials each student required for mastering the activity, the number of activities attempted, the number of activities mastered for each student and class, and the student's relative class standing. The learning management system provides teachers with considerable flexibility in managing individual and class group progress, courseware placement, assigning and sequencing activities for students and class groups, and in determining the frequency and the types of management reports desired. Management reports can be generated for either individual students or class groups for a specific courseware activity, or multiple activities, or the capabilities also allow districts to correlate their own objectives with the courseware objectives. Teachers can also restructure the courseware curriculum for students and classes to better parallel the classroom instructional sequence.

Advanced Assessment and Testing Features

The integrated learning systems include advanced school assessment and testing capabilities. Computerized predictive assessment tests have been developed from national lists of objectives and from specific state assessment objectives. These predictive assessment tests can be administered at the school's choice any time during the school year. The test results indicate which state assessment objectives each student or group of students has mastered and which objectives are not yet mastered. For objectives that are not mastered, the computerized assessment system also provides prescriptions to appropriate textbook pages and to courseware lessons. These prescriptions are used by the teacher to more effectively help the student or group of students master the state-mandated objectives. When students initially begin using the courseware, the computerized testing capabilities can help determine their skills in the subject and provide appropriate placement in the courseware lessons.

In implementing these computerized testing programs, the following advantages have been found for the computerized assessment tests over paper and pencil achievement tests.

- standardized administration conditions
- ease of administration and management
- individualized test administration
- immediate scoring and reporting
- nonbiased scoring
- enhanced presentation capabilities (text, graphics, and audio)
- enhanced response capabilities (multiple choice, free response, performance)
- increased testing efficiency
- improved test security

Even more exciting from an educational standpoint than the computerized assessment applications are the pioneering capabilities for delivering computerized adaptive achievement tests. A product of recent research in item response theory and advances in microcomputer technology, computerized adaptive testing provides the capability of delivering tests that can adapt themselves during administration according to student performance on each test item. In a computerized adaptive test, an initial proficiency estimate is made for each student based on the student's grade level, performance on previous tests, and so on. The first item is assigned based on this initial proficiency estimate. If the student answers the item correctly, a more difficult item is assigned; if not, the next item is less difficult. After each response the student's proficiency estimate is updated and a new item is selected at the new estimated proficiency level. The testing process continues until a specified level of reliability or precision is reached and the testing process is terminated. Research results have shown that computerized adaptive tests can significantly reduce the amount of testing time and number of items required by 50 to 75 percent with an equal or greater level of measurement precision.

In implementing these new tests, we have found the following advantages of computerized adaptive tests over standard paper and pencil tests:

- provide more precise measurement with fewer test items than conventional tests
- reduce testing time by 50 to 75 percent
- tests are adapted or tailored to each individual student's responses
- use current procedures and applications of item response theory
- provide equally precise measurement at all ability levels
- test items are carefully selected to match student ability levels
- reduce frustration for low-ability students and boredom for high-ability students

Another innovative application of computerized assessment is in the area of customized test creation and item banking. With a computerized test creation system, districts can prepare customized tests using comprehensive, professionally prepared banks of objectives, items, and instructional prescriptions. The local school district can specify the test design options; select and sequence the objectives, items, and prescriptions to be included in the test; and then automatically create the computerized test to meet local school or district objectives. This means that professional-quality tests can be designed at a local level without requiring teachers to create an entirely new set of test items each time they want to administer a test.

Hardware System Features

Various learning center configurations have been designed to meet the needs of small- to moderate-sized schools using a standard learning center configuration with up to 32 learning stations for school use in schools with up to 350 students. The large school learning center configuration provides up to 64 learning stations for schools with enrollments of 700 students. The smallest school learning center configuration provides either 8 or 16 learning stations and can meet the needs for schools or categorical education programs with up to 175 students. The modular configurations of the learning center system configurations provide for continued expansion of the learning system as the school needs change. All learning centers provide computerized instruction and assessment with high fidelity audio, graphics, and animation. Schools can link popular microcomputers as alternative learning center stations. Current capabilities also allow for centralized management of learning stations that are located in multiple classroom locations.

LEARNING IMPROVEMENT RESULTS FROM INTEGRATED LEARNING SYSTEMS

The World Institute of Computer-Assisted Training's (WICAT) integrated learning systems have been installed in several minority school districts for a period of one to four years. Several of these districts have conducted district evaluations of the outcomes from the learning centers. Most of these evaluations have employed a pretest-posttest evaluation design. The following sections present learning improvement results from the district-sponsored evaluations of integrated learning centers used for minority students. Additional information will be available over the next several years as additional districts implement and evaluate these integrated learning centers.

Pharr–San Juan–Alamo District, Texas

The Pharr–San Juan–Alamo, Texas, school district began implementation of integrated learning systems districtwide at 17 school sites during the 1986–87 school year. The Pharr–San Juan–Alamo Independent School District is located in the Rio Grande Valley of Texas, where the student population is about 90 percent Hispanic. Approximately 40 percent of the school population was limited English proficient at the beginning of the evaluation period. Each of the 17 sites installed a learning center with 32 learning stations along with the reading courseware. Evaluations were conducted with 1,300 to 1,400 students at third- and fifth-grade levels for each of the two implementation years.

The computerized predictive state assessment test was administered in October 1986 and 1987 to all district third- and fifth-grade students. Individual and group reports showing mastery or nonmastery of state assessment objectives were provided to teachers. Teachers also received prescriptions to courseware lessons and textbook pages for all nonmastered state assessment objectives. Teachers implemented the appropriate classroom and learning center prescriptions. The computerized predictive state assessment test was readministered in January 1987 and 1988. Teachers then implemented the appropriate final remedial prescriptions.

An evaluation of the Learning Solution was conducted using the Texas Educational Assessment of Minimum Skills (TEAMS), the Texas state assessment test, which was administered in February 1986, 1987, and 1988. The 1986 results provide a baseline score before the implementation of the integrated learning centers. The 1987 and 1988 results show results after one and two years of implementation of the learning centers.

Table 26.1 presents learning improvement results comparing the percent of students passing the state assessment test for third and fifth grades for each content area and year. Results are included for district and statewide percentages for all district students and for the LEP students.

The relative learning improvement gains for districtwide students (32 to 100 percent gains) are significantly greater than the comparable statewide gains (6 to 52 percent gains). In 1986 the district results were either at or significantly below the state average; in 1987 and 1988 the districtwide results were consistently greater than the statewide averages. The results from the LEP students are even more dramatic—their district learning improvement gains (53 to 253 percent) are significantly greater than the comparable statewide gains (33 to 92 percent). These results indicate that the integrated learning systems were very effective for district minority students and for the LEP minority students.

San Jacinto Elementary School, Goose Creek Independent School District, Texas

An integrated learning system was installed at the San Jacinto Elementary School, which is a Chapter I school. The school population is 86 percent minority, predominantly Hispanic. A learning center with 32 learning stations was installed along with the reading courseware. The learning center

Table 26.1

Students Passing the Texas Educational Assessment of Minimum Skills, Pharr–San Juan–Alamo District, 1986–88

	ALL STUDENTS		LIMITED ENGLISH PROFICIENT STUDENTS	
	DISTRICT	STATEWIDE	DISTRICT	STATEWIDE
GRADE 3				
READING				
1986	55%	74%	29%	30%
1987	75%	79%	56%	42%
1988	88%	84%	76%	51%
2-Year Gain	33%	10%	47%	21%
Relative Gain	60%	14%	162%	70%
MATH				
1986	72%	80%	59%	55%
1987	90%	86%	83%	71%
1988	95%	91%	90%	78%
2-Year Gain	23%	11%	31%	23%
Relative Gain	32%	14%	53%	42%
WRITING				
1986	49%	50%	27%	26%
1987	71%	63%	50%	40%
1988	78%	76%	61%	50%
2-Year Gain	29%	26%	34%	24%
Relative Gain	59%	52%	126%	92%

Table 26.1 (continued)
Students Passing the Texas Educational Assessment of Minimum Skills, Pharr–San Juan–Alamo District, 1986–88

	ALL STUDENTS		LIMITED ENGLISH PROFICIENT STUDENTS	
	DISTRICT	STATEWIDE	DISTRICT	STATEWIDE
GRADE 5				
READING				
1986	57%	83%	27%	40%
1987	84%	83%	64%	46%
1988	84%	88%	63%	53%
2-Year Gain	27%	5%	36%	13%
Relative Gain	47%	6%	133%	33%
MATH				
1986	62%	80%	37%	51%
1987	89%	86%	76%	65%
1988	93%	89%	83%	70%
2-Year Gain	31%	9%	46%	19%
Relative Gain	5%	11%	124%	37%
WRITING				
1986	41%	64%	17%	29%
1987	83%	68%	64%	31%
1988	82%	79%	60%	43%
2-Year Gain	41%	15%	43%	14%
Relative Gain	100%	23%	253%	48%

Table 26.2
Educational Outcome Results Performance on the Texas State Assessment Test, San Jacinto Elementary School, Texas, Spring 1986–Spring 1987

SUBJECT	GRADE	SCHOOL RESULTS	STATE RESULTS
READING	3	61% passing (1986)	74% passing (1986)
		89% passing (1987)	79% passing (1987)
		28% Gain	5% Gain
MATHEMATICS	3	83% passing (1986)	80% passing (1986)
		96% passing (1987)	86% passing (1987)
		13% Gain	6% Gain
WRITING	3	51% passing (1986)	50% passing (1986)
		76% passing (1987)	63% passing (1987)
		25% Gain	13% Gain

was used by 101 third-grade students for 30-minute sessions, three to four times a week. The computerized predictive state assessment test was administered as described above for the Pharr–San Juan–Alamo District. The TEAMS was administered to all students in third grade during February 1986 and February 1987. The February 1986 results are prior to implementing the learning centers. Table 26.2 presents the learning improvement results. These results show significantly greater achievement growth for the school (13 to 28 percent gains) than the comparable state results (5 to 13 percent).

Blackstock Junior High School, Oxnard, California

An integrated learning system was installed in the Blackstock Junior High School during the 1984–85 school year. Blackstock is a sixth- through eighth-grade junior high school with a total enrollment of 810 students; 60 percent are minority students with the largest group being 44 percent Hispanic. A learning center with 30 learning stations was installed along with the reading and mathematics courseware. Students used the learning center for 15-minute periods five times a week for reading and five times a week for mathematics. An evaluation was conducted for 112 sixth-grade students using the Comprehensive Test of Basic Skills administered during the spring of 1983, 1984, and 1985. School percentile scores and gains were compared

Table 26.3
Educational Outcome Results, Blackstock School, Oxnard, California,
Comprehensive Test of Basic Skills, Spring 1983–Spring 1985

SUBJECT	GRADE	NATIONAL PERCENTILE
READING	6	48 (1983)
		61 (1985)
		13 Percentile Gain
MATHEMATICS	6	47 (1983)
		77 (1985)
		30 Percentile Gain
LANGUAGE ARTS	6	49 (1983)
		60 (1985)
		11 Percentile Gain

for spring 1983 and spring 1985. The spring 1983 scores were prior to implementing the Learning Solution. Table 26.3 presents the learning improvement results. These results show learning gains of 11 to 30 percent over the two-year period.

Zenos Colman Elementary School, Chicago, Illinois

An integrated learning center was installed at the Zenos Colman School during the 1985–86 school year. Colman School is a K–8 school with an enrollment of 950 students. Nearly all of the students (98.5 percent) live in public housing projects. The entire student population is Black. The school installed a 32-station learning center with reading and mathematics courseware. A total of 233 students from first through sixth grades used the learning center for 90 minutes a week in reading and 60 minutes a week in mathematics. The Iowa Test of Basic Skills was administered to first-grade students

Table 26.4
Educational Outcome Results, Zenos Colman School, Chicago, Illinois

		GRADE 1 N=71	GRADE 2-6 N=162
MATHEMATICS	LC	7.7 months gain in five months	9.8 months gain in nine months
	CI	3.9 months' gain prior year	4.4 months' gain prior year
READING	LC	9.1 months gain in five months	9.5 months gain in nine months
	CI	6.9 months' gain prior year	4.5 months' gain prior year

KEY: LC = Learning Center Instruction
        CI = Classroom Instruction

in November 1985 and April 1986, and to second- through sixth-grade students in April 1985 and 1986. Table 26.4 presents the learning improvement results. These results show grade equivalent gains nearly twice as large from the learning center compared with prior achievement gains using standard classroom instruction.

McCorkle Elementary School, Chicago Illinois

An integrated learning system was installed in the McCorkle Elementary School during the 1986–87 school year. Located on Chicago's southside, McCorkle is a preschool–eighth grade school with an average enrollment of 600 students. Approximately 90 percent of the students live in public housing projects. The student population is 100 percent Black. A learning center was installed with courseware for reading and mathematics. The students used the learning center for five 35-minute periods, three times a week in reading and two times a week in mathematics. The Iowa Test of Basic Skills was administered to 400 students in fourth through eighth grades during April 1986 and 1987. Table 26.5 summarizes the learning improvement

Table 26.5
Educational Outcome Results, McCorkle Elementary School, Chicago, Illinois

GRADE 4-8

N=400

MATHEMATICS	LC	8.1 months' gain in five months
	CI	5.7 months' gain prior year
READING	LC	10.6 months' gain in five months
	CI	4.2 months' gain prior year

KEY: LC = Learning Center

         CI = Classroom Instruction

results. These results show grade equivalent gains that are significantly greater with the learning center than prior achievement gains with standard classroom instruction.

DISCUSSION

This chapter has described several innovative applications of integrated learning systems and the promising achievement results for minority students. Significant learning improvement gains have been found on state assessment tests and on standardized norm-referenced achievement tests. Learning improvement gains were found across different districts, regional locations, and minority populations. Following are several possible explanations for these significant learning improvement results.

First, the integrated learning system includes computerized, criterion-referenced tests for assessing and targeting specific individualized learning needs. These computerized tests provide for prescriptions and placement into the computerized courseware as well as in classroom textbooks to help students master the identified instructional objectives. These computerized tests can be administered as often as needed to provide assessment and prescriptive remediation based on student progress on specific instructional objectives.

Second, the comprehensive courseware provides an effective educational supplement to the traditional classroom instruction. The courseware has sufficient scope and breadth to meet the needs of students from kindergarten through twelfth grade in mathematics, reading, and language arts areas. These individual learning needs can be met for mainstream students, remedial students, at-risk students, and for gifted and talented students. The courseware also teaches higher order thinking and problem-solving skills along with the basic skills instruction. The courseware thus provides individualized instruction with an unlimited number of example and practice trials using a combination of text, graphics, high-quality audio, and animations. Minority students may benefit significantly from the quality courseware design, step-by-step presentation, interactive example and practice opportunities, and the graphics and audio instructional supplements.

Third, the integrated learning system provides teachers with a comprehensive instructional management system for monitoring and tracking individual student and class progress. These management reports indicate student progress on test objectives and courseware instruction. Teachers can readily modify the student courseware assignment lists to better meet individual student needs. As teachers continue to integrate the courseware instruction with their classroom instruction, the student's learning achievement should improve accordingly. With previous individualized instructional systems, the teachers were often overwhelmed with the amount of paperwork and management time required to provide individual assignments, lessons, and assessments for each student. With the computerized courseware, the teacher can easily do the management work required for individualized instruction. Teachers also provide instructional support and individual help to students in the computerized learning center.

Fourth, the minority students themselves report significant value from using the computerized courseware and assessment activities. The students report liking the individualized, one-on-one instruction that the courseware provides, the interactive practice and feedback exercises, and the high-quality development of the text, graphics, and audio instruction. Students like to keep track of their own progress through the courseware lessons and testing activities. As shown above, the use of the integrated learning system also produces significant student achievement and learning gains for minority students on state assessment tests and standardized achievement tests.

In summary, this chapter highlights several benefits from using integrated learning systems for minority students. These learning improvement results

offer significant promise for improving current and future learning of underachieving minority students.

NOTE

1. N. S. Cole, "Future Directions for Educational Achievement and Ability Testing," in B. S. Plake & J. C. Witt, eds., *The Future of Testing* (Hillsboro, NJ: Lawrence Erlbaum, 1986), pp. 84–86.

PART IV

Collaborative Arrangements

TWENTY-SEVEN

Successful Collaborations

EUGENE COTA-ROBLES

The earlier contributions to this book have made a fundamental point: the minority community itself must take an important role in improving achievement among minority youngsters. That aside, we still have to work with the schools in order to improve the education of underachieving minorities. We think this is possible in a number of ways.

Improving education requires the strengthening of certain activities. First, we must improve and strengthen instructional strategies that are effective for all students. Second, we must improve and strengthen the curriculum, particularly in schools that have large minority enrollments. We must also strengthen positive contributions by parents and other family members. We must improve the organizational ability of schools and other educational institutions. We must strengthen assessment tools and practices and we must strengthen students' expectations of themselves. Finally, we must strengthen the cultural and social support systems that students require to succeed in school. Our goal is to have full participation by minority students in the educational process. Until we achieve that goal, special efforts will be required in each one of the contexts outlined above. What may be less clear, however, is that special efforts are also needed to achieve and enhance effects across these different contexts.

One way to talk about these efforts is to talk about forging collaborations. The need for this kind of collaboration is generated by cultural discontinuity. Students learn and develop as whole individuals, and the background of their work in the school is participation in a larger world. We have to find ways, then, to bridge this discontinuity.

Generally, reform efforts deal only with the part of the student that is in school, and therefore deal only with part of the student's world. For example, some reform efforts focus on the development of skills but ignore problems created for students by unclear, ambiguous, or unreasonable class assignments. Others focus on improving the curriculum without involving in those efforts the classroom teachers who will have to implement these new reforms. Still other efforts are designed to improve the skills of individual teachers without addressing problems of school organization that keep teachers from being more effective. So reform movements are valuable, but frequently, unless they work across the system, they are not particularly useful. Reform effort has been very helpful for individual teachers, but substantial long-lasting improvements in the education of minority students will require that we find ways to broaden the objectives of these programs and increase collaboration among them, as well as within.

Let me tell you about a few University of California case histories in bridging K–12 and higher education. When implemented, these programs had a sharp focus, but as they achieved some success, the focus of each expanded and they have had to develop associations and collaborations in a broader context. The first of these examples is a program we call MESA: mathematics, engineering, science, and achievement.

This particular program was started in Berkeley in 1970 through the School of Engineering. Faculty members were interested in finding ways in which more Black students could attend engineering school. The program moved slowly until it became clear to industrial engineers that there was a real need to help and participate in this program. They started to work with the university, and in doing so, established connections between companies and the School of Engineering at Berkeley and with the schools in Oakland. MESA limped along at first, but now is very, very successful. MESA recently graduated 40 engineers from the University of California at Berkeley who are Black and Chicano youngsters, youngsters who probably would not have been able to go through the system without the help of MESA. In addition, from those 40 who went through the minority engineering program, 14 are going on to graduate school and preparing themselves for advanced training. Can you imagine the pressure these young minority engineers felt to take immediate employment? Working together permitted them to set higher goals and, perhaps, to work toward contributing their talents to faculties of the University of California. I feel that one of the most important things required to improve schools is that the faculties be diversified.

Other collaborative activities that are now being directed toward minority achievement are the California Writing Project and the California Mathematics Project. In these two programs, the university is working with teachers to upgrade their skills in writing and mathematics. Part of the focus of these programs is on teachers in minority schools, and the programs stress that the teachers who go back to those minority schools have a responsibility to help the other teachers. We are interested in improving the skills of teachers, but we also are interested in these teachers acknowledging that they have additional responsibilities, and one is to work intensively to upgrade the education that minority youngsters receive.

We are working on two other projects through the university that are types of collaborations. One is the linguistic minority project, which funds faculty to conduct research on the education of linguistic minority youngsters. One of our faculty who works in this area, Lillie Wong-Filmore, recently gave some staggering information to the University of California Regents.[1] She reported that the grade point average of Asian students at the University of California at Berkeley is inversely proportional to the length of time they have spent in California schools. She also pointed out that quality of teaching is crucial to the education of minority youngsters. Black and Hispanic youngsters, particularly, walk away from schools where instruction is inadequate. Asian students, on the other hand, acknowledge and accept that inadequacy and work harder to obtain high GPAs. The cultural context is very important. These are the kinds of studies that university faculty are contributing to the efforts to upgrade minority education.

The final study that I want to mention is the Black Eligibility Study, which has been generated primarily through the interest of individuals in the university such as Winston Doby and Joe Watson. They have convinced President Gardner that we must make an extended examination of why Black students show a decline in eligibility for the university. This must not be just a long-range view, we must also develop some short-term intervention strategies.

There are three kinds of collaboration. One is collaboration among similar professionals. An example would be the California Mathematics Project, a collaboration of teachers working together, teacher-to-teacher. The Achievement Council is a principal-to-principal collaboration. The Black Eligibility Study is heavily faculty-to-faculty. These kinds of collaborations are very useful.

Collaborations among individuals who occupy very different positions within the educational enterprise are a second kind. For example, the work we have done in MESA with teachers, counselors, parents, and students has permitted us to develop collaborations that are very effective. A very specific example of this kind of cross-collaboration is the project PUENTE. A collaboration between the community colleges and the university, PUENTE is an expansion of the Writing Project. It uses mentors from the Hispanic community to advise not only the students in California community colleges but the counselors as well.

A third type of collaboration is among different institutions, and this is necessary to insure that change is structural and longstanding. An example is Project TEAMS, Teaching Excellence and Achievement in Minority Schools. In this program, the Math Project, the Writing Project, the Achievement Council, and the UCLA effort in staff development are all tied together to make one entity with a focus on pushing excellence and achievement in minority schools.

It is important to remember that the students, their parents, and their friends can remain relatively untouched by our more ambitious efforts to bring collaboration. In fact, if we fail to provide increased opportunities for students to work more effectively with those immediately involved in their education—their peers, teachers, parents, and other family members—the best of our efforts, no matter how hard we try, will be ineffective.

One of the most important types of collaboration that we should encourage is collaboration in the classroom, collaboration between students. Classrooms must be redesigned so that minority students want to participate in school. They must have numerous opportunities to participate, and their participation and academic pursuits must be rewarded consistently. Collaboration in the classroom between students and teachers, and among the students themselves, is the key to this kind of participation, not only for minority students, but for the rest of the world as well.

Classroom collaboration is not something everyone is involved with directly on a daily basis, but we can certainly keep it in mind as we think about opportunities and proposals for increasing collaboration among the institutions and projects with which we are directly involved.

NOTE

1. L. Wong-Filmore, *Preparing for the Future Student Body of the University,* invited testimony to the Regents of the University of California. Presented at "Preparing for Population Changes in the State of California," San Diego, June 1987.

TWENTY-EIGHT

Forging Collaborations

WINSTON DOBY

We have a great challenge ahead of us if we are going to take the lineup of recommendations presented in this book and make them work for the betterment of the schools. Now is the time to move beyond the sharing of knowledge and insights and to begin deliberations on strategies to apply these concepts to the betterment of schools that serve minority youngsters. To begin that process, I suggest that an important first step is the creation of networks or infrastructures among those of us who share a common goal. Making schools work for underachieving minorities will require the successful collaboration of those who want to see it happen.

One of my favorite words is "synergy": the whole is greater than the sum of its parts. In medical terms, drugs are said to have synergistic effects when they increase the effects of each other. In team sports, some coaches and players have the ability to make the team better than the simple sum of the individual talents represented on the team. I believe that successful collaborations depend on several factors, and I will point out two examples to try to identify some of these factors.

The Los Angeles Lakers, in my view, represent the most recent example in sports. The Lakers had a common vision, to be the best in the National Basketball Association. They had excellent leadership from both the owner and what I would term a synergistic coach, a coach capable of getting his players to accept their roles and thereby making the Lakers a stronger team. They had talented players who agreed to accept these roles and who believed in themselves, who believed in their coach and in the Lakers system. Of course, they had Magic Johnson, the supreme synergistic agent.

Another example of a successful collaboration is the organization that created the conference from which this book evolved, the Center for Research on Evaluation, Standards, and Student Testing. CRESST is a creative national organization. It works because the stakeholders share a common belief in the importance of testing and the importance of evaluation in improving schools and informing public policy. The CRESST team of established researchers serves as the catalyst for bringing together educators, education practitioners, researchers, and policy makers, and they do it at all levels. Clearly, this volume is an excellent example of a successful collaboration.

I'm involved in yet another collaboration. This is a group whose goal is to increase the number of Black students in Los Angeles County who are eligible to attend selected county colleges and universities. The stakeholders in this collaboration represent 26 community organizations, 7 school districts, over 100 colleges and universities, and several major companies in the Los Angeles area. They are working in collaboration on behalf of over 2,000 ninth-grade Black youngsters. One organization, the 100 Black Men of Los Angeles, serves as the community catalyst to forge the collaboration necessary to make it all work.

Still a very young program, it has generated nearly $1 million from community support. It involves over 1,000 community leaders and role models, and it has all of the ingredients of a successful collaboration: a common vision, a catalytic agent, stakeholders who are committed and involved, and, most importantly, a belief that in working together we can make a greater difference than working separately. It is this last factor on which I would like to encourage you to concentrate.

There are many educators who have the opportunity to begin a collaboration of their own on behalf of the youngsters served in minority schools. Only by working together can we make such schools work for underachieving minority students. Educators who are aware of the status of our underachieving minority students are the synergistic agents who can make the schools make a difference. We must take on that challenge.

PART V

Making Schools Work for Underachieving Minority Students

TWENTY-NINE

An Ambitious Critical Agenda

Joan L. Herman and Josie G. Bain

Contributors to *Making Schools Work for Underachieving Minority Students* eloquently articulate the national dilemma that continues to confront us. Each acknowledge that we have yet to realize the dream of making it possible for all students to gain sufficient education to become productive and contributing members of our society. The depth and severity of this dilemma, the consequences if it is not resolved, and some key dimensions of potential solutions were carefully explored by the keynote speakers (the authors of chapters in Part I of this volume), Samuel Betances, James Comer, and Henry Levin. Other chapter authors/conference participants then explored with great enthusiasm and optimism promising programs and innovative practices that could brighten the future for currently at-risk students. In the final session of the conference, participants were divided into small working groups under the leadership of Dr. Norma Cantu, Director of the Mexican American Legal Defense and Education Fund; Dr. Gary Peterson, Director of Research and Evaluation, Milwaukee Public Schools; Dr. Grace Pung Guthrie, Research Associate, Far West Regional Laboratory; Dr. Linda Davis, Deputy Superintendent, San Francisco Unified Schools; and Dr. Gary Estes, Program Director, Northwest Regional Laboratory. These working groups considered the conference proceedings in relation to four major questions:

1. What are the most important keys to improving education for underachieving minority students? Are there common ideas, factors, or processes that appear to characterize various promising practices?

2. What are the most significant impediments to implementing these key ideas?

3. What federal, state, and/or local actions (other than only money) would most help?

4. How could R&D in educational testing and/or evaluation best contribute to solutions? Are there important testing and/or evaluation issues that need to be
addressed? What kinds of testing and/or evaluation information, if any, could
help improve educational opportunities for minority students?

The major findings of the conference, based on a synthesis of working group
deliberations and conference presentations, are structured by these same
questions. These findings suggest an important and ambitious agenda for
continued work to help resolve a critical national problem.

WHAT ARE IMPORTANT KEYS TO IMPROVING EDUCATION FOR UNDERACHIEVING MINORITY STUDENTS?

Recommendations for improving education for minority students focused
on five areas (1) instructional development, (2) the professional development
and training of teachers, (3) school climate, (4) community and parental
involvement in the education of minority children, and (5) educational research and evaluation.

Recommendations for Instructional Development

*Effective instruction must be linked with a focused assessment of school
outcomes and sound diagnosis of student needs and abilities.* In essence, a
dynamic model of assessment and instruction must be developed that allows
for the following activities: improved diagnosis and prescription; varying
instructional strategies and materials in response to individual and group
needs; continually monitoring and improving the quality of school programs;
and setting high expectations for all students and all schools. In addition,
R&D is needed to enable better matching of teaching strategies with student
learning styles.

Recommendations for Teacher Development

*Particular attention must be paid to the training and professional devel-
opment of teachers.* Further research is necessary to increase our understanding of the key dimensions and indicators of excellent teaching; these
in turn need to be incorporated into strong preservice and inservice training
programs. Because teachers must also understand the culture of minority
students to improve their education, teacher education and administration
programs should develop cultural awareness, encourage the value of cultural
diversity, and develop positive attitudes among their students.

There is also a need to recruit minority candidates into teacher training
programs and to utilize practitioners in these programs who can serve as

strong role models (e.g., Black mentors who have recently taught in inner city schools). These actions will lead to the recruitment and training (and retraining) of a culturally sensitive and culturally enriched teaching and administrative workforce.

Finally, the empowerment of teachers is necessary to support a strong teaching profession and a profession to which the best are attracted. Empowerment will also promote efficacy and responsibility, encouraging teachers to explore a wider variety of techniques, collaborative teaching strategies, and other innovations to build students' basic and problem solving skills.

Recommendations for School Climate

Elements of the school climate are essential to successful educational improvement. In particular, the conference reaffirmed characteristics associated with effective schools as identified in the literature. Leadership is a central element in promoting a productive school climate, with the principal functioning as a strong and committed instructional leader. It is crucial to have a school climate that encourages high expectations, quality relationships among and between teachers and students, order, articulated goals and equity.

Recommendations for Community/Parental Involvement

The creation of broad based efforts that involve all members of the community (business, church, parents) in the education of children is highly recommended for improving the education of minority students. To promote active involvement in and reinforcement of their students' learning, minority parents and significant others in the child's life must begin to feel a sense of possibility and hope for the future as well as a change in their perception that schools are "not for us or our children." Efforts must be directed to bring about and build an atmosphere of concern, high expectations, and positive perceptions.

Recommendations for Research and Evaluation

The bridging of research, evaluation, and practice is a critical element in bringing about change. Applied research and evaluation can assist school planning, focus outcomes, and help support effective policy making at various levels. Concrete plans of action for individual schools and school systems need to be established, then systematically monitored and evaluated for both summative and formative purposes.

WHAT ARE THE SIGNIFICANT IMPEDIMENTS TO IMPLEMENTING KEY IMPROVEMENTS FOR MINORITY EDUCATION?

Conference participants identified what they deemed the most significant impediments to implementing innovations that could improve education for minority students. The areas most troublesome included those related to (1) school management and bureaucratic constraints, (2) attitudes, and (3) problems in research and development.

Impediments Related to School Management and Bureaucratic Constraints:

Bureaucratic constraints and problems in how schools are managed appear to present serious obstacles to reform and innovation. Some of the problems cited include: government mandates without resources to implement them; restrictions in the use of special funds; inflexibility in schools organization and management (e.g., structure of school time); and a lack of support for risk taking and innovation in implementing new ideas to help minority achievement. Further, in some cases, school management is not held accountable for the use of funds targeted to particular groups, making it difficult to get resources where they are most needed.

Another aspect of the problem related to management is the scarcity of minority role models in leadership positions and the lack of serious commitment at all management levels. The latter means insufficient leadership for mobilization and change efforts within the schools. Exacerbating the problem is an increasingly diverse population, which makes it difficult to set and mount a unified effort toward common objectives.

Impediments Based on Attitudes

Public attitudes and racism are major impediments to recognition and resolution of the problems of minority achievement. Changes in attitudes/ perceptions must occur before significant gains for minority education are possible, yet changing entrenched attitudes and dispelling fears and stereotypes is a recalcitrant problem. Among the most difficult is changing attitudes from "those children can't learn" to "all children can learn and should be encouraged to do so." The lack of will, the lack of real commitment to improve minority achievement continues to plague us. These negative attitudes have been communicated to students, creating learner apathy and lack of motivation, inspiration, and hope. If attitudes do not change, students must be taught to reject rejection.

In the view of some, schooling functions to sort individuals into successes and failures, thereby assuring that there will always be low achievers. This

role is clearly detrimental to minorities. The current federal attitude toward
minorities also shortchanges the needs of these communities.

Impediments Related to Testing and Evaluation

*Inappropriate use of evaluation and testing methods was noted as a par-
ticular problem.* Impediments in the area of testing include a heavy reliance
on standardized test scores and narrow kinds of assessment data that have
been used to confirm stereotypes and limit opportunities. Tests must be
designed to fairly assess student capabilities and accomplishments and evaluations must be sensitive to a full complement of school goals. Testing and
evaluation should serve as bridges rather than barriers to better programs.

WHAT FEDERAL, STATE, AND LOCAL ACTIONS (OTHER THAN MORE MONEY) WOULD HELP IMPROVE EDUCATION FOR MINORITIES?

Conference participants envisioned (1) actions that could and should be
undertaken at all legislative and administrative levels, and (2) a few recommendations that were particularly salient to the federal, state, or local
level.

Recommendations for Action at All Levels

*Sustained commitment and focused policy direction are necessary at all
levels to maximize efforts to educate ALL students.* Serious commitment
requires attention, direction, and allocation of scarce resources. Yet all too
often regulations and mandates come from various levels—federal, state, or
local—without adequate resources to implement them. In order to better
address the problem, all levels should recognize the full complement of
quality resources and supports that are needed to improve education for the
underachieving. A next step would be to focus the best available resources
(e.g., teachers, instructional materials, etc.) on those with the greatest needs.
This is but one way in which commitment to the improvement of education
for all can be sustained and supported without the expenditure of new funds.

*Sustained commitment involves actions that facilitate the participation of
minorities at all levels, especially in leadership roles.* Such a task may be
carried out in part by providing incentives to bring more minorities and
women into management, higher education and research, and/or networking
with and among minority groups regarding an appropriate research and
action agenda. Another part of this task may require assigning sanctions to
those that neglect affirmative action.

*All levels must also be committed to improving the collection and sharing
of information.* Dissemination of information on promising practices to prac-

titioners and policy makers can be the first step leading to the refinement and replication of successful programs to improve minority achievement. All levels should also consider better communication with the public, particularly using the media to educate the public about successes.

Recommendations for Action at the Federal Level

There must be sustained federal commitment to the improvement of minority achievement. Federal actions that would help bring about change include: promoting federal regulations that allow more flexibility and creativity in designing and implementing compensatory programs; and enforcing equity policies in federally supported programs. In the latter regard, it appears that enforcement has weakened in recent years. Affirmative action must be pursued vigorously, promoting equal access in the private as well as public sector.

Also of prime importance, federal policies must explicitly support multicultural efforts and assure serious attention to the special needs of limited English proficient and bilingual students. The promulgation of fair and unbiased information about the impact of bilingual education was another immediate need. Sustained financial commitment to existing programs that work was another obvious requirement.

Recommendations for Action at the State Level

State-level actions should include innovations directed at teachers, instructional improvement, testing and incentives for change. For example, in the area of teacher preparation, the states must assure that teacher training incorporates a truly multicultural curriculum. States also should consider policies that encourage local program adaptation and community involvement. State agencies specifically need to avoid regulations or statutes that reduce the flexibility of local districts and schools to respond to local needs and contexts.

Other state-level innovations that would help support change include: the development of a core curriculum to be taught to all in the schools; the development of more efficiency in testing; and the refocusing of testing directives to assure both the assessment of significant skills and attention to a more comprehensive range of quality indicators. In the latter area, state assessments should consider the strengths that can serve as building blocks to success rather than paying exclusive attention to weaknesses that identify schools as failures. Flexible collaborations with local districts should encourage experimentation and new programming innovations to support learning, such as alternative learning and homework centers in neighborhood areas (e.g., malls, churches).

Recommendations for Action at the Local Level

Needed action at the local level involves strong collaboration between local school districts and their communities to secure a strong network of support for the education of minority youth. The establishment of strong partnerships between home, business, church, and each school campus was widely advocated to strengthen school programs and reinforce the attainment of educational goals and expectations. The activities of individuals involved in reducing the dropout rate, of groups like the 100 Black Men and Young Black Scholars program in Los Angeles, and of programs sponsored by the National Urban League and the National Council of La Raza are examples of initiatives whose success can be monitored and replicated in other communities. Volunteer task forces established by local districts and community representatives can assist in making schools work for underachieving minorities.

In addition to engendering community support, school administrations at the local level must be held accountable for the delivery of equitable educational services. Therefore, local districts must put into place valid and reliable evaluation and accountability systems, including a variety of quality indicators, to monitor and support school improvement efforts.

WHAT ARE THE IMPLICATIONS FOR RESEARCH AND DEVELOPMENT IN EDUCATIONAL TESTING AND/OR EVALUATION?

Specific recommendations were made under the general topics of (1) testing, (2) evaluation, and (3) bringing research into the schools.

Recommendations for R&D in Testing

In the area of test development, removing test bias and seeking alternatives to standardized testing and reporting remain concerns with considerable advocacy. Curriculum-based testing and criterion-referenced measures as well as alternatives to a multiple-choice format are highly recommended. A new testing technology is needed to better diagnose student needs and enable students to demonstrate their talents. Test developers need to involve more minority persons (researchers and practitioners) in the development of improved tests.

Responsibilities for appropriate test use fall on the shoulders of both the user and test developer. Test developers and users must debunk myths about particular standardized tests and actively discourage their inappropriate use for LEP and other students. The diagnostic and instructionally relevant purposes of testing should be emphasized, with better integration of testing with instruction. For example, new arrivals to a district should be tested upon entry in order to assess their educational needs and posttested later on curriculum-based skills to assess the real impact of education in the new district. Users must also improve the quality of their decision making by cross-validating any testing data they receive against alternative sources of information. Users must understand that test results are imperfect and an insufficient basis for decision making.

Test reporting must also improve. In reporting data about schools, demographic data such as SES, language and ethnic characteristics, and community context should be reported alongside testing data. School performance should be reported in a way to hold schools accountable for the progress of every ethnic group, but such reports should simultaneously take into account both SES and ethnicity.

Training in appropriate test interpretation and use must improve. A particular area of identified need was training for testing personnel and school counselors to assure that test results are not misused to limit students' opportunities. Evaluation mechanisms may be needed to assess the attitudes of counselors and others who administer and interpret tests since their attitudes may affect test-takers' performance and subsequent life changes. Parents also need more knowledge about the meaning of test results and their appropriate interpretation.

Recommendations for R&D in Evaluation

Research and development must continue to develop sensitive evaluation designs and reporting practices that support the use of evaluative data to help minority students and their communities. In designing evaluations, researchers should develop workable SES measures; broaden the range of indicators used to assess quality and equity; and use approaches that promote fair and productive use of evaluation findings. In the latter area, a balanced combination of top-down policy relevant measures and bottom-up locally ideographic measures was recommended. Innovative program evaluation models must be designed and more creative ways to assess teachers must be developed; both need to be sensitive to unique local circumstances but capable of generating comparable results. Evaluations should attempt to identify strengths that can serve as a foundation for improvement.

Research and development should take community politics and public interest into consideration through independent evaluations and publications of reports in concise, understandable language. Districts must give priority attention to disseminating results throughout their districts and to analyzing and addressing findings. Researchers must assist in the interpretation of findings with explicit advice on what can and cannot be generalized from the results. Researchers and practitioners must improve the use of data at the local, state, and federal levels.

Recommendations for Bringing Research into the Schools

Strategies must be devised to bring research into the schools to be used more effectively by teaching and administrative personnel. Districts should establish a policy on disseminating and applying research results. Dissemination efforts must include teachers. In fact, there are many who advocate the development of the "reflective practitioner"—one who uses research to reform action and decisions. Users (and nonusers) need to understand testing and evaluation and how it is appropriate or inappropriate to use in assessing outcomes, determining policies, and designing instructional improvement strategies.

School-based planning models and data-based decision making need to be more effectively utilized, an effort that will require better training of teachers and principals. These actions can make evaluation data an important tool in the improvement of educational opportunities for minorities.

A final recommendation from the groups advised wide dissemination of this conference report through the Educational Commission of the States, the Council of Chief State School Officers, the National School Boards Association, the National Urban League, the National Council of La Raza, the Council of the Great City Schools, the National Council of State Legislators, the National Governors' Association, the Business Roundtable, minority organizations, and the U.S. Department of Education.

THIRTY

The Course Ahead

EVA L. BAKER, JOAN L. HERMAN, AND
JOSIE G. BAIN

The issue of minority educational achievement must be spotlighted, and productive approaches need continued review, trial, and improvement. This book, and the conference upon which it was based, brings together shared interest in contributing to this area. Authors and conference participants had two things in common: their commitment and their own achievement. They also sounded a recurrent theme: that minority achievement problems grow from broader societal sources. Poverty, and its limiting effects on positive experience, goals, time, and know-how, can be only partially assuaged by productive school environments. Continually reaffirmed, however, was the view that individual action, someone caring about students, does make a difference. The challenge is to mobilize the deep concern within the community to a level where most children receive the encouragement they need.

Conferences are frequent professional events, and books of proceedings are likewise common enterprises. A good conference is one that is well-organized, stimulating, and engaging, and one where opportunities for informal contact are provided. A good book shares many of these same features. By such measures, our effort was a good one. But a useful endeavor is one that has effects beyond the time and place of the meeting and stimulates action beyond reading. How our endeavor rates on that dimension is more difficult to assess at this early date. However, CSE/CRESST has taken some concrete steps toward longer range impact.

In collaboration with the National Council of La Raza and the National Urban League, CRESST has developed a study group whose goal is to produce evaluation tools that can be adapted and used by community groups to assess the impact of their many programs directed toward improving minority educational options. We hope that the final product will be used and widely disseminated to community groups, churches, and school districts, to provide the impetus and alternatives for assuring that their programs are making a difference.

Within the CRESST family, the conference helped to reaffirm a rich agenda for research in testing and evaluation, an agenda that we will pursue seriously. We will contribute at a number of levels. At the policy level, we will help to assure that local, state, and federal policy makers pay attention to indicators of equity in their assessments of school quality and will help to formulate what those indicators should be. At the school and local program levels, we will help to devise better and more useful evaluation models to support local problem-solving and program improvement for minority students. At the classroom and student levels, we are developing alternatives to traditional testing and are preparing diagnostic testing techniques that better support student learning. At all levels, we will continue to serve as a consumer advocate on behalf of our students, keeping watch over the actual use of tests and their potential misuses. In partnership with the involved communities, we look for our efforts to make significant impact on the quality of education for minority students.

References

Acher, C. (1985). Raising Hispanic achievement. In *Make something happen: Hispanics and urban high school reform. ERIC/CUE Digest*, 26 (April).

American Association of Colleges of Teacher Education. (1983). *AACTE Briefs*, May. Washington, DC.

———. *AACTE Briefs*. June. Washington, DC.

Anrig, G. R. (1986). Teacher education and teacher testing: The rush to mandate. In S. Packard, ed., *The leading edge* (pp. 79–91). Washington, DC: American Association of Colleges of Teacher Education.

Applebee, A., Langer, J. A., & Mullis, I.V.S. (1986). *The writing report card: Writing achievement in the American schools*. Princeton, NJ: Educational Testing Service.

Bachman, J. G. (1971). *Dropping out: Problem or symptom?* Ann Arbor: University of Michigan, Institute for Social Research.

Baker, E. & Herman, J. (1985). Educational evaluation: Emergent needs for research. *Evaluation Comment, 7*(2) (December).

Banks, J. A. (1983). Multiethnic education and the quest for equality. *Phi Delta Kappan, 64*(8), 582–85.

Baratz, J. C. (1986). Black participation in the teacher pool. Paper for the Carnegie Forum's Task Force on Teaching as a Profession.

Barro, S. M. (1987). *Who drops out of high school?: Findings from "High school and beyond."* Washington, DC: National Center for Education Statistics.

Bell, D. (1983). Learning from our losses: Is school desegregation still feasible in the 1980's? *Phi Delta Kappan, 64*(8), pp. 572–75.

Bennett, W. J. (1986). *First lessons: A report on elementary education in America*. Washington, DC: U.S. Department of Education.

Bernal, E. M. (1986). Increasing the interpretative and practical utility of Hispanic children's scores on tests of maximum performance. Paper presented at the Minority Health Conference, Ohio State University, Columbus.

Bloom, B. S. (1984). The two sigma problem: The search for methods of group instruction as effective as one-to-one tutoring. *Educational Researcher*, June/July, 4–16.

Bodmer, W. F. & Cavalli-Sforza, L. L. (1970). Intelligence and race. *Scientific American*, October, pp. 19–29.

Borich, G. D. (1984). *Needs assessment and program planning techniques.* (Available from Gary D. Borich, College of Education, The University of Texas at Austin, 78712.)

Brandt, R. (1982). On school improvement: A conversation with Ronald Edmonds, *Educational Leadership*, 40(3), 4–11.

Brown, T. J. (1986) *Teaching minorities more effectively.* Lanham, MD.: University Press of America.

Bruffee, K. A. (1982). Liberal education and the social justification of belief. *Liberal Education, 68*, 95–114.

Bruner, J. S. (1960). *The process of education.* Cambridge, MA: Harvard University Press.

Carnegie Foundation for the Advancement of Teaching. (1988). *The condition of teaching: A state-by-state analysis.* Princeton, NJ: Princeton University Press.

Charters, W. W., Jr. & Jones, J. E. (1973). On the risk of appraising non-events in program evaluation. *Educational Researcher, 2*, 5–7.

Chase, C. (1980). Three views in the complex controversy on the origin of intelligence. *Phi Delta Kappan, 61* (11), 217–18.

Cole, N. S. (1986). Future directions for educational achievement and ability testing. In B. S. Plake & J. C. Witt, eds., *The future of testing.* Hillsboro, NJ: Lawrence Erlbaum.

Coleman, J. S. (1966). *Equality of opportunity.* Washington, D.C.: U.S. Government Printing Office.

Comer, J. P. (1980). *School power: Implications of an intervention project.* New York: Free Press.

———. (1988). *Maggie's American dream: The life and times of a Black family.* New York: New American Library.

Congressional Budget Office. (1986). *Trends in Educational Achievement.* Washington, DC: Author.

Cooper, C. C. (1986). Strategies to assure certification and retention of black teachers. *Journal of Negro Education.* 55(1), 46–55.

Crain, R. L., Mahard, R. E., & Narot, R. E. (1982). *Making desegregation work.* Cambridge, MA: Ballinger.

Cropper, A. & Nomura, K. (1987). PPST report: Current status and plans for the future. Unpublished manuscript, Northern Arizona University, Center for Excellence in Education, Flagstaff.

Cuban, L. (1983). Transforming a frog into the prince: Effective schools research, policy, and practice at the district level. National Institute of Education Report.

Cummins, J. (1981). The role of primary language development in promoting educational success for language minority students. In *Schooling and language minority students: A theoretical framework.* Los Angeles: California State University, Evaluation, Dissemination, and Assessment Center.

———. (1984). *Bilingualism and special education.* San Diego: College Hill Press.

———. (1986). Empowering minority students: A framework for intervention. *Harvard Educational Review, 56*(1), 18–35.

Daniels, R. S. & O'Neil, C. (1979). The reverse RFR. *Educational Evaluation and Policy Analysis, 1,* 43–44.

Diaz, S., Moll, L., & Mehan, H. (1986). Sociocultural resources in instruction: A context-specific approach. In *Beyond language: Social and cultural factors in schooling language minority students* (pp. 197–230). Sacramento: Bilingual Education Office, California State Department of Education.

DiPardo, A. & Freedman, S. W. (1987). *Historical overview: Groups in the writing classroom* (Tech. Rep. No. 4). Berkeley: Center for the Study of Writing.

Dorr-Bremme, D. W. & Herman, J. L. (1986). Assessing student achievement: A profile of classroom practices. *CSE Monograph Series in Evaluation, No. 11.* Los Angeles: Center for the Study of Evaluation.

Duckett, W., Strother, D., & Gephart, W. (1982). Evaluating the evaluator. *Practical Applications of Research,* March, p. 1.

Duran, R. (1986). Improving Hispanics' educational outcomes: Learning and instruction. Unpublished manuscript, University of California, Graduate School of Education, Santa Barbara.

Eder, D. (1982). Differences in communicative styles across ability groups. In L. C. Wilkinson, ed., *Communicating in the classroom.* Orlando, FL: Academic Press.

Edmonds, R. (1979). Effective schools for the urban poor. *Educational Leadership, 37*(1).

Eisner, E. (1985). *The art of educational evaluation: A personal view.* Philadelphia: The Falmer Press.

Eysenck, H. J., & Kamin, L. (1981). *The intelligence controversy.* New York: John Wiley.

Feistritzer, C. E. (1985). *Cheating our children.* Washington, DC: The National Center for Educational Information.

Finn, C. E., Jr. (1987). The high school dropout puzzle. *The Public Interest,* Spring.

Flaugher, R. L. (1971). *Minority versus majority group performance on an aptitude test battery* (Project Access Report No. 3). Princeton, NJ: Educational Testing Service. (Research Bulletin No. 71–48.)

Foster, R. W. (1983). Desegregation in Denver: Down for the count? *Phi Delta Kappan, 64*(5), 331–33.

Franklin, J. H. (1947). *From slavery to freedom: A history of Negro Americans.* New York: Alfred A. Knopf.

Fullan, M. (1982). *The meaning of educational change.* New York: Teachers College, Columbia University.

Galambos, E. C. (1986). Testing teachers for certification and recertification. In T. J. Lasley, ed., *Issues in teacher education, Volume II: Background papers from the National Commission for Excellence in Teacher Education* (pp. 153–62). Washington, DC: American Association for Colleges for Teacher Education.

Gallimore, R., Boggs, J. W., & Jordan, C. (1974). *Culture, behavior, and education: A study of Hawaiian-Americans.* Beverly Hills, CA: Sage Publications.

Gallimore R. & Howard, A. (1968). Hawaiian life style. In R. Gallimore & A. Howard, eds., *Studies in a Hawaiian community: Na Makamaka O Nanakuli* (pp. 10–

16). Pacific Anthropological Records, No. 1. Honolulu: Department of Anthropology, Princess Bernice Pauahi Bishop Museum.

Garcia, E. (1987). Instructional discourse in effecting bilingual classrooms. Working paper No. 3, Bilingual/Bicultural Education Center, Arizona State University.

Garcia, E. & August, D. (1988). *Language minority education in the U.S.: Research, policy and practice.* Chicago: Thomas Publishing Company.

Garcia, P. A. (1985). *A study on teacher competency testing and test validity with implications for minorities and the results and implications of the use of the Pre-Professional Skills Test (PPST) as a screening device for entrance into teacher education programs in Texas.* Washington, DC: National Institute of Education.

Gay, G. (1983). Multiethnic education: Historical developments and future prospects. *Phi Delta Kappan, 64*(8), 560–63.

Giroux, H. A. & McLaren, P. (1986). Teacher education and the politics of engagement: The case for democratic schooling. *Harvard Educational Review, 56,* 213–38.

Glass, G. V., & Ellwein, M. C. (1986). Reform by raising test standards. *Evaluation Comment,* December. Los Angeles: UCLA Center for Research on Evaluation, Standards, and Student Testing.

Goldenberg, C. (1984). Roads to reading: Studies of Hispanic first graders at risk for reading failure. Unpublished doctoral dissertation, Graduate School of Education, University of California, Los Angeles.

Goldenberg, C. & Gallimore, R. (1987). The social context of emergent home literacy among Hispanic children. Paper presented at the Institute on Literacy and Learning, Linguistic Minority Project, University of California, Santa Barbara.

Goodman, Y. (1980). The roots of literacy. In M. P. Douglass, ed., *Reading: A humanizing experience.* Claremont, CA: Claremont Graduate School.

Gould, S. J. (1981). *The mismeasure of man.* New York: W. W. Norton.

William T. Grant Foundation. Commission on Work, Family, and Citizenship. (1988). The forgotten half: Non-college youth in America. Washington, DC: Author.

Gutierrez, K. & Garcia, E. (In press). Academic literacy in linguistic minority children: The connections between language, cognition, and culture. In O. Saracho, ed., *Cognitive styles in early childhood.* London: Gordon & Breach Science Publishers.

Hakuta, K. (1986). *Mirror of language: The debate on bilingualism.* New York: Basic Books.

Hall, G. (1979). The concerns-based approach to facilitating change. *Educational Horizons, 57*(4) (Summer), 202–8.

Hall, N. (1987). *The emergence of literacy.* Portsmouth, NH: Heinemann Educational Books.

Hammack, F. M. (1986). Large school system's dropout reports: An analysis of definitions, procedures, and findings. *Teachers College Record, 87*(5), 324–41.

Heath, S. B. (1981). Toward an ethnohistory of writing in American education. In M. Farr-Whitman, ed., *Variation in writing: Functional and linguistic-cultural differences.* Vol. 1 of *Writing: The nature, development, and teaching of written communication* (pp. 225–46). 2 vols. Hillsdale, NJ: Lawrence Erlbaum.

———. (1986). Sociocultural contexts of language development. In *Beyond language: Social and cultural factors in schooling language minority children*. Sacramento: Bilingual Education Office, California State Department of Education.

Hodgkinson, H. L. (1985). *All one system: Demographics of education, kindergarten through graduate school*. Washington, DC: Institute for Educational Leadership.

———. (1986). *Higher education: Diversity is our middle name*. Washington, DC: National Institute of Independent Colleges and Universities.

Howard, B. C. (1987). *Learning to persist and persisting to learn*. Washington, DC: Mid-Atlantic Center for Race Equity.

Howard, J. & Hammond, R. (1985). Rumors of inferiority. *The New Republic*, September 9, pp. 17–21.

Howe, H. & Edelman, M. W. (1985). *Barriers to excellence: Our children at risk*. Boston: The National Coalition of Advocates for Students.

Hundley, M. G. (1965). *The Dunbar story: 1870–1955*. New York: Vantage Press.

Jenifer, F. G. (1984). How test results affect college admissions of minorities. In C. Daves, ed., *The uses and misuses of tests* (pp. 91–106). San Francisco: Jossey-Bass.

Jensen, A. R. (1960). How much can we boost I.Q. and scholastic achievement? *Harvard Educational Review*, Winter, pp. 1–123.

———. (1981). *Straight talk about mental tests*. (1981). New York: Free Press.

Jones, F. C. (1981). *A traditional model of educational excellence: Dunbar high school of Little Rock, Arkansas*. Washington, DC: Howard University Press.

Jones, L. (1987). Achievement trends for black school children, 1970–1984. Paper presented at a collegium on Black Families and Public Policy, Historical and Contemporary Perspectives, May, Yale University.

Joyce, B. & Showers, B. (1980). Improving inservice training: The messages of research. *Educational leadership, 37*(5), 379–85.

Ladner, J. (1986). Teenage pregnancy: The implications for black Americans. In *The State of Black America, 1986*. New York: National Urban League.

Lanasa, P. J. III & Potter, J. H. (1984). Building a bridge to span the minority-majority achievement gap. Paper presented at the National Conference on Desegregation in Postsecondary Education, October.

Lemann, N. (1986). The origins of the underclass. *The Atlantic Monthly*, June, pp. 31–55.

Lenning, O. T. (1977). *The outcomes structure: An overview and procedures for applying it in postsecondary institutions*. Boulder, CO: National Center for Higher Education Management Systems.

Lenning, O. T., Munday, L. A., Johnson, O. B., Vander Well, A. R., & Brue, E. J. (1974). *The many faces of college success and their nonintellective correlates: The published literature through the decade of the sixties*. Iowa City, IA: American College Testing Publications.

Levin, H. M. (1986). *Educational reform for disadvantaged students: An emerging crisis*. Washington, DC: The National Education Association.

Little, J. W. (1981). School success and staff development: The role of staff development in urban desegregated schools. Paper presented at the annual meeting of the American Educational Research Association, Los Angeles.

Machado, L. A. (1980). *The right to be intelligent*. New York: Pergamon Press.

Martinez, R. (1986). *Minority youth dropouts: Personal, social, and institutional reasons for leaving school.* Colorado Springs: University of Colorado, Center for Community Development and Design.

Mayeske, G. W. & Beaton, A. E., Jr., (1975). *Special studies of our nation's students.* Washington, DC: U.S. Government Printing Office.

McDill, E., Natriello, G., & Pallas, A. (1985). Raising standards and retaining students: The impact of the reform recommendations on potential dropouts. *Review of Educational Research, 55*(4) (Winter).

McGhee, J. D. (1985). The black family today and tomorrow. *The state of black America 1985.* New York: National Urban League.

Mercer, J. R. (1979). In defense of racially and culturally non-discriminatory assessment. *School Psychology Digest, 8*(1), 89–115.

Mercer, W. (1984). Teacher education admission requirements: Alternatives for black prospective teachers and other minorities. *Journal of Teacher Education, 35*(1), 26–29.

Messick, S. (1984). Assessment in context: Appraising student performance in relation to instructional quality. *Educational Researcher, 13*(3), 3–8.

Moll, L. C. & Diaz, E. (1982). *Bilingual communications in classroom text.* Final Report. Washington, DC: National Institute of Education.

———. (1983). Toward an interactional pedagogical psychology: A bilingual case study. San Diego: Center for the Study of Human Information Processing, University of California.

Morine-Dirshimer, G. (1985). *Talking, listening and learning in elementary classrooms.* New York: Longman.

Mullin, S. P. & Summers, A. A. (1983). Is more better: The effectiveness of spending on compensatory education. *Phi Delta Kappan, 64*(5), 229–343.

Nairn, A. and Associates. (1980). *The reign of ETS: The corporation that makes up minds.* Washington, DC: Ralph Nader.

National Academy of Education, Commission on Reading. (1985). *Becoming a nation of readers: The report of the Committee on Reading.* Pittsburgh: National Academy of Education.

National Assessment of Educational Progress. (1976). *Functional literacy and basic reading performance.* Washington, DC: Office of Education, U.S. Department of Health, Education and Welfare.

———. (1985). *The Reading Report Card: Progress toward excellence in our schools: Trends in reading over four national assessments, 1971–1984.* Princeton, NJ: Educational Testing Service.

———. (1986). *The writing report card: Writing achievement in American schools.* Princeton, NJ: Educational Testing Service.

National Center for Education Statistics. (1983). *The condition of education, 1983 edition: A statistical report.* Washington, DC: U.S. Department of Education, National Center for Education Statistics.

National Commission on Excellence in Education. (1983). *A nation at risk: The imperative for educational reform. A report to the nation and the secretary of education.* Washington, DC: U.S. Department of Education.

Natriello, G., (1986). *School dropouts: Patterns and policies.* New York: Teachers College Press.

Oakes, J. (1986). Tracking, inequality and the rhetoric of reform: Why schools don't change. *Boston University Journal of Education*, 168(1).

———. (1987). *The distribution of excellence: Indicators of equity in precollege mathematics, science, and technology education*. (National Science Foundation Contract No. WD–2919/3–1–NSF). Santa Monica, CA: Rand Corporation.

Oakland, R., ed. (1977). *Psychological and educational assessment of minority children*. New York: Brunner/Mazel.

Ogbu, J. & Matute-Bianchi, M. E. (1986). Understanding sociocultural factors: Knowledge, identity, and school adjustment. In California State Department of Education, ed., *Beyond language: Social and cultural factors in schooling language minority students*. Los Angeles: California State University, Evaluation, Dissemination, and Assessment Center.

Ornstein, A. C. (1982). The education of the disadvantaged: A 20-year review. *Educational Research*, 24(3), 197–210.

Orum, L. S. (1986). *The education of Hispanics: Status and implications*. Washington, DC: National Council of La Raza.

Page, E. B. & Stake, R. E. (1979). Should educational evaluation be more objective or more subjective? *Educational Evaluation and Policy Analysis*, 1, 45–47.

Peitzman, F., ed. (in press). *The power of context*. Los Angeles: UCLA Center for Academic Interinstitutional Programs.

Phillips, B., ed. (1973). *Assessing minority group children*. New York: Behavioral Publications.

Pugh, G. E. and Krasmakevich, J. (1971). *School desegregation with minimum busing*. Arlington, VA: Lambda Corporation.

Rodman, B. (1985). Teaching's 'endangered' species. *Educational Week*, 5(3) (November), 1, 11–13.

Rodriguez, A. M. (1980). Empirically defining competencies for effective bilingual teachers: A preliminary study. In R. V. Padilla, ed., *Theory in bilingual education* (pp. 372–87). Ypsilanti: Eastern Michigan University.

Saphier, J. & Gower, R. (1982). *The skillful teacher*. Carlisle, MA: Research for Better Teaching.

Schlechty, P. (1985). District level policies and practices supporting effective school management and classroom instruction. In R. Kyle, ed., *Reaching for excellence: An effective schools sourcebook*. Washington, DC: U.S. Government Printing Office.

Scribner, S. & Cole, M. (1981). Unpackaging literacy. In M. Farr-Whiteman, ed., *Variation in writing: Functional and linguistic-cultural differences*. Vol. 1 of *Writing: The nature, development, and teaching of written communications*. (pp. 71–88). 2 vols. Hillsdale, NJ: Lawrence Erlbaum.

Sizemore, B. A. (1985). Pitfalls and promises of effective schools research. *The Journal of Negro Education*, 54(3).

———. (1986). The limits of the black superintendency: A review of the literature. *The Journal of Educational Equity and Leadership*, 6(3) (Fall).

———. (1987). The effective African American elementary school. In G. W. Noblit & W. T. Pink, eds., *Schooling in social context: Qualitative studies*. Norwood, NJ: Alex Publishing Corporation.

———. (1989). Curriculum, race and effective schools. In H. Holtz, I. Marcus,

J. Dougherty, J. Michaels, & R. Peduzzi, eds., *Education and the American dream*. Granby, MA: Bergin and Garvey Publishers.

Sizemore, B. A., Brossard, C. A., & Harrigan, B. (1983). *An abashing anomaly: Three high achieving predominantly black elementary schools*. National Institute of Education, Grant #G–80–0006.

Slavin, R. (1986). Best-evidence synthesis: An alternative to meta-analysis and traditional reviews. *Education Research, 15*(9), 5–11.

Smith, G. P. (1984b). Minority teaching force dwindles with states' use of standard tests. *AACTE Briefs, 5*(9) (November), 12–14.

Smith, G. P. (1984a). The critical issue of excellence and equity in competency testing. *Journal of Teacher Education, 35*(2), 6–9.

Southern Regional Education Board (SREB). (1986). *Measuring Student Achievement*. Atlanta: Author.

Sowell, T. (1972). *Black education: Myths and tragedies*. New York: David McKay.

Spradley, J. P. (1971). Cultural deprivation or cultural innundation? *Western Canadian Journal of Anthropology, 2*, 65–82.

Staples, R. (1987). Social structure and black family life: An analysis of current trends. *Journal of Black Studies, 17*(3) (March), 267–87.

Steinberg, S. (1981). *The ethnic myth: Race, ethnicity, and class in America*. New York: Atheneum.

Stickney, B. D. & Plunkett, V.R.L. (1982). Has Title I done its job? *Educational Leadership, 39*(5), 378–83.

Suchman, E. (1967). *Evaluative research*. New York: Russell Sage Foundation.

Tharp, R. (1989). Psychocultural variables and constants: Effects on teaching and learning in schools. *American Psychologist, 44*(2), 1–11.

Tharp, R. & Gallimore, R. (1988). *Rousing minds to life: Teaching, learning and schooling in social context*. Cambridge: Cambridge University Press.

Tikunoff, W. J. (1983). Effective instruction for limited English proficient students. Paper presented at the 12th Annual Conference of the National Association for Bilingual Education, February, Washington, DC.

Tough, J. (1982). Language, poverty, and disadvantage in school. In L. Feagans & D. C. Farran, eds., *The language of children reared in poverty* (pp. 3–18). New York: Academic Press.

Trueba, H. (1987). *Success or failure? Learning and the language minority student*. Cambridge, MA: Newbury House.

Trueba, H. & Delgado-Gaitan, C. (1988). *School and society: Learning content through culture*. New York: Praeger Publishers.

U.S. Bureau of Labor Statistics. (1985). The employment situation. In *Current Population Survey*. Washington, DC: Author.

U.S. General Accounting Office. (1986). *School dropouts: The extent and nature of the problem*. Washington, DC: Author.

Van Sertima, I. (1976). *They came before Columbus*. New York: Random House.

Vygotsky, L. S. (1962). *Thought and language*. Cambridge, MA: MIT Press.

———. (1978). *Mind in society*. Cambridge, MA: Harvard University Press.

Walsh, C. (1987). Language, meaning, and voice: Puerto Rican students' struggle for a speaking consciousness. *Language Arts Journal, 64*, 196–206.

Webb, M. B. (1986). Increasing minority participation in the teaching profession. *ERIC/CUE Digest*, No. 31 (April).

Weisner, T., & Gallimore, R. (1985). The convergence of ecocultural and activity theory. Paper read at the annual meeting of the American Anthropological Association, Washington, D.C.

Weisner, T., Gallimore, R., & Jordan, C. (1988). Unpackaging cultural effects on classroom learning: Native Hawaiian peer assistance and child-generated activity. *Anthropology and Education Quarterly, 19*, 327–53.

Weiss, C. H. (1973). Between the cup and the lip. *Evaluation, 1* 49–55.

Wheelock, A. (1986). Dropping out: What the research says. *Equity and Choice, 3*(1) (Fall).

Wildavsky, A. (1972). The self-evaluating organization. *Public Administration Review*, September/October, pp. 509–20.

Williams, C. (1974). *The destruction of black civilizations*. Chicago: Third World Press.

Williams, R. (1974). Black pride, academic relevance, and individual achievement. In R. W. Tyler and R. M. Wolf, eds., *Crucial issues in testing*. Berkeley, CA: McCutchan.

Wilson, R. and Melendez, S. (1985). *Minorities in higher education: Fourth Annual Status Report*. Washington, DC: Office of Minority Concerns, American Council on Education.

Witty, E. P. (1982). *Prospects for black teachers: Preparation, certification, employment*. Washington, DC: ERIC Clearinghouse on Teacher Education, ED 213 659.

Wong-Filmore, L. (1983). Effective instruction of LEP students. Paper presented at the 12th Annual Conference of the National Association for Bilingual Education, February, Washington, D.C.

———. (1987). Preparing for the future student body of the University. Invited testimony to the Regents of the University of California. Presented at "Preparing for Population Changes in the State of California," San Diego, June.

Wood, F. et al. (1982). Practitioners and professors agree on effective staff development practices. *Educational Leadership*, October, pp. 28–31.

Wright, S. J. (1980). The survival of black public school teachers. A challenge for black colleges and universities. In E. Witty, ed., *Proceedings of the national invitational conference on problems, issues, plans, and strategies related to the preparation and survival of black public school teachers*. Norfolk, VA: Norfolk State University School of Education. ED 212 565.

Name Index

Subject Index

Absenteeism, 72, 231, 233, 235
Academia del Pueblo, 92–94, 98
Accelerated instruction, 9–11
Accelerated Schools for the
  Disadvantaged, 9–11
Accountability, 142, 171, 225, 273–74
Achievement, 105, 161, 216–18; and
  testing and evaluation, 186; of
  disadvantaged, 3–4; of high school
  graduates, 113, 115, 122; of limited
  English proficient students, 138, 247;
  on national assessments, 127, 175–76
Achievement, Black student, 2, 44–45,
  47–48, 86; on standardized tests, 54,
  127, 207, 222–24, 231–33, 251–52
Achievement, Hispanic student, 83,
  86–88, 138; on standardized tests,
  54, 127, 224, 232–33, 247, 250
Achievement, programs for improving,
  55–58, 73–74, 105–8; for bilingual
  education, 138–40; for Black
  students, 21–22, 44, 47–49; for
  college eligibility, 109–11, 116–24;
  for disadvantaged, 7–11; for Hispanic
  students, 92–101; in effective
  schools, 161–62, 177–79, 236–39; in
  school-based planning, 202–211,
  using computers, 242–46; with

community organizations, 76–82. See
  also Instructional strategies
Achievement gap, 7–9, 45, 54, 147,
  160, 172, 217–18; narrowing of, 221–
  24, 229, 231–33, 239
Achievement Goals Program, 197
Administrators, 157–58, 162, 203, 209–
  10; number of Hispanic, 88; staff
  development for, 163; training of, 16,
  140, 203. See also District
  administration; Leadership;
  Principals; Superintendent
Adult education. See Parent education
Affirmative action, 271–72
African American students. See Black
  students
Alienation, 72. See also Self-esteem
Alternative schools, 72
American Association for the
  Advancement of Science, 95
American Association of Colleges of
  Teacher Education, 147–48
American College Testing program
  (ACT), 107, 148, 170
American Indian students, 131;
  achievement of, 113, 233; dropouts,
  223; in special programs, 234;
  number in schools, 114

Center for the Study of Evaluation,
  100, 277–78
Centralized programs, 216. *See also*
  Organization
Chapter I, 73–74, 75, 162, 183, 233–35
Charles Rice Elementary School, 48
Child care, 90. *See also* Extended-day
  programs
Child development, 16–18, 98
Churches. *See* Religious institutions
Cities in Schools, 90
Citizenship, 23, 30, 171
Civil Rights Movement, 20, 141
Classroom management, 244–45, 254
Classroom Management Training
  Project, 205–6
Class size, 178, 191, 196
Climate, school, 73, 133, 161; in
  effective schools, 41, 179, 238, 229;
  programs to improve, 23, 78
Collaborations: between state and
  district, 272; for dropout prevention,
  73–74; with businesses, 32–33, 73,
  77, 95; with colleges and
  universities, 107, 109–11, 116–24,
  156, 260–62, 264; with community
  organizations, 73, 76–78, 81–82, 92–
  101, 264, 273; with Hispanic
  organizations, 84–85, 90–101; with
  social service organizations, 77–78;
  within schools, 261–62. *See also*
  Partnerships
College enrollment: in California, 114,
  118, 122; of Black students, 75, 109,
  122, 207; of Hispanic students, 83–
  84, 122. *See also* Higher education
Colleges and universities: programs
  sponsored by, 9, 57, 78, 107, 109–
  11, 114–24, 155–58; staff
  development sponsored by, 77, 260–
  61. *See also* Higher education
Commission on Work, Family, and
  Citizenship, 86
Communication: among teachers, 56,
  99, 156–57; between school and
  parents, 56, 76–78, 88, 224
Community involvement, 14–15, 224,
  238–39, 259, 269, 277–78; in dropout

prevention, 73; in effective schools,
  178; in school-based planning, 203–4,
  206, 216; programs that increase,
  119–20, 228–29, 235–36
Community organizations, programs
  sponsored by, 76–78, 81–82, 84–101
Compensatory education, 75, 127, 238;
  drawbacks of, 7–9, 57, 86, 100, 108,
  131; evaluation of, 181–82, 185–86;
  Federal support for, 272; Hispanic
  students in, 86; in higher education,
  5
Competency testing: of students, 6,
  142, 179, 207, 217, 226; of teachers,
  106, 142, 148–49, 183, 185. *See also*
  Graduation requirements
Computer-assisted instruction, 7, 97,
  172, 241–44, 246–54
Computer-assisted testing, 184, 226–
  27, 242–54
Computer education, 92, 94, 162
Conflict resolution, 81–82, 97–98
Congressional Budget Office, 222
Connecticut, programs in, 21–23
Constitutional Rights Foundation, 95
Continuing education, 155–58, 260–61.
  See also Staff development; Teacher
  training
Contracts between parents and school,
  9–10, 80, 92, 95
Cooperative learning, 7, 10, 64, 93, 95,
  97, 132
Core curriculum, 55–56, 107–11, 141,
  272
Council of Chief State School Officers,
  191–93, 275
Council of the Great City Schools, 275
Counseling services, 206, 210; and
  testing and evaluation, 191; for Black
  students, 49; for career planning, 78,
  80–81, 94–97; for college, 116–17; for
  dropouts, 73, 96–97; for Hispanic
  students, 87, 90, 94, 261
Courseware, computer, 242–44, 247,
  250–52, 254
Critical thinking skills, 48, 155. *See
  also* Higher order thinking skills;
  Problem-solving skills

About the Editors and Contributors

JOSIE G. BAIN is a CRESST project director at the UCLA Center for the Study of Evaluation. She is a past member and vice-president of the California State Board of Education and a member of the State Personnel Board. Prior to this, Dr. Bain served as an elementary school teacher, vice-principal, principal, area coordinator, area superintendent, and associate superintendent of instruction in Los Angeles city schools. Her current interests focus on improving educational opportunities for at-risk and underachieving minority students.

JOAN L. HERMAN is Associate Director of the UCLA Center for the Study of Evaluation and a project director for CRESST. She directs research projects on the effects of testing on teaching and learning and on the effects of technology on the reporting and use of evaluation information at the district and school levels. She is particularly interested in the role of testing and evaluation in school improvement. A former teacher, Dr. Herman has been active in teacher training and has directed a number of large-scale evaluations of educational reform.

ED C. APODACA is Director of Admissions and Outreach Services for the University of California.

EVA L. BAKER is Associate Dean of the Graduate School of Education and Director of the Center for the Study of Evaluation at the University of California, Los Angeles.

ERNESTO M. BERNAL is Director of Research Services for the Center for Excellence in Education at Northern Arizona University.

SAMUEL BETANCES is Professor of Sociology at Northeastern Illinois University.

JAMES COMER is the Maurice Faulk Professor of Child Psychology at Yale Child Study Center and the Associate Dean for the Yale School of Medicine.

ERIC COOPER was Associate Director of Program Development for the College Board. He is currently Vice-President of In-Service Training and Telecommunications for Simon and Schuster.

EUGENE COTA-ROBLES is Assistant Vice-President of Academic Affairs for the University of California.

WINSTON DOBY is Vice-Chancellor of Student Affairs for the University of California, Los Angeles.

TODD ENDO is Director of the Office of Research and Evaluation for the Fairfax County Public Schools.

JOSE GALVAN was Director of Foreign Language Programs for the Center for Academic Interinstitutional Programs.

KRIS GUTIERREZ is Assistant Professor at the University of California, Los Angeles, Graduate School of Education.

WALTER HATHAWAY is Director of Research and Evaluation for the Portland Public Schools.

KATI HAYCOCK was Executive Director of the Achievement Council. She is currently Vice-President of the Children's Defense Fund.

LESTER W. JONES is Professor of Math at Xavier University of New Orleans.

HENRY LEVIN is Director of the Center for Educational Research and a professor at Stanford University.

DANIEL LEVINE is Professor of Education at the University of Missouri at Kansas City.

ROGER D. MITCHELL is Project Director for the National Urban League.

CHARLES MOODY is Vice-Provost for Minority Affairs at the University of Michigan.

JAMES B. OLSEN is Director of Testing at the World Institute of Computer-Assisted Training.

LORI S. ORUM is Director of Project Excel and the Los Angeles Program Office for the National Council of La Raza.

BONNIE RUBIO is Regional Administrator of Operations for the Los Angeles Unified School District.

ANA MARIA SCHUHMANN is Interim Dean of Education at Kean College.

RAMSAY SELDEN is Director of the State School Assessment Center at the Council of Chief State Schools Officers.

BARBARA SIZEMORE is a professor at the University of Pittsburgh.

TWYLA STEWART is Assistant to the Director for the Center for Academic Interinstitutional Programs.

FRED TEMPES is Assistant Superintendent of the Instructional Support Services Division of the California State Department of Education.

SHIRLEY THORNTON is Deputy Superintendent of the Specialized Programs Branch of the California State Department of Education.

MICHAEL TIMPANE is President of Teachers College at Columbia University.